Gift from Richard Jeske 1973

AFTER THE COUNCIL

AFTER THE COUNCIL

EDMUND SCHLINK

Translated by **Herbert J. A. Bouman**

FORTRESS PRESS
Philadelphia

This book is a translation of *Nach dem Konzil,* published by Siebenstern Taschenbuch Verlag, Munich and Hamburg, in 1966.

Library of Congress Catalog Card Number 68-12327

5962H67 Printed in U.S.A. 1-96

Foreword

On December 8, 1965, the Second Vatican Council was brought to a solemn close. An impressive variety of themes had been considered. The resolutions are now before us. The story of this Council, however, has not come to an end, for an integral part of the story is what happens afterward. Realization of the Council's resolutions will take time, and, as the history of councils demonstrates, it will not everywhere come to pass at the same time or in the same way. In this sense the close of the Council is only "the beginning of the beginning" (Karl Rahner). At the moment nothing definitive can be said concerning its significance. This will be possible only after many years.

Nevertheless, the rest of Christendom cannot confine itself to awaiting further developments, since in this Council the Roman Catholic Church has executed an astonishing turn in the direction of other churches. The Decree on Ecumenism has opened up possibilities of exchange and cooperation with the "separated brethren" that had hitherto been denied Catholic Christians. Making these possibilities a reality, however, depends not only on the Roman church but also on the manner in which other churches assess the altered situation and the kind of stance they take in relation to the Roman church. The other churches will have to study the resolutions of the Council with great care, become clear on their implications, and, at least tentatively, seek to evaluate the significance of this Council for the common life of all Christians.

Observers at the Council had the privilege of following the course of events at St. Peter's at very close range. Having served as official observer for the Evangelical Church in Germany and having participated in all four sessions, I could not evade the assignment to present a public report from an Evangelical perspective on the results of these four years. In popular language and without scholarly apparatus, I propose to present an introduction to the most important resolutions of the Council, to attempt an analysis of the changed situation since the Council, and then to consider how we must now act in relation to the Roman Catholic Church. In this connection we dare not overlook the fact that, by virtue of its membership in the World Council of Churches, the Evangelical Church in Germany is linked not only with other churches of the Reformation but also with the Eastern Orthodox church. Therefore, the many points of view of the latter will also find expression here. In what follows I generally refer to the Roman Catholic Church as the "Roman church." This way of formulating that church's self-designation is simply to recognize the fact that most other churches also regard themselves as catholic churches or even call themselves by that name.

Observers at the Council were instructed to report to their sponsoring bodies on the events at the Council and also to inform the Council Fathers and theologians about the positions of their own churches. A fruitful dialogue developed, above all in the framework of the joint sessions with the Secretariat for the Promotion of Christian Unity. There the texts currently being debated in the Council were discussed and observers were expressly asked for their critiques. Cardinal Bea was especially responsible for the atmosphere of frankness and confidence in which this dialogue was carried on. This book, too, should be regarded as an expression of gratitude. How else should we express our gratitude than by acknowledging that the resolutions of this Council involve us, and by carefully testing, with the eyes of hope, the possibilities presented for the common life of Christians in the future.

Table of Contents

Acknowledgments

Excerpts from the Constitutions, Decrees, and Declarations of the Ecumenical Council are taken from *The Documents of Vatican II*, published by Guild Press, America Press, Association Press, and Herder and Herder and copyrighted 1966 by The America Press. Used by permission.

Grateful acknowledgments are also due to the following for permission to quote:

To Herder & Herder, Inc., for quotation from *Herder-Korrespondenz*, Volume 15 (1961).

To B. Herder Book Co., for quotations from *The Church Teaches* (1955), edited and translated by John F. Clarkson, *et al*.

1

The Awakening of Christendom

The accomplishments and significance of the Second Vatican Council cannot be understood if considered in isolation and exclusively in the context of the history of the Roman Catholic Church. Events in this century have changed the situation for all Christendom and have confronted all churches with new problems and decisions. Such changes are still taking place, moving on at a precipitous and breathtaking tempo.

The Loss of Security in Christendom

The past decades comprise some of the most dramatic epochs in the entire history of the church. Forms that had grown for centuries, and through which Christianity had as a matter of course become imbedded in the surrounding culture and political order, have become questionable or have been shattered. In the tumult of events, entire churches have been pushed off the public stage and relegated to an almost invisible existence. The invasion of traditionally Christian nations by anti-Christian forces has largely reduced Christians in those countries to a minority, a state of affairs that can only be compared with the inroads of Islam into the church's territories in the Near East and northern Africa since the seventh century. Furthermore, the number of people who have been killed in our century because of their church membership far exceeds the number of victims in the persecutions during the early centuries of the church. Many others have defected from the Christian faith under pressure of persecution. Churches of all confessions have been affected by these upheavals. Every denomination has suffered great losses in members, influence, and freedom.

To make the two world wars, together with the concomitant revolutions, responsible for this state of affairs would be to take no more than a surface view. The wars did not cause these conditions; they only released them. They only uncovered that which had already happened previously in long intellectual transformation, without as yet suspending the legal guarantees of the churches. Apart from North America and the independent churches of England, nearly all churches as late as the nineteenth century still conceived of themselves in terms of the national church, the establishment of which had been completed under Justinian and which had been maintained by the Byzantine and Holy Roman Empires after the schism between the Orthodox and the Roman churches and even by the Evangelical territorial princes following the separation of the Reformation churches from the Roman church. This conception of the unity of Christian faith, culture, and political order, however, had long ago become questionable. The emergence of the natural sciences and the Enlightenment, the estrangement of the educated world and labor from the church, and the aloofness of the church over against the new scientific, social, and political necessities, meant that this unity had already been gutted and had become a mere facade, even where it was still formally observed. It only remained for the tumult of world events in this century to bring about a complete collapse. It became apparent, however, that where the old order had been supplanted by a religionless order, post-Christian man, who had once learned to know the freedom in Christ and had then renounced Christ, could not permanently remain in the neutrality of agnosticism. Rather, he gives birth to new meanings and world-views by means of which he seeks to master the questions of the age over against the Christian faith and develops comprehensive systems and sees them through. But these systems enslave men in a manner similar to the enslavement exercised by the powers and authorities spoken of in the New Testament. It is no accident that some leaders of anti-Christian movements have come out of Christian schools and seminaries.

Corresponding to these processes in traditionally Christian countries are the profound changes taking place in those areas where Christianity first began to be propagated. As late as the nineteenth century a missionary enterprise originating in Europe and America had worked so intensively in Africa and Asia that for the first time in its history Christianity spanned the entire globe and the goal of a Christianized humanity seemed within view. To the non-Christian world, however, the two world wars appeared to be fratricidal wars among Christian nations, and led to such a weakening of moral prestige and power for the participants that the non-Christian nations were able to rebel, throw off the yoke of colonialism, and constitute themselves as sovereign states. In the process they discovered a reserve of strength in their own religions, especially in Hinduism, Buddhism, and Islam. Believed to be spent, these religions were renewed with an astonishing force and now proceeded to exert a world missionary thrust of their own. Deprived of the legal and economic privileges granted them by the colonial powers and exposed to the onslaught of nationalism and the non-Christian religions, the churches in these lands are today isolated and their further expansion is seriously restricted. Entire regions are now altogether closed to the Christian message. Added to this is the eruption of thousands of syncretistic sects, especially in Africa where nationalistic pagan groups separate themselves from the Christian churches.

In view of these changes, we must move beyond a consideration of the disintegrating factors of the world wars and the end of colonialism. Here, too, these factors are only in the foreground. Christianity got into this difficult situation in these lands only because its expansion had been too intimately and too obviously associated with Western civilization, Western thought forms and ways of life, and Western educational methods. As a result, Christianity had penetrated to the real self of the Asiatic and African peoples far less than had seemed to be the case under the pseudo-transformation of these peoples during the colonial period. To these people, the Father of Jesus Christ proclaimed in the missionary message appeared to be more the mighty God of the white race than the universal Father of all men and thus *their* Lord and Father. It was therefore inevitable that, in the national upsurge of those peoples, the Christian churches would be suspected of being the representatives of foreign political powers and for that reason were restricted and in part even persecuted and exterminated.

Thus in a peculiar way Christendom has today lost its security. In many areas the Christian church has become a persecuted church, while in other places it is barely tolerated. But even where the church still appears to be determining the total life of a nation and enjoying governmental guarantees, its position is being largely undermined. This is true not only of Roman Catholic countries like Italy, Spain, and those of South America, but also of West Germany, Scandinavia, and England. Largely bereft of cultural and political supports, Christians have in a new way again become strangers and pilgrims in this world. It is true that the number of baptized exceeds the number of adherents of any other religion, and that the number of Christians continues to increase. Nevertheless, in the midst of the totality of a rapidly multiplying humanity, Christendom is a steadily diminishing minority. The totals for Christendom are even less when the statistics are figured on the basis of those who actually attend church rather than the number of baptized.

Renewal from the Source

Christendom has reacted in sharply different ways to its loss of security. Some looked upon those who deprived them of their security as enemies whom they must fight with all possible weapons. In a virulent battle they sought to salvage what they could and even clung to what was beyond saving as their goal. Even if their weaknesses have meanwhile been exposed, they press their claims with renewing energy and seek to restore what was lost as soon as a new political situation permits it. Examples of this kind are found not only in the events in Spain.

Others recognized in this loss of security the activity of a God who uses even the enemies of the church as his instruments. In the stormy events of world history they recognized the power of God who jolts and shakes the tree of Christianity so that the dry leaves and dead branches may fall by the tempest of his chastisement, and so that those parts of the tree which draw their vital strength from the roots might be tested and strengthened. In the hostility of their environment and in the apostasies they recognized the effects of a church that had become secure and smug, a church that had seemed to many a prop for outmoded world-views and social and political systems rather than a light of the world and a helper of the poor. They regarded their losses as vanished illusions, while in these tempests the reality of the church came to light anew and her proper tasks disclosed themselves once again. Men learned that Christ's strength manifests itself in the weakness of Christians and that the sufferings of witnesses to the faith are sufferings together with Christ through which his cross becomes a triumphant reality in the midst of this world. Here the church's loss of security and her status of stranger and pilgrim were affirmed. The dominant theme became not fighting the enemies of the church but wrestling with God for his forgiveness and his guidance for further obedience.

Thus in the most disparate parts of Christendom a new searching of the Holy Scriptures was begun. With the end of the Constantinian era the situation of the church in many areas had in a surprising way again become similar to the situation of the primitive church. This led to an elementary search for the answers to today's questions in the New Testament witness of the apostles and the primitive church on the basis of proximity to the once-and-for-all saving deed of God in Christ. The Old Testament writings, as witnesses to the way God leads his people, also came alive again and became relevant as warning, consolation, and guidance for the present. Thus in many churches, often independently of each other, theologians and laymen studied the Scriptures together and produced one of the most potent Bible movements in the church's history, a movement that resulted in many Bible translations and biblical commentaries.

At issue was not only an historical interest in biblical writings but also a desire to hear what God has to say to us today. The chief concern was, therefore, not only reading the word of Holy Scripture but also expounding and proclaiming its promise and its demands, so that it might be accepted in faith, prayer, and worship. The concern was not simply for God's saving deed, completed once and for all, but also for God's saving activity today on the basis of that unique act. Jesus Christ is indeed "the same yesterday and today and for ever" (Heb. 13:8). In many churches this led to the rise of a liturgical movement, not primarily determined by historical and aesthetic interests but rooted in a basic hunger for the living word of God and for the sacramental participation in Christ's death and resurrection, and in the yearning of men to present themselves to God as sacrifices of praise in the fellowship of the faithful.

This biblical and liturgical awakening stirred up a new interest in the church's confession of its faith, for in such confession the believer affirms the center of the great variety of biblical statements. In confession the believer surrenders himself to the Christ who died once and for all, as to the present Lord. All affirmations of faith are concentrated in such confession: witness and prayer, teaching and worship. At the same time the person confessing does not remain an individual but joins in the confession of the church—of the brothers who are his contemporaries and of the fathers who have preceded him in faith. In this way the church's dogma in its gathering, strengthening, and actualizing function was looked at with a new awareness.

In the process the church, her nature, her task, her form, began to be considered in a new light. Her former possibilities for activity had been largely changed. The more strongly alien inroads questioned or destroyed the form of the church, however, the more significant became the identity of the church of all ages, her calling to be not of this world, the universal priesthood of the believers, and the solidarity of God's pilgrim people with the host of the perfected saints. Thereby the ancient church became important once again, not only the church before Constantine, persecuted in this world and perchance tolerated, but also the church in temporal proximity to the primitive community, in which the abiding structures of the church on the apostolic foundation began to assume their first comprehensive historic form. In an unexpected way the century in which the church lost her security became "the century of the church" (O. Dibelius). Moreover, the horizon was broadened beyond the boundaries of denominations. Churches like the Russian Orthodox, regarded in the West as ossified, began through their martyrdom to send out brilliant beams of light and to shame and arouse other churches that had considered themselves strong.

Thus, in the midst of the loss of security in our time, a renewal of Christendom based on its source had been set in motion.

Responsibility for the World

These impulses could not be called renewal if they merely served as religious self-gratification and introverted security for Christians who by this means sought compensation for their lost external security. It speaks for the genuineness of the renewal movement that a new turn in the direction of the world followed upon the biblical movement, the liturgical movement, and a new understanding of the church's essence, a turn motivated by the experience of divine worship and by reflection upon the church's task. The church has not only been called by God to be not of the world; the church is also the people of God sent out into the world. In essence, the church does not live only in the movement away from the world but also in the movement toward the world.

The more intensively Christians thought back to their origins, the greater their freedom from the accustomed cultural and political ties to which the church's tradition had bound them. Men and women arose who consciously declined to meet the objections and attacks of the church's enemies by means of the customary weapons of apologetics. On the contrary, they paused, humbled themselves under the judgment of the divine word, and from this perspective thought through the catastrophes and upheavals of our time. They were not ashamed to confess the guilt of a Christendom for which the message of Christ had become a systematized Christian world-view, and for which Christian discipleship had become the affirmation of traditional social and political orders. As a result, Christendom had largely misunderstood the ethos of the modern sciences, the validity of the labor movement and the rights of colonized peoples, as well as the dangers inherent in the imperial claims of the European nations. In this way the church had been guilty of driving to unbelief many to whom the gospel addresses itself in particular, those who hunger and thirst and seek after truth and righteousness. But now the obligation to serve the world was realized anew.

This service consists at all times and above all in bearing witness to Jesus Christ. Christ died for all and as the Risen One he has been set as Lord over all. To everyone he has become both brother and Lord. This must therefore be called to the attention of all men. Christ desires to come to everyone through the call of the gospel. This message is not new, but it had to be presented in a new way so that Christians would not conceal the universality of their Lord. Christians needed again to take seriously the words of Paul: "For though I am free from all men, I have made myself a slave to all, that I might win the more. To the Jews I became as a Jew, in order to win Jews; . . . To the weak I became weak, that I might win the weak. I have become all things to all men, that I might by all means save some" (I Cor. 9:19 ff.). Christians must not only proclaim the message of Christ's self-abnegation; they themselves must follow his self-abnegation. In this vein, new methods of witnessing were undertaken by pastors and laymen in a variety of ways.

This witness could not be confined to the word of God. It must also be extended to areas where the word could not yet be received or where it was forbidden. Also, an entrance into the totality of the labor, the circumstances of life, and the needs and questions of others can become a witness to Christ that elicits new questions and hopes. In this and a variety of ways, living churches came into being with new forms, churches conscious of their responsibility to their de-Christianized and even pagan surroundings.

This responsibility is also valid over against the upheavals of world society, the conflicts between social strata, nations, and races, the problems of emerging nations and the population explosion, and the suppression of the weak and the arrogance of the mighty. The message concerning Christ is the primary task of Christendom. God desires, however, not only the sinner's justification by faith. He also wants civil righteousness, in which all men may live together in peace. It is characteristic of the awakening Christians today that many no longer defend their own security and the traditional order but have instead begun to think in a revolutionary way of their fellow men and to raise their voices with a new freedom on behalf of the suppressed, undaunted by unpleasant reactions to public warnings addressed to their own governments. They know that their responsibility obligates them to promote the cause of all nations and peace among men and that it cannot stop at the borders of their own countries.

Thus, paradoxically, precisely through loss of security in this world, a dimension of the world has been opened up anew for Christendom. The collapse of the political order and the traditional security in European culture has led to the church's transition from her European epoch to the epoch of humanity. The patronage relationship between European and American churches on the one hand and the mission fields on the other has now been supplanted by the fellowship of churches with equal rights from all continents, races, peoples, and cultures.

This renewal from the source in part already determines the consciousness of entire areas of the church, while in part it has just begun. It treads a tension-filled path over against traditional church resources. In only a few churches, however, are the signs of the awakening entirely missing. It is not always the same persons and groups who espouse the Bible movement, the liturgical movement, the missionary proclamation, and social responsibility and world peace. Yet wherever the new life has stirred, these different concerns were not understood as opposites but as coherent functions of the same churchly life which finds its fulfillment as a community of differing charismatic gifts and services.

The Ecumenical Movement

As Christendom bestirred itself it became conscious of the scandal of its divisions. How can the world acknowledge Christ as the one Lord when the churches bearing witness to him are not one? How can the world expect peace from Christ as long as he has not even brought mutual peace to those who confess him? The disgrace of separation was recognized before God and men as the guilt of Christendom.

In general, the biblical and liturgical movements, responsibility for civil righteousness, etc., have come to life in the various churches spontaneously and independently of others. However, this parallel awakening could not remain hidden from the separated churches. They recognized the activity of the same Christ even beyond the boundaries of their own churches, and the walls between the churches became transparent. This led to encounters among members of different churches, to joint work-programs, to meetings between official representatives of churches, to large conferences, and finally to inclusive organizations in which the churches cooperate.

The ecumenical movement of our age sprang from many fountains and became a stream encompassing all churches. It was no accident that the first strong impulses came from the Christian student movement and from missions. Nowhere is the separation of the churches felt more keenly than in the missionary witness. Since no union is possible without a settlement of the dogmatic, liturgical, and church-political differences, a world conference on Faith and Order was planned alongside the International Missionary council even before the First World War. However, it was not until after the convulsions caused by the First World War that a meeting of that world conference could be arranged, a meeting which concerned itself with the burning issues of practical fellowship in prayer and world service among the churches. This meeting was the first Universal Conference on Life and Work, held in Stockholm in 1925. From this conference came impressive statements expressing the churches' contrition for not fulfilling their obligations and their responsibility for infiltrating all areas of human life with the gospel, and these statements determined the further course of this endeavor. Two years later, in Lausanne, marked the first of the world conferences on Faith and Order, in which the churches by means of careful comparisons became aware of what they had in common in their differences. In 1948, at Amsterdam, both ecumenical movements were joined together in the World Council of Churches, and in 1961 at New Delhi the International Missionary council was merged with the World Council.

The ecumenical movement began within the churches of the Reformation. Very soon, however, it found a most responsive echo in the Orthodox churches of the East. Of pioneer significance for the structuring of the movement was the letter of the Ecumenical Patriarch of Constantinople, January 20, 1920, addressed to "all the churches, wherever they may be." In this letter the Patriarch called upon the churches, in spite of existing doctrinal differences, to create an alliance for mutual support, to refrain from proselytizing, and to seek community of action. Thus, the Orthodox churches, with the exception of the Russian, participated in the world conferences from the beginning. It is true that after the Second World War as well the other Orthodox churches under Communist rule were temporarily kept from further participation, although the Bulgarian and Roumanian churches, especially, had made fruitful contributions to the ecumenical movement in the past. Since 1961, however, all, including the Russian Orthodox church, are members of the World Council of Churches and constitute a living fellowship with the old non-Orthodox oriental churches (Monophysite and Nestorian), with the Lutheran, Reformed, Anglican, Methodist, and other churches of the Reformation, as well as the Old Catholic Church. Today all denominations on earth with the exception of the Roman Catholic Church are represented in the World Council of Churches.

"The World Council of Churches is a fellowship of churches which confess the Lord Jesus Christ as God and Saviour according to the Scriptures and therefore seek to fulfill together their common calling to the glory of the one God, Father, Son, and Holy Spirit" (Constitution of the World Council, I). Agreement with this "Basis" is a prerequisite for membership. Within the work of the World Council it is the specific task of the Faith and Order Commission

> to proclaim the essential oneness of the Church of Christ and to keep prominently before the World Council and the churches the obligation to manifest that unity and its urgency for world mission and evangelism [and also] to study questions of faith, order and worship with the relevant social, cultural, political, racial and other factors in their bearing on the unity of the churches (Constitution, VI, 2).

The member churches of the World Council are not yet united. Again and again, however, they have experienced and publicly attested their unity in Christ, and they seek union on the basis of this oneness. In the certainty of unity in Christ the many churches are no longer in a state of opposition to each other but more and more in a state of being joined together. The fullness of the riches of the same grace and the guidance in history by the same Lord is beginning to transcend the differences in the churches' traditions. The churches are assisting each other in surmounting the barriers of their differences in order that the poor and the harassed among them may experience further development in freedom and in accord with their individuality. Thus the churches support one another by counsel and deed in their missionary concern; they take a common position over against the problems of rapid social upheaval, the emerging nations, racial tensions, economic and political exploitation, etc.; they lend a helping hand to the distressed and issue appeals to governments and nations. Above all, however, the World Council of Churches is a fellowship of faith, prayer, and witness. A great thing has happened when churches which for centuries carried on their separate existence and often fought each other can say together:

> We confess Jesus Christ, Savior of men and the light of the World; Together we accept his command; We commit ourselves anew to bear witness to him among men; We offer ourselves to serve all men in love, that love which he alone imparts; We accept afresh our calling to make visible our unity in him; We pray for the gift of the Holy Spirit for our task (*The New Delhi Report,* ed. W. A. Visser 't Hooft [New York: Association Press, 1962], p. 54).

The World Council of Churches

The ecumenical movement resulted in a conciliar event which finds concrete expression in the plenary assemblies of the World Council.

Representatives of churches from all peoples, races, and nations and from a broad range of ecclesiastical traditions assemble here. They are not only the leaders and theologians of these churches but also lay people, men and women. In these assemblies all churches have equal rights and all their representatives are seated and given the rights of the floor without discrimination. In freedom these assemblies determine their constitution, order of business, program of topics, and they elect their presidents and the chairmen and members of committees. In freedom they discuss the issues and reach their conclusions. The assemblies are greatly enriched by the fact that not only the clergy but also the free charismatic gifts and services of the laity are involved in the deliberations and decisions, and also that laymen may be chosen as presidents of the World Council. As a result, there is an exchange and a common concern for the witness to Christ before the world involving spiritual experiences and impulses not only on the part of different churches and countries, but also on the part of diverse areas of responsibility, the official work of the church, free evangelism, education, social work, economics, political activity, etc.

All deliberations are imbedded in the common worship. They proceed from worship and point toward worship. Just as in the councils of the ancient church as well as in the Roman church, the worship services are not merely the external framework; in a decisive manner they determine and permeate the deliberative and implementing activity as a whole. The chief topics of deliberation are the unity of the churches in Christ and a united witness to Christ in the world of today. Since the representatives of the churches come from the most diverse peoples, races, and countries among whom there are in part considerable tensions and contrasts, further topics suggest themselves. They arise out of the obligation to give thought to the responsibilities which God's loving will imposes upon believers in the midst of the real tensions of today's world, and the obligation to consider the paths which Christians must walk in order to promote peace and help for the oppressed.

These assemblies are ecumenical, on the one hand, in the sense that all churches on earth are invited to participate as full-fledged members of the World Council without any demand for change in their doctrinal, liturgical, or constitutional peculiarities. These assemblies are ecumenical, on the other hand, because of their common concern for the unity of all churches in accordance with the will of the church's Lord. In this endeavor, however, no church can be compelled by a majority vote to deny her insights and to change her identity. If an assembly of the church can be called ecumenical only if all churches on earth are represented in it, then the assemblies of the World Council are not ecumenical since the Roman church in particular is not represented. Yet they are ecumenical as assemblies that are open to all churches and that by a common faith in Christ seek the unity of all churches.

The assemblies of the World Council have many similarities to the structure of the synods of the ancient church. However, even apart from the fact that the ecumenical councils of the ancient church were convoked by the emperor and hence were not free synods, there are such far-reaching differences that the World Council of Churches has never claimed to be a continuation of the ecumenical councils. The most important difference consists in the fact that among a number of member churches there is no communion fellowship at all, or only a limited one, and no mutual recognition of each other's ministry. In the assemblies of the World Council, churches that are separated and in part do not recognize each other as churches in the full sense are joined together in prayer and deliberation. The synods of the ancient church, on the contrary, were supported by a given, though oft imperiled, visible unity of the churches, and for that reason possessed *a priori* a greater authority.

The assemblies of the World Council of Churches therefore represent something new in the history of the church. What constitutes their newness? The synods of the ancient church proceeded from the existing unity of the church and sought to protect and strengthen this unity against threatened disruption in questions of doctrine and order. The assemblies of the World Council, however, presuppose a fragmented Christendom. It is true that they, too, proceed from a unity, namely, the confession of the one Christ as God and Savior. But this oneness in Christ is still concealed under the disunity of the churches. The assemblies *seek* that unity in which this oneness will become visibly manifest and be realized in full church fellowship. They are thus an adventure of faith, of love, and of hope. The plenary sessions of the World Council do not presume to anticipate and represent the desired unity. They do not regard themselves as the guiding instrument for all of Christendom. They only desire to serve and help in the growth of the unity which God creates through his Holy Spirit when and where it pleases him.

2

The Awakening of the Roman Church in the Vatican Council

The processes leading to the loss of security had affected the Roman Catholic Church also. Here, too, many had responded by giving new thought to the church's origins, a response which bore fruit in the liturgical movement, in the rediscovery of the Bible, and in a new consideration of the church and its social responsibility. In many ways these movements were also supported by the church's teaching office. Until recently, however, the Roman church kept herself officially aloof from the ecumenical movement.

On May 16, 1919, a delegation of bishops from the Anglican communion (the Protestant Episcopal Church in North America) visited Pope Benedict XV in order to present an invitation to the Roman church to participate in the first planned ecumenical conference on Faith and Order. While the pope personally gave them a friendly reception he declined their invitation in no uncertain terms, stating that the doctrine and practice of the Roman Catholic Church with regard to the unity of the visible church was well known to everyone, and that hence the Catholic church could not possibly participate in the planned conference. After the World Conference on Faith and Order had been held in 1927, attended by representatives of all denominations except the Roman Catholic Church, Pope Pius XI, in his encyclical *Mortalium Animos* in 1928, reiterated the Roman church's rejection of the ecumenical movement:

> There may be many non-Catholics who loudly promote the brotherly fellowship in Jesus Christ, but there is surely no one who would conceive of submitting himself to the teaching and ruling office of

> the Vicar of Christ. Meanwhile they emphasize that they would gladly negotiate with the Roman church, but only on the same legal basis and only as equals. If, however, such negotiations were arranged, they would doubtless negotiate with the purpose of protecting themselves by contractual agreement from the necessity of yielding those views on the basis of which they continue to this day to roam around aimlessly outside of Christ's only sheep fold. In this state of affairs it is obvious that the Apostolic See can under no circumstances participate in their meetings and that Catholics can under no circumstances favor or promote such endeavors. Thereby they would only increase and strengthen the prestige and influence of a totally false Christian religion which is far removed from the one church of Christ. . . .

In the encyclical *Mystici Corporis* (1943), Pius XII was equally negative about the ecumenical movement. In this encyclical the boundaries of the mystical body of Christ are made identical to the legally constituted Roman church. In 1948 some Catholic theologians, whose hearts yearned for fellowship with non-Roman Christians, wanted to participate as guests and observers at the world conference of churches in Amsterdam, where the World Council of Churches was established. However, they were forbidden by the competent church authority to do so. Shortly thereafter, on December 20, 1949, the Instruction of the Holy Office concerning the ecumenical movement explicitly warned against the dangers of irenics and indifferentism and permitted interdenominational meetings only if there was well-founded prospect of success, that is, of bringing the separated back to the Roman church. Otherwise, such meetings were to be promptly adjourned. When in 1954 some Catholic theologians had traveled to Evanston to participate as observers at the assembly of the World Council, they were forbidden even to enter the city limits. Coupled with such prohibitions were occasions when pointed slights were administered to prominent Roman theologians who had embraced the cause of ecumenism. This is all the more startling since the Roman church, too, had experienced severe losses in influence, security, and membership, and was confronted by the same new problems as the other churches. Nevertheless, in spite of many parallels between the renewal movements on both sides, direct contact between them was confined almost entirely to personal relationships that were generally regarded with suspicion by Rome. These contacts could not develop into open cooperation. This extremely negative attitude of the Roman church rested on the conviction that it was in itself already the one holy catholic and apostolic church.

A thoroughgoing change in attitude toward other churches was brought about by Pope John XXIII, who is remembered with admiration and love by many non-Roman Christians too. He established the Secretariat for Promoting Christian Unity and under the leadership of Cardinal Bea gave it so many possibilities for success that non-Catholic visitors at the Vatican soon became aware of a change in atmosphere. Pope John sent Roman Catholic observers to the plenary assembly of the World Council at New Delhi in 1961. He assigned extremely important tasks to the Secretariat for Christian Unity in preparation for Vatican II and he invited non-Roman churches and the World Council to send observers to the Vatican Council. He summoned Catholic theologians who were open to ecumenism but had previously been under suspicion to serve as Council theologians, and he made ecumenism the theme of the Council. At the Council he created an atmosphere of fraternal openness which led to an objectively fruitful and humanly felicitous exchange between the observers and many Council Fathers and theologians.

Convoking and Preparing for the Council

A few months after his election as successor to Pope Pius XII, John XXIII, on January 25, 1959, amid general surprise, announced the convoking of an ecumenical council which, according to his intention, was not only to serve the edification of the Catholic church but was also to be an invitation to the separated churches to join in the search for unity. This announcement was widely understood to mean that non-Roman churches, especially the Orthodox, were to be invited to participate in a union council. It soon became clear, however, that the pope had in mind only a council of bishops of the Roman church, which was nevertheless termed an ecumenical council because, as the Roman church sees things, all its councils are designated as ecumenical. In spite of this limitation concerning those who could vote and enjoy full privileges of the floor, the goal which the pope had in mind for this council was not restricted to the Roman church.

The Council's task was to be, above all, the renewal and strengthening of the Roman church herself, and during the time of preparation Pope John XXIII in ever new turns of speech kept reminding all participants of this task. This renewal was to proceed not in further dogmatic delimitations against heresies but in positively developing the faith, in turning toward the man of today and adapting to him (*aggiornamento*).

> In the modern era of a world with sharply altered features, a world that had difficulty maintaining itself over against the enchantments and dangers of an almost exclusive striving for material goods . . . , there is more at issue than retracing this or that doctrine or discipline back to the pure sources of revelation and tradition; at issue is the substance of human and Christian thought and life for which the church is the *guardian and teacher and must again be* made effectual and shining.[1]

Of the common worship services, deliberations, and decisions of the Council, however, John XXIII expected not only a new flowering of the spiritual life in the Roman Catholic Church, a new Pentecost, but also an impact on other churches and on the world. He wanted the Council to be a "remarkable display of truth, unity and love"—"a display which those who are cut off from this Apostolic See will observe. We sincerely hope that they will receive it as a gentle invitation to seek and to acquire that unity which Jesus Christ prayed for so ardently to His heavenly Father."[2]

[1] Address to the members and advisers of all commissions preparing for the Council, November 14, 1960. *Herder-Korrespondenz*, 15 (1961), 167.

[2] Encyclical, *Ad Petri Cathedram,* 1959, Part 3; in Ann Freemantle (ed.), *The Papal Encyclicals in Their Historical Context* (New York: New American Library, 1963), p. 320.

Hence the Council was also planned with the other churches in view.

The reasons for convoking this Council have been sought in the external situation of the Roman church—in her extensive isolation from the modern world, in the social backwardness of many Catholic countries, in the menace of communism, in the church's isolation from other churches which, including the Orthodox churches, had meanwhile joined together in the World Council of Churches. However, the controlling motive for announcing the Council is to be looked for elsewhere. According to John XXIII, the idea of the Council was not the result of lengthy premeditation. Rather, the idea came to him as a divine impulse while he was at prayer, as an inspiration, as if he had suddenly been touched by God.[3] This stimulus led the affectionate outreach to men, so characteristic of him, to determine the tasks of the Council and what he expected of the Council—the creation of a new fellowship with the separated brethren and, beyond them, a fellowship with all who are yet afar off.

Preparations for the Council were quickly begun in a comprehensive manner. The bishops of the world, as well as the boards of the Roman Curia, and the superiors of religious orders and Catholic faculties, were asked to list frankly the problems which they felt should be taken up at the Council. These replies were published in many volumes—eight of them for the bishops' replies alone—to be of use in the internal preparation for the Council. The replies were then worked through in a systematic way. Attention was given to overlapping proposals and an attempt was made to make the selection of desired topics as comprehensive as possible. On Pentecost Monday, 1960, ten preparatory commissions and three secretariats, including the Secretariat for Promoting Christian Unity, were established, and the topics for the Council were distributed among the commissions which would

---

[3] Cf. *Acta et Documenta Concilio Oecumenico Vaticano II Apparando* (Rome, 1960).

work out the proposals to be placed before the Council (*schemata*). These commissions dealing with the various themes were subordinated to a central commission which was to review and approve the *schemata* prepared by the separate commissions before they were given to the Council Fathers. Beyond question, it was in this way that the Council was prepared most comprehensively and carefully. Before the Council got under way some seventy *schemata* had been worked out, but only seven of them reached the Council Fathers as bases for discussion before the first sessions. A second volume with two additional *schemata* was published in November, 1962.

The Structure of a Council of the Roman Church

Pope John's proclamation of an ecumenical council evoked so much surprise primarily because of the widespread opinion since the end of the First Vatican Council (1870) that future councils of the Roman church would henceforth be unnecessary, perhaps even impossible. Vatican I had defined the primacy of the bishop of Rome as consisting of supreme and plenary power over the church and the infallibility of his definitive decisions in matters of faith and morals. According to Canon 218 of the Codex of Canon Law, the Roman pontiff possesses "not only a primacy of honor, but the supreme and plenary power of jurisdiction over the entire church, both in matters of faith and morals as well as in matters that concern the discipline and government of the church scattered over the entire globe." This had made a council of the Roman church superfluous in principle. In the case that a council is convened, it is henceforth completely dependent on the greater or lesser willingness of the pope to listen to the voice of the bishops. The pope alone has the right to convene a council, to determine the program and order of business, to appoint the preparatory commissions and the presiding officers, and to lend authority to the decisions of the council fathers. Only by his consent and promulgation do the decisions become the official resolutions of the council. On the basis of these considerations there arose not only the question whether a council of the Roman church was still necessary, but even whether under these presuppositions genuine conciliar activity was still possible, since one individual member of this church had been granted such all-embracing power over the entire church.

Because of this constitutional structure, a council of the Roman church differs from the councils of all other churches. Such a dominant position of the bishop of Rome was also unknown to the ancient church councils. As the Second Ecumenical Council of Constantinople (381) demonstrates, the presence of the bishop of Rome or his legate was not essential for the concept and the validity of an ecumenical council of the ancient church.

In the more recent history of Roman councils a profound change has also come over the composition of the council. While in a number of medieval councils large numbers of laymen still participated, the delegates today are exclusively clerical. Participants with seats and voices in the council are now limited to the bishops, or more accurately, to cardinals, patriarchs, primates, archbishops, bishops, certain abbots, and other representatives of the upper clergy. In contrast to the so-called Apostolic Council (Acts 15), the synods of the first centuries, and also the synods of the Reformation churches and some of the Orthodox synods, the church's laity is completely excluded. They can be given a hearing only indirectly, to the extent that the bishops make the concerns of the laity their own. In the formulation of decisions, the cooperation of the lower clergy is also excluded.

Furthermore, a council of the Roman church differs from the councils or synods of other churches in that it calls itself an "ecumenical council," even though seat and voice in the council are granted only to bishops of the Roman church, not to those of the Orthodox church and the non-Roman churches of the West. This title is claimed even when it is not a union council and when the council program concerns itself in no other way with the reunion of the separated churches. The Roman church calls her general councils ecumenical because, in principle, she recognizes no other church as a church in the true and full sense of the word. According to her self-understanding the Roman church is already in herself the one holy catholic and apostolic church on earth. In contrast, all other churches, including both the Reformation churches and the Orthodox churches, have refrained from calling their own synods ecumenical councils, because of the divisions in the church. Accordingly, no other church recognizes the general councils of the Roman church as ecumenical. This is one of the reasons that the Orthodox churches were so hesitant about sending observers to Vatican II. Also, in calling themselves ecumenical the councils of the Roman church differ from the ecumenical councils of the ancient church, which could rightfully claim that title because the Eastern and Western churches were united.

Thus, in comparison with the councils of the ancient church, the councils of the Roman church, too, are a novelty in the history of councils. Our view of this state of affairs must not be clouded by the idea that the councils have become what they are today as a result of a process of historical evolution, and thus preserve the appearance of a continuity. Yet this evolution, which went through considerable zigzagging during the late Middle Ages, has resulted in profound changes from the structure of the ancient church councils.

The councils of the Roman church are, indeed, a novelty in a sense quite different from, yes, even opposite to, that of the assemblies of the World Council of Churches. While the latter have their starting point in the fragmented state of Christendom, the Roman councils disregard all churches not under the pope and proceed from the premise of the internal visible unity of the Roman church. The assemblies of the World Council seek to embrace all Christendom and, on the basis of a confession of Christ shared by all participants, seek to push forward to joint declarations on questions of faith and order, and beyond that to joint work and visible unity; the way of the Roman councils, on the contrary, has been determined by the will of an increasingly dogmatic and canonical guarantee and confirmation of the church's own existing visible unity, which non-Roman Christians were then invited to join. While the danger threatening the World Council of Churches lies in its member churches confining themselves to the busyness of joint work, instead of achieving visible unity, the Roman church is in danger of shutting herself up in a self-centered solipsism, instead of recognizing the catholic fullness of Christ active on earth.

The First Period of the Council

Following the solemn processional of far more than two thousand bishops through the portals of St. Peter's and after the Mass celebrated with the invocation of the Holy Spirit, Pope John XXIII opened the Council with an impressive address which gave the Council Fathers a significant orientation and at the same time permitted them full freedom in treating the topics before the Council. Particular attention was given to the pope's warning against a pessimistic assessment of this present age and the admonition to distinguish between "the substance of the ancient doctrine of the deposit of faith [*depositum fidei*] . . . and the way in which it is presented." The Catholic doctrine must be set forth "through the methods of research and through the literary forms of modern thought,"[4] and above all with a pastoral application. The church meets the needs of today "by demonstrating the validity of her teaching rather than by condemnations [of heresies]."[5]

In the first business session on the next day there was to be an election of the members of the Council's ten commissions on the basis of suggested slates which listed primarily the members of the preparatory commissions. On a motion of Cardinals Lienart and Frings, the election was postponed to give the Council Fathers an opportunity to discuss suitable persons. Circles within the Council drafted their own slates, and the election results

[4] *The Documents of Vatican II,* ed. Walter M. Abbott (New York: Guild Press, 1966), p. 715. Hereafter cited as *Documents.*

[5] *Documents,* p. 716.

showed not only the Council's independence over against the Curia and its nominees but also its desire to secure the progressive forces their proper place in the activities of the Council.

This step, which created a sensation, was taken because the Council was disappointed in the issues worked out by the preparatory commissions, especially by the theological commission standing close to the Holy Office. In view of the status of Catholic theology, particularly in France and Germany, the proposals laid before the Council were astonishingly behind the times. Thus, for example, if the *schema* of the Constitution on the Sources of Revelation had been followed, modern Catholic exegetes could not possibly have continued their work. Again, the *schema* of the Constitution on the Purity and Preservation of the Faith so indiscriminately coordinated the rejections of various errors of our time that it failed completely to reflect the pastoral goals of the Council. Equally backward was the manner in which a *schema* on marriage had been developed. It was obvious that the representatives of a new Catholic theology had not succeeded in making their point in the preparatory commissions in opposition to the prevailing conservative forces. Added to this was the fact that in advance of the Council many of these deficiences had been criticized in the central commission but in spite of the criticisms had not been rectified before the texts were sent to the Council Fathers. In this state of affairs the fathers detected an arbitrary procedure on the part of the circles around the Curia and they were not willing to yield to them. Further sources of irritation, including some of long standing, also played a role.

This first independent decision of the Council blazed a trail for the freedom in which the deliberations and the alignments among the Council Fathers then proceeded. It is not our purpose at this point to offer a detailed history of the Council. We are most interested in the content of its decisions and their significance for the rest of Christendom. Yet in this chapter we must picture the impressive dynamics of the entire process. We must see the breakthrough achieved by the progressive forces, the growth of these forces, and their restraint in the presence of the obligation to reach joint decisions in cooperation with the forces of retardation.

The Council's discussion began with the *schema* of the Constitution on the Sacred Liturgy. This *schema* was the most advanced and its subject matter must have been closest to every bishop's heart from the start. For this reason it was best suited to create a proper synodical atmosphere in a short time. It was by no means obvious that the more than two thousand bishops would experience a synodical solidarity so quickly. The questions broached in this *schema* concerning the vernacular and the liturgical laws of the territorial bishops' conferences were already of great significance, especially since important questions regarding views on the church were already involved in the questions dealing with liturgical practice. Especially prominent was the understanding of the unity of which the common use of the Latin liturgical language had hitherto been a component. What is the relationship of unity, uniformity, and variety? In the course of this discussion, the interest in a pastoral outreach to the man of today and his capacity for understanding, an interest of great importance for the further course of the Council, began to grow quickly and to assert itself against the traditional liturgical order. The dramatic aspects of the discussion were heightened in connection with the *schema* on the Sources of Revelation. This *schema* was directed against modern Catholic biblical scholarship and moved along the lines of recent attacks in Rome on the work of the Pontifical Biblical Institute. The *schema* also rejected an interpretation of Trent that attempted to upgrade the Holy Scriptures by viewing them as the source of the total revelation, not only a part of it. Also highly dramatic were the objections—especially on the part of the Melchitic Patriarch Maximos—to the *schema* for a Constitution on the Unity of the Church which contained the conditions for reunion of the Orthodox church with the Roman church. These conditions were regarded by the Orthodox as offensive rather than inviting.

There was more at stake in these and other discussions than the texts themselves. What happened here was a loosening up of the Council, and the dynamics of this fact rightfully made a deep impression outside the Roman church as well. By means of an impressive self-criticism there was strong pressure for a renewal of the church. The Council Fathers demanded dynamic activity instead of a static self-understanding, moving ahead instead of standing still, the courage to be poor instead of insistence on the guarantees of power and glory, an openness toward the separated brethren instead of isolation based on the desire to defend oneself. Beyond this was the demand for a new approach to the world. More and more of the Council Fathers were seized by this new stance, and before long the others became a minority and were pushed back on the defensive. It became evident that elementary spiritual forces are alive in the Roman church, forces which had often remained hidden under ritualistic, juridical, and scholastic forms and which now came to the fore by means of the encounter within the Council. These forces attempted to batter the walls in order to serve God and man in a new and direct way. The press repeatedly spoke of a battle between the "progressive" and the "conservative" forces of the Council. However, apart from the fact that even during tense moments the deliberations were conducted in a dignified and objective way, these labels are misleading. The "progressives" have very little in common with modernism or liberalism; on the contrary, they are oriented in a new way toward the theology of the ancient church fathers and are therefore really representatives of the old. The "conservatives," on the other hand, are really the modernists in the church's history since they support the positions of the Catholicism developed since the Counter-Reformation, positions fortified in the last century by means of the theology of neo-scholasticism. At stake in the upsurge of the "progressives" was, therefore, an ecumenically significant reconsideration of the biblical and creedal foundations which all churches have in common. From this perspective, the "progressives" sought in a new way to come to grips with the problems and tasks confronting Christendom today.

The rapid spread of this movement could not have succeeded without the theologians who were assembled in Rome either as theologians of the Council or as theological advisers of their bishops. Pope John XXIII had not hesitated to call on the most determined sponsors of the new theology, men who under his predecessor were kept back and continued to be suspect by the Holy Office. Thus John had made it possible for representatives of all theological schools of thought in the Roman church to be present at the Council. What such forward-looking theologians as, for example, the Germans Karl Rahner, Küng, and Ratzinger, and the Frenchmen Congar, Daniélou, and de Lubac accomplished, can hardly be overestimated. It is true that their contributions could not be given expression directly in the assembly hall, since only bishops had seats and voices in the Council. Yet in many addresses at conferences of bishops, and in countless conversations, they provided insight into their view of the problems discussed in the *schemata.* Many bishops still held captive by the scholastic theology of their student days came to see that the new theology, which at first seemed strange to them, opened up the possibility of grasping the problems of our time more aptly than could have been done by the scholastic theology with its thought patterns so foreign to the thinking of today. This in effect led to conversions in theological thinking during the Council, and in increasing number the bishops entrusted themselves to the advice of precisely these "progressive" theologians as they worked out their formal opinions for the discussions.

This upheaval also exerted its influence on the relationship between the Council Fathers and the observers representing non-Roman churches. There were, of course, cardinals, bishops, and theologians who shook their heads at the pope's ecumenical interests and consented only because it was their duty to obey. Perhaps this consent was made easier by the thought that the presence of the official observers and guests from the various churches might appear to the world as a gathering of all churches around the pope. They treated the observers with a carefully accented politeness while maintaining their reserve. Others enthusiastically believed that they could leap over the existing differences among the churches and the history of separation among the churches. Moreover, they expected that the impact of the Council would arouse in the observers an irresistible pressure for a return to the Roman church. They approached the observers with an embracing certainty of victory. There were also, however, those who took seriously the reasons for the separations and the conscientious position of Christians separated from Rome; these felt the existence of other churches as a genuine question addressed to the Roman church. They had no firm conception of the way to union but began by asking in fraternal openness about the truths by which the others live, and in turn witnessed to them the truth by which they themselves live. Here there were genuine encounters and here grew ecumenical insights which give promise of bearing fruit. The number of those who sought such frank conversation with the observers increased, and as a result there was an exchange in depth concerning the proposals before the Council. In promoting these encounters the Secretariat for Promoting Christian Unity achieved outstanding success. Every week the Secretariat invited men to a joint meeting with the observers and expected these to subject the texts currently under consideration to a critical review. Many of the opinions of the observers were then referred by the Secretariat to the proper commissions of the Council for consideration. More than once ideas expressed by observers were incorporated in the opinions of the Council Fathers or in the editing of the texts.

Pope John deserves the chief credit for the fact that the Council was able to develop in this freedom. His intervention in the affairs of the Council became apparent only twice: once when he interrupted the discussion on the liturgy and insisted on the inclusion of St. Joseph in the canon of the Mass, and again when he set aside the *schema* on the Sources of Revelation as a basis for discussion. Here, however, the pope decided in favor of the majority of the Council Fathers, who by themselves had not commanded two thirds of the vote. Thus the Council began as a magnetic field with three poles: Pope, Council, and Curia, or, more accurately, the pope, the Curia together with the "conservative" bishops, and the "progressives," who included only a few representatives of the Curia. In contrast to the First Vatican Council and the Council of Trent, the pope and the Curia did not form a single pole. Only in this way it was possible for the progressive majority of the Council to defeat the backward forces of the Curia in many ballots.

The Second and Third Periods of the Council

John XXIII was sincerely revered and loved far beyond the borders of the Roman church and his passing was equally mourned. Anxiously, questions were asked: Who will succeed him? Will he continue the Council? How will he go about it? When Cardinal Montini, formerly secretary of state under Pius XII and archbishop of Milan, was elected, he ascended the papal throne as Paul VI. He quickly confirmed the Council and in a letter to Cardinal Tisserand, chairman of the Council Praesidium, he tightened up the organization of the Council's program in several important ways, and also admitted several of the laity as auditors to the Council sessions (at first only men, but later also some women).

In his address at the beginning of the second period of the Council the new pope fully affirmed the task imposed on the Council by his predecessor. Speaking directly to the deceased he said:

> Conscious of the church's teaching office, you have revived the conviction that Christian doctrine is to be not only a truth which is investigated by a reason illuminated by faith, but also a word which creates life and action, and that the authority of the church dare not confine itself to the condemnation of heresies conflicting with the faith, but must also extend to the proclamation of those positive and vital doctrines by which faith is fruitful.

Beyond this Paul VI added depth to the program of his predecessor. In an extremely urgent manner he set Christ before the assembly as the starting point, the way, and the goal of the Council's total program. The four themes of the Council—the self-understanding of the church, the reformation of the church, the reunion of all Christians, and the church's dialogue with the world of today—were to be treated in a christocentric way. In connection with the presentations on the third theme, the Pope addressed the observers from non-Roman churches as follows:

> If we are in any way to blame for this separation, we humbly beg God for forgiveness and we also ask the brothers who feel offended by us to forgive us. As for us, we are ready to pardon the insults that have struck the Catholic church and to forget the pain that has been inflicted upon her in the long course of disagreements and separations.

The Pope's references to guilt are conditional and the dogmatic decisions of the Roman church are excluded from this confession of guilt. Nevertheless, this fact must not keep us from recognizing the fifth petition of the Lord's Prayer in these words, nor from responding in an appropriate way. The Pope movingly assured the observers of the sincerity of his approach to them and of his respect for "the original and common religious heritage that was preserved among the separated brethren and was in part well developed by them."

The forces of renewal in the Council were able to interpret this address as an encouragement. Hence, in their discussion on the church and ecumenism they continued to push forward topics which during this period had the focus of attention together with religious liberty and Israel. The dynamics of the first sessions were given greater theological depth as the rather conservative *schema* on the church was criticized and as the ecumenical idea, new to most of the fathers, was accepted. More and more emphasis was laid on a view of the church and her relation to the world in terms of salvation history and eschatology. Explicitly biblical concepts were preferred to the thought patterns of a scholastic dogmatics of the schools. These presuppositions led to an increasing receptivity for God's saving activity beyond the boundaries of the Roman church as well. The non-Roman churches were drawn into the deliberations from new perspectives and there was a constantly increasing awareness of the dimensions of variety within the church's unity. The dynamics of the Council began to assert themselves in methodical and basic conceptions.

Also during the second period, more and more aligned themselves with the progressive approach to the Roman church's renewal, and the forces of retardation appeared to have become a still smaller minority. At the same time it became clear that this minority clung to its position and could not be overcome, especially since it had a strong reserve in the Curia. Furthermore, especially in the discussions concerning collegiality, it became clearer than in the first period that the authoritative dogmatic and canonical obligations of the Roman church imposed limits on every renewal of that church, and that the forces of resistance could with some justification appeal to this fact. In addition, the slow pace at which the work of the Council proceeded was increasingly felt to be oppressive. At the end of the second period only the Constitution on the Sacred Liturgy and a rather superficial Decree on the Instruments of Social Communication (press, radio, television) could be released. And even though the original seventy *schemata* had been condensed into seventeen, there were still a large number of proposals which had not yet been accepted as a basis for discussion or which needed to be reworked because of the widely divergent opinions expressed in the discussion. Also, some texts had not yet been given to the Council Fathers. These facts may well have influenced the Pope's addresses at the close of the second period and at the beginning of the third. His remarks were more cautious than his first address and they could no longer be interpreted as an incentive for the progressive forces.

The third period of sessions demonstrated that these forces had by no means been immobilized. In the questions concerning the relationship of Scripture and tradition, and also, particularly, in the concern for a new relationship to the world of today, significant advances were made. At the same time there began in increasing measure a search for compromises which would have a chance of being adopted. This became especially evident in the discussions on the Marian theme. In spite of the obviously negative impact which this course of action would have on non-Roman churches, "progressive" bishops now began to minimize their objections to the demand of the "conservatives" that Mary be designated "Mediatrix," while the counterpart seemed no longer, as in the past, to insist on the demand that Mary be designated "Mother of the Church." These and other compromises made it possible for the *schemata* on the church and on ecumenism to be adopted by large majorities in the voting on their individual paragraphs.

It became clear at the end of the third period, however, that the minority sought to achieve its goals not only by its contributions in the sessions and in the commissions, but also by exerting hidden pressures on the procedures of the Council and by laying claim to the papal authority. On November 16, surprisingly, a "guiding explanatory note" (*nota explicativa praevia*) to chapter iii of the *schema* on the church was distributed. This note, which claimed permanent validity, defined the freedom of the pope over against the college of bishops and thus shifted the accents in the text which had already been voted on and adopted by the Council. On November 19, a previously scheduled vote on the *schema* on religious liberty was surprisingly put aside and a petition to the Pope, sponsored by American bishops and supported by many hundreds of signatures in a few hours, was rejected. Furthermore, the highest authority made nineteen textual changes in the Decree on Ecumenism, which had already been adopted in detail by the Council. Several of these changes clearly weakened the intended ecumenical thrust of the document. These interventions caused great consternation and dejection among most of the Council Fathers, since a different "collegial" understanding of the relationship between pope and bishops had meanwhile established itself. Finally, in the public closing session on November 21, the Pope proclaimed Mary as "Mother of the Church," although in its Marian text the Council had deliberately avoided the use of this title.

There can be no doubt that in accordance with the structure of a council in the Roman church the Pope was justified in intervening as he did. Yet it is difficult to understand why he acted as he did. His interventions damaged the prestige of the Council in world opinion and undermined confidence in the Council's synodical freedom. Did the Pope want to come to the aid of the minority and prevent a repetition of what happened at Vatican I—now, however, involving not the opponents but the supporters of the definition of primacy as then formulated? Did he wish to appease the Curia since he had to rely on its cooperation in a special way? Did he see in the trends of the progressive bishops a threat to his own primacy and power? In any case, the constellation of forces at the end of the third period had undergone a change over against the first period. The Pope now appeared to be making common cause with the Curia and the conservative minority, and the tripolarity of forces appeared to have become bipolar.

The Close of the Council

The sessions of the fourth period produced no new advances, not even in the treatment of the *schema* on the Church in the Modern World, still the most controversial *schema*. It was now a matter of bringing the Council to a close. Apart from the questions of celibacy and birth control, the Pope imposed no limits on the discussions. It was reported that his wishes for changes were submitted not as decisions of the Pope but as opinions of the bishop of Rome, which should be treated in the same way as the opinions of other bishops. Yet he did attach importance to a formulation of the definitive texts in such a way that in the final balloting there might be as few opposing votes as possible. In this way the conservative minority was given greater weight than its number warranted. As a result, the resolutions were undoubtedly watered down in a number of cases. But the significance of this must not be overestimated. A comparison of the final official texts with the first drafts clearly demonstrates what great advances were made and how many of the new departures were retained in spite of compromise formulations. A joke, which did not originate among the observers, compared the Council with a dance that went one step forward, one step backward, one step left, and one step right, and everybody turns himself around. It is only fair to add that the forward steps were much larger than the backward steps.

The fourth period of sessions was characterized especially by the editorial work of the committees and the many votes taken. In this period, eleven proposals were adopted and proclaimed by the Pope. Only with the highest admiration can one think of the excellent work which the commissions accomplished in these extremely difficult final revisions. For some of the *schemata* there were thousands of proposed amendments which in part were quite contradictory. Every proposal had to be carefully examined in the light of the total thrust of the past discussion, and its ultimate adoption or rejection had to be precisely justified. All this was accomplished with admirable care and in great loyalty to all the Council Fathers so that to the very end further clarifications were achieved.

The fact that the proposals before the Council were almost all adopted by an overwhelming majority is due to the work of the commissions. This consensus was not the result of weariness nor of an act of obedience to a formal obligation to unity but the fruit of a cooperative endeavor in the course of which the matters were objectively debated and a meeting of minds was achieved. Looking back on the fourth period of sessions, one can say that, within the limitations of a council of the Roman church, Vatican II provided a genuine synodical experience, more so than Vatican I. Papal diplomacy was responsible for the apparent absence of victors and vanquished at the close of the Council.

In spite of all advances, a great gap still exists between the separated churches. This became clear toward the close of the Council in the statements on the question of indulgences, which provided the occasion for the Reformation and which are rejected also by the Orthodox church. In spite of many pointed Catholic criticisms of the indulgence practice, there was hardly a voice that questioned indulgences as such. This state of affairs is reflected in the specifications of the apostolic constitution *Mirificus Eventus* in which the Pope proclaimed a council jubilee in connection with the institution of the holy year.

On December 7 and 8 the Council was brought to its brilliant close. Several days earlier a joint service was held in St. Paul's Basilica Outside the Walls, in which the Pope, the bishops, and the observers participated. Lections and prayers were read alternately by Catholic theologians and non-Catholic observers, and the Pope gave a warmhearted farewell address to the representatives of non-Roman Christendom. On December 7 the Pope proclaimed the last four resolutions of the Council. Furthermore, a papal brief was read and presented to the legate of the Ecumenical Patriarch Athenagoras. In this brief the Pope expressed his regret concerning the excommunication of the Patriarch Cerularius in 1054 and the consequences of this act for both the Roman and the Orthodox churches. This was an impressive gesture of a willingness to be reconciled. On December 8 the Pope concluded the Council in a public and solemn ceremony in St. Peter's Square. All sixteen resolutions were implemented as being perpetually valid and the bishops promised to maintain them for ever. At the same time the universality of the Roman church was demonstrated by means of words of greeting to the sick, laborers, artists, and others.

3

The Resolutions of the Council

The great number of resolutions of the Council, the variety of topics, and their unusual total scope correspond to the comprehensive task of the *aggiornamento* which Pope John XXIII had assigned to the Council, as well as to the comprehensive consideration of the questions which the bishops had requested of the Council. The total volume of documents far exceeds that produced by any of the ancient ecumenical councils, any of the later councils of the Roman church, or even by the Council of Trent, whose sessions covered a span of eighteen years (1545-63).

Constitutions, Decrees, Declarations

As late as the third period of sessions the Council was still dealing with five categories of *schemata,* namely, constitutions, decrees, declarations, propositions, and a *votum* on the sacrament of marriage. In the final results, however, only three categories of conciliar resolutions were distinguished. The sixteen resolutions are listed below in chronological order within each category, including the Latin words by which they are known and the date of their solemn promulgation by the Pope.

Constitutions:

Constitution on the Sacred Liturgy (*Sacrosanctum Concilium*), December 4, 1963.

Dogmatic Constitution on the Church (*Lumen Gentium*), November 21, 1964.

Dogmatic Constitution on Divine Revelation (*Dei Verbum*), November 18, 1965.

Pastoral Constitution on the Church in the Modern World (*Gaudium et Spes*), December 7, 1965.

Decrees:

Decree on the Instruments of Social Communication (*Inter Mirifica*), December 4, 1963.

Decree on Eastern Catholic Churches (*Orientalium Ecclesiarum*), November 21, 1964.

Decree on Ecumenism (*Unitatis Redintegratio*), November 21, 1964.

Decree on the Bishops' Pastoral Office in the Church (*Christus Dominus*), October 28, 1965.

Decree on Priestly Formation (*Optatam Totius Ecclesiae Renovationem*), October 28, 1965.

Decree on the Appropriate Renewal of the Religious Life (*Perfectae Caritatis*), October 28, 1965.

Decree on the Apostolate of the Laity (*Apostolicam Actuositatem*), November 18, 1965.

Decree on the Church's Missionary Activity (*Ad Gentes*), December 7, 1965.

Decree on the Ministry and Life of Priests (*Presbyterorum Ordinis*), December 7, 1965.

Declarations:

Declaration on Christian Education (*Gravissimum Educationis Momentum*), October 28, 1965.

Declaration on the Relationship of the Church to non-Christian Religions (*Nostra Aetate*), October 28, 1965.

Declaration on Religious Freedom (*Dignitatis Humanae Personae*), December 7, 1965.

How do these three categories of conciliar resolutions differ from each other? The answer to this question would not be easy if one tried to formulate definitions on the basis of how these terms were used in the history of the church. The word "constitution" had been used in various ways in the past, and the words "decree" and "declaration" have also, in the course of church history, been applied to very heterogeneous decisions and documents. In Vatican II the Constitutions are those resolutions in which a leading theme comprising many individual questions is treated in a fundamental way. The Decrees provide guidance for specific themes—frequently with explicit reference to basic decisions made in the constitutions. The Declarations on Religious Freedom and on the Relationship of the Church to non-Christian Religions are basic explanations of specific themes. The Declaration on Christian Education could also have been designated a decree.

Among the constitutions themselves there are further differences in nomenclature. The Constitutions on the Church and on Revelation are explicitly named "Dogmatic Constitutions," and the one on the Church in the Modern World is called a "Pastoral Constitution," while the Constitution on the Sacred Liturgy, without further qualification, establishes the principles underlying liturgical reform. The last two constitutions also proceed from dogmatic considerations, the Pastoral Constitution, in particular, proceeding from the doctrine of man, while the Constitution on the Sacred Liturgy proceeds from the perspective of the ecclesiological significance of worship. On this foundation the fundamental directives for the common life in human society are provided in the Pastoral Constitution, and the directives for further efforts in liturgical reform are given in the Constitution on the Sacred Liturgy. The Dogmatic Constitutions on the Church and on Divine Revelation do, however, occupy a pre-eminent place because these two present a fully articulated dogmatic treatment of the doctrine. This was also the case in the Vatican I Dogmatic Constitutions on the Catholic Faith and on the Church (papal primacy). It is noteworthy that, in contrast to the Council of Trent and Vatican I, the dogmatic constitutions of Vatican II contain no canons, that is, no anathemas of heterodox teaching. There is no precedent for the designation "pastoral" constitution in conciliar history. For further discussion see Chapter 8.

As to the degree of binding authority, the two dogmatic constitutions should be given first rank. The other two constitutions deal to a greater extent with statements subject to change. Indeed, not the foundation but the shape of the liturgy and certainly the world situation are historically subject to change. The same could be said of many statements in the decrees. The significance of the declarations is of more limited scope than that of the constitutions. The pre-eminent rank of the two dogmatic constitutions is further enhanced by the fact that they are repeatedly cited as authoritative foundation for the decrees and even for the pastoral constitution. This is true particularly of the Constitution on the Church.

Are the dogmatic constitutions to be designated as dogma in the strict sense of the word? This question was raised repeatedly and was answered by the pertinent commission on the doctrine of faith and of morals in this way: "In accordance with the sense of conciliar custom and with the pastoral goal of this Council" only what the Council explicitly featured as a defined dogma is to be acknowledged as such. Hence the dogmatic constitutions as a whole are by no means dogma in the formal sense of an irreformable and infallible decision. Rather, they are specific statements explicitly featured as dogmatic definitions. Most of the Council theologians are of the opinion that such definitions are lacking altogether, as indicated also by the absence of condemnatory formulas. Consequently, the Council kept to the pastoral task assigned to it by John XXIII and avoided the establishment of new dogmas by which the gap between the Roman church and others would have been widened. This is of special ecumenical significance in view of statements in the Constitution on the Church concerning Mary as Mediatrix. For although this title goes beyond the official Marian dogmas of the Roman church, it is itself not yet a dogma. Evidently this does not deny that the dogmatic statements of the Council are extremely significant and lay a claim on the members of the Roman church more binding than the papal encyclicals.

An Attempt to Present the Decisions of the Council in Systematic Order

At first glance, the themes treated in the Council documents and mentioned in their titles appear to present a bewildering variety. This is the result of the large number of themes suggested by the bishops for consideration and the adoption of the sixteen texts reduced from the original number of more than seventy *schemata.* Although it is true that the comprehensive scope and variety of the themes is most impressive, it must be remembered that many overlappings and repetitions have resulted from this development. Furthermore, many things which belong together were separated and distributed among various documents, as, for example, the juxtaposition of the Decree on the Church's Missionary Activity and the Declaration on Non-Christian Religions. The same is true of occasional discrepancies. Thus, the defining of the relationship between church and world as expressed in the Constitution on the Church and in the Decree on Missionary Activity appears to be closer to the New Testament material than the corresponding statements in the Pastoral Constitution on the Church in the Modern World.

In attempting to arrange the many conciliar decisions in systematic order based on their content, it must be borne in mind that it was no accident that the proposals on the sacred liturgy were discussed and adopted first of all. It is true that even in its first draft this document was in a more advanced stage than the other *schemata.* Yet the structure of themes suggested that this matter be considered first. In a unique way the life of the church is concentrated in the practice of worship. In worship God's manifest saving activity for man takes place; here men are built up into the church through Christ's present activity; here those who have been called out of the world are sent by God back into the world. Here men respond to God's saving deed as they praise, invoke, and confess him, surrender themselves to him, proceed into the world to bear witness to him, and present their bodies in his service as "a living sacrifice, holy and acceptable to God" (Rom. 12:1). The life of the church is concentrated in the act of worship as a fellowship of the gathered in reciprocal receiving and serving, and at the same time as a fellowship of all worshiping assemblies on earth with the liturgy of those who have reached the goal and who preceded us in the faith, and with the song of praise offered by the whole of creation.

Beginning our systematization with the Constitution on the Sacred Liturgy, we may then view the Dogmatic Constitution on Divine Revelation as the result of reflection on God's manifest saving activity, and the Constitution on the Church as the result of reflection on the worshiping assembly.

Some of the decrees must then be understood as explications of the dogmatic statements in the Constitution on the Church concerning the structure of God's people on earth. The Decree on Eastern Catholic Churches advances on the statements in chapter ii of the Constitution on the Church concerning the individual churches; the Decree on the Bishops' Pastoral Office proceeds from the discussion of Articles 18-27 in chapter iii, while the Decree on the Ministry and Life of Priests proceeds from Article 28 of the same chapter. The Decree on the Apostolate of the Laity is a further treatment of chapter iv, and the Decree on the Appropriate Renewal of the Religious Life is an additional explication of chapter vi. The Declaration on Christian Education is of a more general nature.

The systematic arrangement of the rest of the Council's resolutions is suggested by an illustration repeatedly used by Pope Paul VI. He spoke of concentric circles within which the Roman Catholic Church is to carry on her dialogue with others: the innermost circle, representing the Roman church with the pope in the center, is surrounded by a circle representing non-Roman Christians, which is surrounded by a circle representing non-Christian religions, and finally the outer circle representing all of humanity (so, e.g., in the encyclical *Ecclesiam Suam*). Corresponding to these three concentric circles surrounding the Roman church are the Secretariats for Promoting Christian Unity, for Non-Christian Religions and Unbelievers, and the projected Secretariat for the Promotion of International Social Justice, all recently established by the Pope. In line with this structure are also the astonishing trips which Pope Paul VI took during the Council. The trip to Jerusalem (at the close of the second period of sessions) led to a meeting with the Ecumenical Patriarch Athenagoras of Constantinople; the trip to Bombay (after the third period of sessions) led to an encounter with non-Christian religions, and the trip to New York (during the fourth period of sessions) brought the Pope together with the United Nations.

Directives for the relationship of the Roman church to non-Roman Christendom are found among the conciliar resolutions in the Decree on Ecumenism. Directives for encounter with non-Christian religions are found in the Decree on the Church's Missionary Activity and in the Declaration on the Relationship of the Church to Non-Christian Religions. Directives for the church's attitude toward the basic problems of humanity as such are contained in the Pastoral Constitution on the Church in the Modern World and in the Decree on the Instruments of Social Communication. The Declaration on Religious Freedom is significant for all three areas, that is, not only for the dialogue with non-Roman Christendom and non-Christian religions, but also for the fundamental relationship between the Roman church and the power of the state.

This inner coherence is to determine the structure of the following chapters, in which, however, there will be a change in order. The Constitution on Divine Revelation will be placed at the end because in this chapter observations on the use of Holy Scripture in the rest of the Council resolutions will be summed up. Thus in the following chapters we shall treat the reform of worship (Chapter 4); the self-understanding of the Roman church (Chapter 5); the Council and non-Roman churches (Chapter 6); the Council and non-Christian religions (Chapter 7); the Council and the modern world (Chapter 8); and Holy Scripture, tradition, and teaching office (Chapter 9).

Preliminary Remarks on Hermeneutics

There is no intention of offering a commentary on the resolutions of Vatican II, nor an *Examen Vaticani secundi* (a critical review of Vatican II) of the kind produced by Martin Chemnitz in the situation created by the Counter-Reformation, when he subjected the decisions of the Council of Trent to an examination (*Examen Concilii Tridentini,* 1565-73). What is intended here is simply a general survey of the events of the Council in order to determine what these signify for non-Roman churches and what the attitude of these churches toward the Roman church ought to be. In spite of this limitation of scope, a survey of the documents calls for a preconsideration of the principles according to which the adopted and promulgated documents are to be interpreted. Such a hermeneutical consideration is all the more important since both within and outside the Roman church the resolutions of the Council are appraised in widely divergent ways. As an extreme on the one hand we may point to the optimistic utterances according to which all essential hindrances have now been removed and the unification of Christendom is imminent. The other extreme is represented by the pessimistic judgments that basically nothing has changed and even that the ecumenical program of the Roman church has made the relationship among the churches more difficult. Between these extreme positions there is a large variety of opinions which are more or less confident or perhaps reserved. Without a doubt, the reason for this great difference in evaluating the resolutions of the Council is to be found to a considerable degree in the absence of a clarification of the principles of interpretation. Since non-Roman Christendom is especially interested in the Decree on Ecumenism, we will begin our hermeneutical reflections at this point and attempt to gain several general viewpoints that are also important for the other decisions.

(a) The Decree on Ecumenism is often interpreted in isolation, as though it were itself the theme of the Council. Ecumenism is, however, only one theme among many others. The Decree on Ecumenism is surrounded by numerous other constitutions, decrees, and declarations which the Council Fathers took no less seriously. The topics treated in these other documents are in part so closely related to the Decree on Ecumenism that the latter cannot be correctly interpreted apart from the former. This is particularly true in regard to the Dogmatic Constitutions on the

Church and on Divine Revelation, and the Decree on Eastern Catholic Churches (i.e., churches in fellowship with Rome). Great ecumenical significance, however, attaches also to the Decrees on the Apostolate of the Laity and on the Church's Missionary Activity, the Declarations on Religious Freedom and on the Relationship of the Church to Jews and Non-Christian Religions, and, not least, the voluminous proposals on the presence of the church in the modern world. The connection between the Decree on Ecumenism and these other texts must under no circumstances be ignored, for the answers which the same Council gives or does not give in those other documents—for example, answers to the questions of religious freedom or mixed marriages or Christian cooperation on the mission field—must be regarded as authentic interpretations of the ecumenical program. Obviously, the statements in the Constitution on the Church about the position of the pope and his relationship to the bishops are of special ecumenical significance. In general, we must follow the rule that the individual document is correctly understood and interpreted only in the context of all the conciliar resolutions.

(b) The Decree on Ecumenism is frequently given more weight than other decisions of the Council. This is true above all with respect to the Dogmatic Constitution on the Church, since this constitution is still and to a larger degree under the influence of the conservative theologians and presents a narrower view of the church than does the Decree on Ecumenism. During the second period of sessions a higher estimate was often placed on this decree, and this was justified by saying that the question of the relative authority of a constitution or a decree had not been clarified. At the same time, there was from the beginning much in favor of assigning a higher rank to a dogmatic constitution than to a decree, and, in fact, during the third period of sessions the relationship between the Decree on Ecumenism and the Dogmatic Constitution on the Church was clearly decided in favor of the latter. The statement (*relatio*) accompanying the submission of the second draft of the *schema* on ecumenism to the Council designated the dogmatic affirmations of the constitution as the determinative presuppositions for ecumenism. Furthermore, the adopted version of the decree makes explicit reference to the constitution (chap. i, near the close). Hence the Decree on Ecumenism must be interpreted in the light of the Constitution on the Church and not vice versa. Every document of the Council must be considered in terms of its relationship to, and dependence on, other documents. This applies especially to the resolutions in which the dogmatic bases are enunciated.

(c) The resolutions of the Council are the product of earnest wrestling in the Council and this is reflected in the various formulations of the respective *schemata*. No *schema* was adopted in its original form. The struggle went on in the Council chamber as the Council Fathers expressed their opinions, and was continued as the commissions of the Council endeavored to evaluate these opinions and produce new texts. In the process, the objections and wishes of every preceding opinion had to be taken into account. The revised version thus produced was resubmitted to the plenary together with printed replies and an introductory essay which took note of the most important points of view governing the revision. Even while the issue was being voted on amendments could still be proposed, and these in turn had to be considered by the commissions. This work, which in the case of some documents went through four periods of sessions (e.g., the Constitution on Divine Revelation), must certainly be considered in the interpretation of the Council's resolutions. Since the earlier drafts, the opinions, and the reasons for textual revisions have not yet been released they can be adduced here only to the extent that they were made public by Council theologians and especially by the daily reports of the Council's press corps.

(d) The Council is more than its resolutions. One who knows only the resolutions of the Council has not yet grasped the conciliar event as a whole. The Council produced the breakthrough of a dynamic that is more comprehensive and more progressive than is expressed in the conciliar resolutions. Since the majority of the delegates were open to the forward-looking impulses, many find the significance of the resolutions, which are not to be regarded as official and irreformable dogmatic definitions, in the fact that these decisions opened hitherto closed doors and officially granted further new advances in the Roman church the right to exist. For such a dynamic view, the wording of the documents as such seems less significant, because these in part lag considerably behind the far more progressive impulses as well as insights and goals of the ecumenical avant-garde and the youth of the Roman church following in its train. The caution and reserve of the Decree on Ecumenism, for example, is then accounted for by saying that its first concern was to win the whole Roman church for the ecumenical idea. In this sense the decree is understood less as a document than as an historical process on the way to further ecumenical development.

Without doubt the conciliar decisions are correctly interpreted only if they are interpreted against the background of the whole conciliar event. It is not easy, however, to obtain a precise grasp of these forward-looking impulses, and it is impossible to predict with certainty how these newly arising impulses will fare after the close of the Council and how much support the conservative minority will receive from the church membership and the Curia.

As we take another look at the Decree on Ecumenism, we see clearly how the newly arising impulses have led to numerous improvements in the original draft. Altogether, four versions of this decree were presented to the Council for deliberation and action. The second and third drafts grew out of previous discussions and opinions. In digesting thousands of such expressed opinions, the Secretariat for Unity performed an outstanding task resulting in a number of noteworthy improvements of the original text in both the second and the third forms.

On the other hand, it must not be overlooked that, in addition to these improvements in the sense of further ecumenical openness, the second draft also contained some significant qualifications which adapted and subordinated the originally less precise, and therefore ecumenically more open, understanding of the church in the decree to the narrower view of the church in the Constitution on the Church. Above all, many bishops and observers were aroused when, at the last minute, by means of an intervention which claimed the supreme authority of the pope for itself, several changes were made in the third draft which the Council had already voted on point by point and whose three chapters the Council had already adopted by an overwhelming majority. This action disappointed many ecumenical expectations. This is particularly true regarding the toning down of statements about the Eucharist in the churches of the Reformation and about the products of their biblical studies. Further surprising interventions in the work of the Council during the last days of the third period made clear that the conservative forces are stronger than many had assumed.

Thus it is true that the conciliar resolutions must be interpreted in the context of the Council's total activity; and yet the context must be seen not only in the emergence of progressive forces but also in the determined battle of the forces of reaction. One who has followed the course of the Council's actions gets the impression with regard to most of the resolutions that in carefully balanced formulations the Council said the utmost that could be said by all the Council Fathers together. What the resolutions say must not be depreciated in favor of hopes or fears for further developments after the Council. In every case the texts must be taken seriously on the basis of what they actually say. The official texts have by resolution of the Council and by papal promulgation received an authority that determines further action in the Roman church.

(e) No text can be interpreted apart from its significance for the interpreter. This is true also of the resolutions, even though it is apparent that not all resolutions are significant in the same way for the respective interpreter. Thus, for the non-Catholic reader there is more significance in the Dogmatic Constitutions on Divine Revelation and on the Church, as well as the Decree on Ecumenism and the Declaration on Religious Freedom, than in the Decree on the Appropriate Renewal of the Religious Life. To do justice to the Council's resolutions, however, it is necessary to distinguish between their significance for the Roman church herself and their significance for other churches. There are many decisions which appear nothing short of revolutionary for the Roman church herself, and therefore their implementation among the people offers considerable problems. The same decisions, such as, for example, the introduction of the vernacular in worship or the recognition of religious liberty, have nothing new to say to most of the other churches. Their significance lies in the fact that here the Roman church is changing her former practice. In the interpretation of the Council's resolutions it is therefore necessary to take cognizance of the position of the Roman church on these same problems in the time before the Council. Only in this way will the significance of the resolutions for the Roman church really become clear.

On the basis of these reflections we shall in the following chapters attempt first of all to evaluate the Council's resolutions against the background of the presuppositions of the Roman church herself. We shall confine ourselves for the moment to an immanent critique of these resolutions on the basis of the Roman church's own presuppositions, among which, admittedly, the Holy Scriptures and the ancient church occupy a special place. Only then (Chapters 10 ff.) will the significance of the Council for non-Roman churches be discussed.

By applying these hermeneutical principles we hope to escape from the confused jumble of evaluations of the Council which are so diverse, enthusiastic, or skeptical, and thus come closer to understanding the Council's true significance.

4

The Reform of Worship

The Constitution on the Sacred Liturgy is a product of the liturgical movement. This movement arose in Benedictine monasteries in Belgium, Germany, and Austria; it elicited a strong response especially in the Catholic youth movement in Germany, and by way of younger priests was brought to a large number of parishes. The liturgical movement, resting on a carefully constructed theological and historical basis, as well as on musical scholarship, has produced strong impulses toward non-Roman Christendom. The popes since Pius X, especially Pius XII, promoted this movement through a series of encyclicals which provided important individual reforms. Sometimes, it is true, they also raised restrictions. It was up to the Council to adopt fundamental principles to guide the future general reform of the Latin rite. Hence, the primary task was not to implement the liturgical reform itself in detail but rather to determine the principles according to which a special liturgical commission could bring about this reform. Of course, this does not exclude the fact that the newly developed principles already contain some direct changes in the accustomed liturgy, and that these changes began to assert themselves on the parish level even before the liturgical commission could complete its post-conciliar task. The renewal of the liturgy is based on the distinction between "unchangeable elements divinely instituted, and elements subject to change."[1]

We are here dealing with a liturgical constitution, not a dogmatic one. The dogmas of the Roman church, especially the teaching concerning the sacrifice of the Mass, continue to be pre-

[1] Constitution on the Sacred Liturgy, Art. 21. *Documents,* p. 146.

supposed as unalterable. Since, however, the liturgy may be understood as an interpretation of the dogma, the question arises whether the liturgical constitution perhaps presents shifts in accent or supplements to the past understanding of the dogma, especially the dogmatic statements about the Mass. We must here confine ourselves to the chief service, the Mass. We desire to fix our attention particularly on those forms of renewal which at the same time involve structural changes in the life of the Roman church.

The Saving Action of God

In the first chapter the Constitution on the Liturgy begins with God's universal saving will and his once-and-for-all completed saving deed in Jesus Christ.

> The wonders wrought by God among the people of the Old Testament were but a prelude to the work of Christ the Lord in redeeming mankind and giving perfect glory to God. He achieved His task principally by the paschal mystery of His blessed passion, resurrection from the dead, and glorious ascension (Art. 5).
>
> To accomplish so great a work, Christ is always present in His Church, especially in her liturgical celebrations. He is present in the sacrifice of the Mass, not only in the person of His minister, . . . but especially under the Eucharistic species. By His power He is present in the sacraments, so that when a man baptizes it is really Christ Himself who baptizes. He is present in His word, since it is He Himself who speaks when the holy Scriptures are read in the church. He is present, finally, when the Church prays and sings, for He promised: "Where two or three are gathered together for my sake, there am I in the midst of them" (Matt. 18:20) (Art. 7).[2]

Thus the constitution is concerned with the present activity of Christ who in his death and resurrection has provided salvation. He is the one who is present and active in the liturgical action of the priest and the congregation. In what follows we shall concentrate on the statements concerning Christ's presence in the Eucharist and in the word.

---

[2] *Documents,* pp. 139 ff.

(a) The teaching of Trent distinguishes in the Eucharist between the distribution of the sacrament (*communio*, Sess. XXI) and the sacrifice of the Mass (*sacrificium*, Sess. XXII). This distinction is not only dogmatic but to a large extent also liturgical. A large number of masses, in fact the majority of them, are celebrated in the Roman church without a reception of the sacrament, except for the celebrant. On the contrary, the sacrament may be offered in other services without consecrating the elements in those services. Previously consecrated wafers are distributed. The Orthodox church and the churches of the Reformation reject such a separation between the sacrifice of the Mass and the communion since this does not conform to the character of the meal as Jesus instituted it. The liturgical constitution still permits low masses without communion, yet there is a shift in accent. Thus, with regard to all liturgical rites, it is taught that "communal celebration involving the presence and active participation of the faithful . . . is to be preferred, as far as possible, to a celebration that is individual and quasi-private." The remark is added: "This rule applies with special force to the celebration of Mass" (Art. 27). "Hearty endorsement is given to that closer form of participation . . . whereby the faithful, after the priest's communion, receive the Lord's body under elements consecrated at that very sacrifice" (Art. 55). In this connection the directives for the common celebration of the Mass by several priests (*concelebratio*) should also be mentioned (Art. 57)[3] since in this way the number of simultaneous masses in the same church is reduced, and, even when the congregation does not receive the sacrament, there is at least a communion on the part of the participating priests.

The extremely animated and fruitful discussion, which the mystery theology of Odo Casel stimulated in the twenties and thirties, particularly in German Catholic theology, received no further consideration in the constitution. Yet perhaps it exerted some influence in that the constitution directed its attention to the

[3] *Documents,* pp. 148, 156 f.

total process of worship. Furthermore, the Mass is here understood not only as representation of Christ's death on the cross, but also in connection with both his death and his *resurrection;* " 'the victory and triumph of his death are again made present' " (Art. 6).[4] Without contradicting the statements of Trent, the constitution also goes beyond them in pointing to the eschatological character of the Eucharist.

> In the earthly liturgy, by way of foretaste, we share in that heavenly liturgy which is celebrated in the holy city of Jerusalem toward which we journey as pilgrims, and in which Christ is sitting at the right hand of God, a minister of the sanctuary and of the true tabernacle. . . . [In the worship] we eagerly await the Savior, our Lord Jesus Christ, until He, our life, shall appear and we too will appear with Him in glory (Art. 8).[5]

The eschatological aspects of the Eucharist are today also more fully emphasized in the churches of the Reformation. As a result of these shifts in accent, the New Testament character of the Eucharist, in accordance with its institution as the Lord's Supper, is again more fully manifested.

The Council of Trent had taught: "If anyone says that each and all the faithful of Christ are by a precept of God or by the necessity of salvation bound to receive both species of the most holy sacrament of the Eucharist, let him be anathema" (Sess. XXI, Canon 1).[6] These words, while not exactly excluding reception of both kinds in the sacrament, did in fact amount to a prohibition, even though reception of both kinds had been customary until the twelfth century and some passing concessions had been made in the sixteenth century. Both the Orthodox church and the churches of the Reformation have rejected this withholding of the cup from the communing laity. Now however, without questioning the validity of the cited Tridentine anathema, the Constitution on the Sacred Liturgy specifies that "communion under both

---

[4] *Documents,* p. 140.
[5] *Documents,* pp. 141 f.
[6] *Canons and Decrees of the Council of Trent,* ed. H. J. Schroeder (St. Louis: B. Herder Book Co., 1941), pp. 134 f.

kinds may be granted when the bishops think fit, not only to clerics and religious, but also to the laity, in cases to be determined by the Apostolic See" (Art. 55). It is true that the example cited to illustrate such a reception by lay people specifically mentions only "the newly baptized in a Mass following their baptism";[7] yet the constitution does in principle also open up the possibility of permitting the distribution of the sacrament under both kinds in other cases. Although this distribution, then, is not envisioned as the rule, there is a shift in accent here, too, and the practice again approaches the Lord's double formula of distribution as recorded in the New Testament.

(b) "Sacred Scripture is of paramount importance in the celebration of the liturgy. For it is from Scripture that lessons are read and explained in the homily, and psalms are sung; the prayers, collects, and liturgical songs are scriptural in their inspiration, and it is from Scripture that actions and signs derive their meaning. . . . [Therefore] it is necessary to promote that warm and living love for Scripture . . ." (Art. 24).[8]

Thus, there is to be "more reading from holy Scripture, and it is to be more varied and suitable" (Art. 35, 1). "The treasures of the Bible are to be opened up more lavishly, so that richer fare may be provided for the faithful at the table of God's Word. In this way a more representative portion of the holy Scriptures will be read to the people over a set cycle of years" (Art. 51).[9] This makes possible a revision of the order of pericopes for worship as well as the selection of several pericope series side by side.

In the structure of the Mass, the sermon is to occupy a fixed place and preaching is to be faithfully provided (Art. 35, 2) both in the service of the Mass and in special Bible services (Art. 35, 4).[10] "By means of the homily the mysteries of the faith and the guiding principles of the Christian life are expounded from the sacred text during the course of the liturgical year. The

---

[7] *Documents*, p. 156.
[8] *Documents*, p. 147.
[9] *Documents*, pp. 149, 155.
[10] *Documents*, pp. 149 f.

homily, therefore, is to be highly esteemed as part of the liturgy itself" (Art. 52).[11]

The liturgical constitution, therefore, lays special weight on the connection between sacrament and word, not only in the sense that the sacrament comes into being through the consecrating word but also in the sense that the reading of Scripture and the sermon are associated with the sacrament. This does not put an end to private masses and masses without preaching, yet here too the accents are shifted in a direction which can only be applauded by the churches of the Reformation and the Orthodox church. In this connection it is significant that the Scripture reading and sermon are there not only to provide instruction on Christ's presence in the sacrament; on the contrary, there is explicit reference to the presence of Christ in the word. This is saying no more than that Christ is present in his word because he himself is speaking when the Holy Scriptures are read. There is here no recognition of the fact that the gospel in its essence is not Scripture and lection but a living word and a concrete address or preaching and is the "power of God" (Rom. 1:16) precisely in this sense. According to the weight assigned by the constitution to the word and the sacrament, the formula would not read "word and sacrament," but rather "sacrament and word." Yet even the significance of the word in the sacrament itself continues to be diminished by the practice of speaking the words of institution over the elements of bread and wine softly, so that the congregation cannot hear them. Still, it is significant that it is said that in not only the sacrament but the liturgy as a whole "God speaks to His people and Christ is still proclaiming His gospel" (Art. 33).[12] Trent had not in this manner presented the word alongside the sacraments as the instrument of Christ's present activity.

The Participation of the Congregation

Since the early Middle Ages the congregation had begun to be silent and was no longer speaking the liturgical responses and

[11] *Documents*, p. 155.
[12] *Documents*, p. 149.

doxologies. More and more the congregation's participation was reduced to adoration and reception of the consecrated host. In general, the action at the altar and the congregation's worship were separate events; everyone prayed in isolation. This was not only an actual development; there were theologians who supported the principle that responses in the service were the exclusive task of the priest's attendant at Mass. The modern liturgical movement has from the beginning opposed this view, and by translations of the Missal it has made it possible for the congregation to follow the order of worship. Already in 1903, Pope Pius X in a *motu proprio* had called for the "active participation" of the faithful in the Mass as an indispensable fountain of the spiritual life. This demand has since then been raised again and again, but putting it into practice presented difficult problems. What is meant by "active participation"? Is it enough to make possible an intelligent but mute participation in the Mass, instead of the aimless prayer of each individual? Or should the congregation go beyond this and be made an active participant in the worship service by having something to say?

The constitution teaches emphatically:

> Liturgical services are not private functions, but are celebrations of the Church, which is the "sacrament of unity," namely, a holy people united and organized under their bishops. Therefore liturgical services pertain to the whole body of the Church; they manifest it and have effects upon it (Art. 26).
>
> The Church, therefore, earnestly desires that Christ's faithful, when present at this mystery of faith, should not be there as strangers or silent spectators. On the contrary, through a proper appreciation of the rites and prayers they should participate knowingly, devoutly, and actively. They should be instructed by God's word and be refreshed at the table of the Lord's body; they should give thanks to God; by offering the Immaculate Victim, not only through the hands of the priest, but also with him, they should learn to offer themselves too (Art. 48).[13]

---

[13] *Documents*, pp. 147, 154.

The service is to be conducted in such a way that within the congregational structure every attendant will perform his proper role in the conduct of the service (Art. 28). This participation is not to be limited to an understanding faith but to become vocal.

> By way of promoting active participation, the people should be encouraged to take part by means of acclamations, responses, psalmody, antiphons, and songs, as well as by actions, gestures, and bodily attitudes. And at the proper times all should observe a reverent silence (Art. 30).

> Such participation by the Christian people as "a chosen race, a royal priesthood, a holy nation, a purchased people" (1 Pet. 2:9; cf. 2:4-5), is their right and duty by reason of their baptism (Art. 14).[14]

In this connection, the re-introduction of the general intercession at the Mass is especially significant. In the course of tightening up the Mass and laying increasingly more weight on the sacrifice of the Mass, this prayer had disappeared from the Mass in the Roman church—in contrast to the liturgy of the Reformation churches and the Orthodox church. The sacrifice of the Mass had in substance replaced the general prayer of the church, except for a few silent intercessions by the priest during the sacrifice. In these prayers the congregation could not participate. Now, however,

> especially on Sundays and feasts of obligation, there is to be restored, after the Gospel and the homily, "the common prayer" or "the prayer of the faithful." By this prayer, in which the people are to take part, intercession will be made for holy Church, for the civil authorities, for those oppressed by various needs, for all mankind, and for the salvation of the entire world (Art. 53).[15]

With all this emphasis on active participation in worship by all the members of the congregation, it is to be noted that the congregation may become vocal only in a liturgically bound way. Its participation is limited to the liturgically prescribed responsories, prayers, and acclamations. Here, then, there is a difference over against the statements of the Apostle Paul regarding the

[14] *Documents*, pp. 148, 144.
[15] *Documents*, pp. 155 f.

variety of spiritual gifts through which every member of the congregation receives from the freedom of the Spirit a special form of service in the congregation. Similarly, there is a difference over against the Apostle's statements regarding the manner in which these spiritual gifts manifest themselves during the congregation's worship in the free word of prophecy, teaching, etc. (I Cor. 12 and 14). This difference, however, is also found in other churches wherever the worship is conducted in set liturgical forms. There, too, the question must be asked whether under such circumstances sufficient opportunity is given for the unhampered witness of the spiritual gifts.

Permitting the Use of the Vernacular

Is it possible for the congregation to participate actively in the conduct of the worship if the liturgy is in a foreign language?

In lively discussions the point was made that the Latin liturgical language belonged to the unity of the Roman church and that this unity would be weakened if the vernacular were permitted. Carrying weight in the background was the further idea that the very inability to understand the words was appropriate to the sacredness of the mystery. However, in order to enable the people to participate actively in the liturgy, it was resolved to extend the limits of the use of the mother tongue and to apply this extension "in the first place to the readings and directives, and to some of the prayers and chants" (Art. 36, 2).[16] Permission was also granted for use of the vernacular in the general prayer of intercession which is to be inserted as part of the liturgy.

At first glance, these directives appear to contradict the Tridentine prescriptions: "Though the mass contains much instruction for the faithful, it has, nevertheless, not been deemed advisable by the Fathers that it should be celebrated everywhere in the vernacular tongue."[17] Accordingly, the missal of unity of 1570, constructed on the basis of the Tridentine decisions, demanded the

[16] *Documents*, p. 150.
[17] Sess. XXII, Chapter VIII; Schroeder, p. 148.

exclusive use of the Latin language. However, the basic dogmatic decision of Trent merely says: "If anyone says . . . that the mass *ought to be* celebrated in the vernacular tongue only . . . let him be anathema."[18] Hence, Vatican II with its introduction of the vernacular does not contradict the basic principles of Trent but merely transcends the latter's actual rejection of the vernacular. At the same time consideration is given to the old regulation by saying that the use of the Latin language is to be preserved in the Latin rites (Art. 36, 1).[19] Furthermore, the Council permitted and recommended, but did not demand, the use of the vernacular, and the parts of the liturgy in which use of the vernacular is explicitly recommended do not include the words of consecration and the prayers in the canon of the Mass. In addition, "steps should be taken so that the faithful may also be able to say or to sing together in Latin those parts of the Ordinary of the Mass which pertain to them" (Art. 54).[20] In spite of this deference to past usage the statements concerning the use of the vernacular represent a very important step.

Permitting Further Adaptations

The constitution goes still further in enabling the congregation to participate:

> Even in the liturgy, the Church has no wish to impose a rigid uniformity in matters which do not involve the faith or the good of the whole community. Rather she respects and fosters the spiritual adornments and gifts of the various races and peoples. Anything in their way of life that is not indissolubly bound up with superstition and error she studies with sympathy and, if possible, preserves intact. Sometimes in fact she admits such things into the liturgy itself, as long as they harmonize with its true and authentic spirit (Art. 37; cf. Art. 38).[21]

Thus "adaptations" are to be made "especially in the case of the administration of the sacraments, the sacramentals, processions,

[18] Sess. XXII, Canon 9; Schroeder, p. 150.
[19] *Documents*, p. 150.
[20] *Documents*, p. 156.
[21] *Documents*, p. 151.

liturgical language, sacred music, and the arts" (Art. 39).[22] In the scholarly research carried on by the liturgical movement it was clearly seen how strongly the liturgy was shaped by late antiquity and the Middle Ages. Increasingly more urgent became the question whether and to what extent this liturgy is suitable for Christians in completely different cultures, to whom the religious and philosophical concepts as well as the rites of the latter part of Graeco-Roman antiquity and medieval Europe are alien. Some very difficult problems came up here, including the question whether the elements of bread and wine should be used since their symbolical significance is not evident in countries where they play no role in the daily nourishment. The constitution excludes any change in the sacraments but does leave room for an adaptation of rites to the presuppositions of other peoples and cultures. This is particularly true of baptism: "In mission lands initiation rites are found in use among individual peoples. Elements from these, when capable of being adapted to Christian ritual, may be admitted along with those already found in Christian tradition" (Art. 65). It is also true of marriage. "The competent territorial ecclesiastical authority . . . is free to draw up its own rite suited to the usages of place and people" (Art. 77). Furthermore, the national traditions of music (Art. 119) and art (Art. 123) are to be given their place in the liturgy, and matters may be adapted "to the needs and customs of their different regions; this applies especially to the materials and form of sacred furnishings and vestments" (Art. 128; cf. Arts. 107 and 110).[23]

In 1742, Pope Benedict XIV vetoed the far-reaching accommodations which the Jesuits had made in eastern Asia. Now the Council once again took up this exceedingly difficult but inescapable problem and created the presuppositions for new attempts at its solution. How pressing a problem this is within the Roman

---

[22] *Documents*, p. 151.
[23] *Documents*, pp. 159, 161, 172, 175, 176.

church is shown by the fact that voices still express the opinion that eastern Asia would be Christian today if in the eighteenth century the pope had not prohibited the accommodations made by the Jesuits.

Liturgical Rights Granted the Conferences of Bishops

Who is responsible for introducing the vernacular and making adaptations? Formerly, questions concerning the liturgy in the Roman church had been decided in Rome. Here the Council brought about a relaxation of the rule. "In virtue of power conceded by the law, the regulation of the liturgy within certain defined limits belongs also to various kinds of competent territorial bodies of bishops legitimately established" (Art. 22, 2).[24] This provision is the basis for leaving questions pertaining to the vernacular and adaptations in the hands of national bishops' conferences or those of larger territories. "It is for the competent territorial ecclesiastical authority . . . to decide whether, and to what extent, the vernacular language is to be used" (Art. 36, 3) and to "consider which elements from the traditions and genius of individual peoples might appropriately be admitted into divine worship" (Art. 40, 1).[25] Resolutions adopted by the bishops' conferences regarding the introduction of the vernacular "are to be approved, that is, confirmed, by the Apostolic See" (Art. 36, 3; cf. Art. 40, 1).[26] The "Instruction for the orderly implementation of the Constitution on the Sacred Liturgy," given on September 26, 1964, furnished precise directives for the composition of the resolutions, the procedure for voting on them, and their presentation to the Holy See. Thus the power of the bishops' conferences is restricted. Yet even though the final decision rests with the Apostolic See, it remains significant that the bishops' conferences are now generally constituted and are granted rights beyond a mere right to make proposals.

---

[24] *Documents*, p. 146.
[25] *Documents*, pp. 150-52.
[26] *Ibid.*

New Structures

Worship is the center of the church's life and it is no accident that the worshiping assembly has put its stamp on the most important concepts concerning the church in the New Testament (*ecclesia*, people of God, body of Christ, temple of the Holy Spirit). The constitution expresses this central function of worship when it calls the liturgy "the summit toward which the activity of the Church is directed; at the same time it is the fountain from which all her power flows" (Art. 10). It is "a sacred action surpassing all others. No other action of the Church can match its claim to efficacy, nor equal the degree of it" (Art. 7).[27]

Because of this central importance no reform of the liturgy can fail to influence the total life of the church. This is not true of each detail of such a reform; but it is true of the basic structures of worship to the extent that they have been newly accented or altered through such a reform. Which are the most important structural changes in the liturgical constitution of Vatican II?

(a) The word of Scripture together with its interpretation in the sermon has been emphasized in a new way over the other traditional parts of the liturgy. They have also been given more prominence alongside the sacraments than was formerly the case.

(b) In the directives for active congregational participation the layman's mouth has been opened for Christian witness in a new way and the universal priesthood of all believers has been given a new significance. Explicitly granting the layman, as his "right and duty" by reason of his baptism, "full, conscious, and active participation in liturgical celebrations" (Art. 14)[28] does not, indeed, remove the difference between the laity and the ordained clergy. Yet all Christians are active in the priestly office. In this involvement the lay people actively surround the priests.

(c) The basic permission to use the vernacular and to adapt the liturgy to the concepts, customs, and rites of the nations has sub-

---

[27] *Documents*, pp. 142, 141.

[28] *Documents*, p. 144.

stituted for liturgical uniformity a different structure of unity of worship in the variety of rites.

(d) By permitting the national conferences of bishops and granting them the right to make liturgical decisions over against papal control, a structural shift has ensued in the direction of recognizing church unity as fellowship. No longer does the pope alone control the worship life of the Roman church; he does this together with the bishops.

These structural changes are of great ecumenical significance. A union of the churches is not possible unless the ancient Christian structure of fellowship and of unity in diversity is recaptured. Above all, it is of fundamental importance for all union endeavors that the Holy Scriptures are given new stature as the authentic transmission of the prophetic and apostolic witness which all churches possess in common.

The principles of liturgical reform were put into practice first of all in those masses celebrated in the assembly hall every morning at the beginning of the session. From the start the concern had been to allow for the variety of the different Latin and Eastern rites, and the Evangelical and Orthodox theologians were pleased to observe that in the Eastern liturgies the eucharistic words were spoken audibly and the sacrament was distributed to a circle of communicants in both kinds. As a rule, however, the Mass was celebrated according to the Roman rite. Over and over the same two biblical texts associated with the Mass of the Holy Spirit were read, the words of consecration were inaudible, the assembly hardly participated actively in the liturgy, and, apart from the celebrating bishop, there was no communion. After the promulgation of the liturgical constitution matters were increasingly different. By means of responsories the assembly took a more active part in the liturgy, the lections became more varied, and the sacrament was regularly distributed to laymen who were permitted to participate in the Council as auditors. In addition, at special occasions there was joint celebration on the part of the Pope and several cardinals, bishops, or priests. It is true that there was no joint communion service for all the Council Fathers. In none of the masses, in fact, not during the entire Council, was there a sermon on a biblical text. The papal addresses in the public sessions at the beginning and at the close of the periods of sessions were of a different character and did not present an exposition of any particular biblical passage.

Since the liturgical constitution validated new structures, its effects cannot be restricted to worship. Rather, as there is theological reflection on the renewed worship event, the implications for the dogmatic understanding of revelation and the church must also be drawn. The question remains whether the structural changes in worship have already been brought into full dogmatic consciousness by the Council or whether the dogmatic formulations are lagging behind.

5

The Self-Understanding of the Roman Church

The church is treated surprisingly late in the history of dogma. The ancient creeds do indeed bring the church into the context of their faith in the Holy Spirit and confess "the holy catholic church" (Apostles' Creed), "one, holy, catholic, and apostolic church" (Nicene Creed), "the communion of saints." The church is furthermore the subject of all dogmatic statements ("we believe," Nicene). Yet in the ancient church the trinitarian and the christological dogmas were the first to be precisely defined. Under the influence of Augustine, Western Christendom next concerned itself with the dogmas of grace. There was always theological reflection on the church and there are elements of an understanding of the church in other dogmas. This is true at least insofar as they contain affirmations about the church's boundaries, as well as regulations concerning the juridical order of the church. Nevertheless, neither the Orthodox church, nor the Roman church, nor the churches of the Reformation have as yet established the dogma of the church in a comprehensive way. Even the important Article VII of the Augsburg Confession constitutes teaching about the identifying marks of the church, rather than offering instruction on the reality of the church in its full dimensions. It is self-evident that the triune God who confronts the church with his gracious activity should become the first theme in the history of dogma. The dogma concerning the church represents a later stage of reflection. At this stage the receiving and confessing fellowship of believers itself becomes the topic of their statements.

It is true that the First Vatican Council had introduced a comprehensive *schema* on the church, comprising fifteen chapters and twenty-four canons (dogmatic statements of rejection). Only chapter ii, on papal primacy, together with a supplement on papal infallibility, was discussed at the time and then subsequently revised, adopted, and promulgated as the constitution *Pastor Aeternus.* The themes neglected at Vatican I were revived for discussion in Vatican II. However, in contrast to Vatican I the second Council, in its Constitution on the Church, did not aim at a dogmatic definition of the church nor a formula of rejection, but confined itself to a description of the church.

The Approach of Salvation History

The Constitution on the Church begins with the "utterly free and mysterious decree" of the eternal Father. "All the elect, before time began, the Father 'foreknew and predestined to become conformed to the image of his Son, that he should be the firstborn among many brethren' (Rom. 8:29)" (Art. 2). According to the free

> decree of His own wisdom and goodness, the eternal Father created the whole world. His plan was to dignify men with a participation in His own divine life. He did not abandon men after they had fallen in Adam, but ceaselessly offered them helps to salvation, in anticipation of Christ the Redeemer, "who is the image of the invisible God, the first born of every creature" (Col. 1:15).
>
> Already from the beginning of the world the foreshadowing of the Church took place. She was prepared for in a remarkable way throughout the history of the people of Israel and by means of the Old Covenant. Established in the present era of time, the Church was made manifest by the outpouring of the Spirit (Art. 2).

The church was established through the mission of the Son who inaugurated the church by preaching the good news of the coming of God's kingdom (Arts. 3 and 5). The church was quickened to life by the Holy Spirit whom Jesus, after his death on the cross and his resurrection, poured out upon his disciples (Arts. 4 and 5).

> Thus, the Church shines forth as "a people made one with the unity of the Father, the Son, and the Holy Spirit" (Art. 4).
>
> While she slowly grows, the Church strains toward the consummation of the kingdom and, with all her strength, hopes and desires to be united in glory with her King (Art. 5).
>
> At the end of time she will achieve her glorious fulfillment. Then . . . all just men from the time of Adam, "from Abel, the just one, to the last of the elect," will be gathered together with the Father in the universal Church (Art. 2).[1]

Through the sacraments the faithful are "fortified by so many and such powerful means of salvation."

> Taking part in the Eucharistic Sacrifice . . . is the fount and apex of the whole Christian life (Art. 11).[2]
>
> As often as the sacrifice of the cross in which "Christ, our passover, has been sacrificed" (I Cor. 5:7) is celebrated on an altar, the work of our redemption is carried on. At the same time, in the sacrament of the Eucharistic bread the unity of all believers who form one body in Christ (cf. I Cor. 10:17), is both expressed and brought about (Art. 3).

In the faithful the Holy Spirit creates prayer and witness and manifold gifts for service in the fellowship. "By the power of the gospel He makes the Church grow, [and] perpetually renews her" (Art. 4).[3]

"The Church, consequently, equipped with the gifts of her Founder and faithfully guarding His precepts of charity, humility, and self-sacrifice, receives the mission to proclaim and to establish among all peoples the kingdom of Christ and of God. She becomes on earth the initial budding forth of that kingdom" (Art. 5).[4] As the Son is sent by the Father, so the church is sent by the Son for the unceasing proclamation of the gospel "towards the full realization of the will of God, who has established Christ as the source of salvation for the whole world" (Art. 17).[5] Hence

---

[1] *Documents*, pp. 15-18.
[2] *Documents*, pp. 29, 28.
[3] *Documents*, pp. 16, 17.
[4] *Documents*, p. 18.
[5] *Documents*, p. 36.

mission work is not added to the activities of the church as one among many; it follows necessarily from the essence of the church, specifically from the essential attribute of her catholicity. The "Catholic Church strives energetically and constantly to bring all humanity with all its riches back to Christ its Head in the unity of His Spirit" (Art. 13).[6]

"Just as Christ carried out the work of redemption in poverty and under oppression, so the Church is called to follow the same path in communicating to men the fruits of salvation" (Art. 8). Thus the church on earth is an exile journeying in a foreign land (Art. 6).

> All the members ought to be molded into Christ's image until He is formed in them (cf. Gal. 4:19). . . . Still in pilgrimage upon the earth, we trace in trial and under oppression the paths He trod. Made one with His sufferings as the body is one with the head, we endure with Him, that with Him we may be glorified (cf. Rom. 8:17) (Art. 7).[7]

This approach and frame of salvation history in the Constitution on the Church represents a significant advance from the *schema* on the church in the First Vatican Council. It even goes beyond the encyclical *Mystici Corporis Christi* of Pius XII (1943). The concepts and lines of thought are now determined far more strongly by the Bible. Consequently, the Constitution on the Church is not directed to a timeless definition of the church and her characteristics; instead, it concentrates on the understanding of the church as the onward-moving, saving, all-inclusive activity of the triune God. Again and again this line of thought is carried through from the beginning with a strong accent on the future consummation. In addition, the eschatological expectation is the special theme of chapter vii, in which, however, the accent lies above all on the unity that already exists between the pilgrim church on earth and the heavenly fellowship of the glorified. In the Constitution on the Liturgy, the Mass was already presented

---

[6] *Documents*, p. 31.
[7] *Documents*, pp. 23, 19 f., 21.

not only in connection with Christ's death but also with his resurrection. Similarly, the Constitution on the Church has presented the relationships of salvation history in their full dimensions and has thereby incorporated, and even largely supplanted, the traditional ontological structure of nature and super-nature into a context of historical thinking. This new approach has also exerted its influence on other resolutions of the Council. It is most welcome and opens up new possibilities for ecumenical dialogue. The great acts of God are the common foundation of all Christian churches. It is only from this perspective that the separated churches can in a new way communicate with each other on the different teachings and rites by means of which the churches treat the realization of God's saving act. The ecclesiological declarations of the World Council of Churches in Amsterdam, Evanston, and New Delhi are likewise determined to a large extent by this trinitarian and salvation-history approach.

The Body of Christ and the People of God

The statements of the *schema* on the church in Vatican I and in the encyclical of Pius XII on the church are shaped by the concepts "mystical body of Christ" and "society." The latter concept had received its impress in the sense of a complete, supernatural, and spiritual society as a result of the post-Tridentine debate with Protestant state churches as well as with modern theories concerning the state. By way of contrast, the Constitution on the Church of Vatican II in a striking way pushes the concept of a society into the background and stresses biblical concepts and images. These are referred to in great variety as flock (sheepfold), vineyard (cultivation, field, olive tree), God's edifice (house, temple, city), the bride of Christ, mother of the faithful (Art. 6). These biblical concepts and images are merely strung together more than they are exegetically developed and made systematically fruitful. The concepts "body of Christ" (Art. 7) and "people of God" (especially chap. ii), however, are developed thoroughly.[8]

[8] *Documents*, pp. 20 ff., 24 ff.

While the concept of "society" is not lacking entirely (cf. Art. 8),[9] it does not play a dominant role. It is noteworthy that the two basic ecclesiological concepts of "body of Christ" and "people of God" are used side by side in the constitution, not indeed without reference to each other but without allowing the one to dissolve in the other or treating the one merely as clarification of the other. In placing these different concepts and images together the mystery of the church is proclaimed.

The decisive elements of the New Testament statements are embraced to a far greater degree in the affirmations about the church as the body of Christ than in the encyclical *Mystici Corporis,* which speaks of the body of Christ on the basis of a preconceived social philosophy regarding a hierarchically structured society and inserts the biblical references into this framework. The Constitution on the Church, however, proceeds in the context of New Testament statements and gives clear expression to the building up of the church as the body of Christ by means of Christ's sacramental body (Art. 7).[10] It was characteristic of the encyclical to play down the references to Christ's exaltation and the outpouring of the Holy Spirit and in this way to create a temporal gap between Christ and the church. This gap must then be bridged by the church's offices in their succession. The constitution, on the contrary, speaks much more strongly of the presence of the exalted Christ and the constantly new activity of the Holy Spirit in the church. Much more emphatically than in the earlier texts, the constitution takes note of the manifold sacramental, organological, eschatological, and even cosmological contexts in which the New Testament speaks of the church as the body of Christ.

In a special way the biblical designation of the church as the people of God demonstrates that salvation history connects the Old Testament Israel and the Messianic-eschatological people of God. The reason for devoting chapter ii to the people of God is,

---

[9] *Documents*, pp. 22 f.
[10] *Documents*, p. 20.

however, not only the salvation-history concern already expressed in chapter i, but also the insight that, before considering the doctrine of the hierarchy as originally planned, the constitution ought to present doctrinal material in which the unity of hierarchy and laity and religious orders is expressed, without thereby denying the difference in task and authority. "Though they differ from one another in essence and not only in degree, the common priesthood of the faithful and the ministerial or hierarchical priesthood are nonetheless interrelated. Each of them in its own special way is a participation in the one priesthood of Christ" (Art. 10). There are corresponding statements concerning the sharing of the whole people of God in Christ's prophetic office (Art. 12).[11] The inclusion of the New Testament statements about the church as a prophetic people and a royal priesthood makes it possible and fruitful for the following chapters, which deal with bishops, priests, deacons, laity, and religious orders, to start with the threefold office of Christ—prophetic, priestly, and royal—and to define the specific character of the church's offices and members in such a way that each office and member participates in its own way in this threefold office. This approach, as a matter of course, creates the possibility of a systematic grouping together of the various grades of the hierarchy, the laity, and the religious orders. Hence, the "obligation of spreading the faith is imposed on every disciple of Christ, according to his ability" (Art. 17).[12] Proclaiming the message to all men is an essential manifestation of the life of the church as a whole because of the mission of the whole people of God and therefore also of each member. This important idea is further developed and emphasized in the Decrees on the Apostolate of the Laity and on the Church's Missionary Activity.

Both the statements about the church as the body of Christ and as the people of God call attention to the variety of gifts and services which the Holy Spirit provides for the benefit of the

---

[11] *Documents*, pp. 27, 29.
[12] *Documents*, p. 36.
[13] *Documents*, pp. 17, 21, 30.

church (Arts. 4, 7, 12).[13] However, not only the variety of the individual members but also the variety of "parts" and "orders" of the church within the unity is recognized. Within the church many different orders are fused together. For that reason,

> within the Church particular Churches hold a rightful place. These Churches retain their own traditions without in any way lessening the primacy of the Chair of Peter. This Chair presides over the whole assembly of charity and protects legitimate differences, while at the same time it sees that such differences do not hinder unity but rather contribute toward it (Art. 13).[14]

This recognition of particular churches as a matter of principle provides the presupposition for the Decree on Eastern Catholic Churches (i.e., those in fellowship with Rome). The decree

> solemnly declares that the Churches of the East, as much as those of the West, fully enjoy the right, and are in duty bound, to rule themselves. Each should do so according to its proper and individual procedures, inasmuch as practices sanctioned by a noble antiquity harmonize better with the customs of the faithful and are seen as more likely to foster the good of souls.
>
> All Eastern rite members should know and be convinced that they can and should always preserve their lawful liturgical rites and their established way of life, and that these should not be altered except by way of an appropriate and organic development. Easterners themselves should honor all these things with the greatest fidelity (Arts. 5 f).[15]

Similarly, there is recognition of the rights of Eastern rite patriarchs (Arts. 7 ff.), the discipline of the sacraments (Arts. 12 ff.), and the liturgy (Arts. 20 ff.).[16] It is true that this variety continues to be limited by the recognition of the papal primacy as well as all the dogmas of the Roman church. No provision is made at this point for a relaxation of uniformity in dogmatic formulations and a movement toward mutual recognition of variety in giving dogmatic formulation to the one faith, a variety characterizing the first centuries of church history.

---

[14] *Documents*, p. 32.
[15] *Documents*, p. 376.
[16] *Documents*, pp. 377 ff.

Corresponding to interest in the variety of churchly traditions, there is more emphasis on the structure of fellowship than on centralization. Yet a recognition of the special rights and orders of particular churches must in no way limit "the pastoral guidance of the Roman Pontiff" (cf. Decree on Eastern Catholic Churches, Arts. 3, 4, 9, *et al.*).[17]

The Structure of the Church

The church is a fellowship of many parts. The Constitution on the Church presents this structure as a hierarchical order embracing all believers and consisting of grades of authority, tasks, and obligations of obedience. The discussion begins at the topmost level. With great care it develops the relationships which connect each level with the others within the unity of the people of God.

(a) Pope and Bishops

Vatican, I, in its dogmatic constitution *Pastor Aeternus,* had adopted a formulation from the Council of Florence in teaching that "to him [the Roman pontiff], in the person of St. Peter, was given by our Lord Jesus Christ the full power of feeding, ruling, and governing the whole Church." To this Vatican I added the assertion that the Roman pontiff "is the supreme judge of the faithful." No one is permitted to pass judgment on the judgment of the Apostolic See.

> Therefore, those who say that it is permitted to appeal to an ecumenical council from the decisions of the Roman Pontiff (as to an authority superior to the Roman Pontiff) are far from the straight path of truth.
>
> And so, if anyone says that the Roman Pontiff has only the office of inspection or direction, but not the full and supreme power of jurisdiction over the whole church, . . . or if anyone says that he has only a more important part and not the complete fullness of this supreme power, . . . let him be anathema (chap. iii). . . .
>
> The Roman Pontiff, when he speaks ex cathedra, that is, when, acting in the office of shepherd and teacher of all Christians, he defines, by virtue of his supreme apostolic authority, doctrine concering faith

---

[17] *Documents*, pp. 374 ff.

> or morals to be held by the universal Church, possesses through the divine assistance promised him in the person of St. Peter, the infallibility with which the divine Redeemer willed his Church to be endowed in defining doctrine concerning faith or morals; . . . such definitions of the Roman Pontiff are therefore irreformable because of their nature, not because of the agreement of the Church (chap. iv).

And though the same constitution stated that this power of the pope did not interfere "with the power of ordinary and immediate episcopal jurisdiction" of the bishops (chap. iii),[18] the impression had widely gained ground that the bishops would henceforth be nothing more than instruments and deputies of the pope.

Chapter three of the Second Vatican Council's Constitution on the Church begins where Vatican I left off. It teaches that "by divine institution bishops have succeeded to the place of the apostles as shepherds of the Church" (Art. 20).

> [To them] by episcopal consecration is conferred the fullness of the sacrament of orders (Art. 21; cf. Art. 26).[19]

> This power, which they personally exercise in Christ's name, is proper, ordinary, and immediate, although its exercise is ultimately regulated by the supreme authority of the Church. . . . Nor are they [the bishops] to be regarded as vicars of the Roman Pontiff, for they exercise an authority which is proper to them, and are quite correctly called "prelates," heads of the people whom they govern (Art. 27).[20]

> Episcopal consecration, together with the office of sanctifying, also confers the offices of teaching and of governing. (These, however, of their very nature, can be exercised only in hierarchical communion with the head and the members of the college.) (Art. 21)[21]

The Constitution on the Church, and especially the Decree on the Bishops' Pastoral Office in the Church, delineate the bishops' duties by expanding on their threefold prophetic, priestly, and royal office. It is to be noted that the task of proclaiming the

---

[18] H. Denzinger (ed.), *Enchiridion Symbolorum*, revised by Karl Rahner (31st ed. [Freiburg: Herder, 1957]), Nos. 1826, 1828, 1830, 1839; translation taken from *The Church Teachers*, ed. and trans. John F. Clarkson, *et al.* (London & St. Louis: B. Herder Book Co., 1955).

[19] *Documents*, pp. 40 f., 50.

[20] *Documents*, pp. 51 f.

[21] *Documents*, p. 41.

gospel is given priority (Art. 25).[22] The bishops' duties over against those of their diocese, the priests, and the laity, and over against those of the pope, the other bishops, and the church as a whole, are set forth in detail. Many of these circumspect pastoral directives may well serve as models even for non-Roman Catholics.

Claiming that by the Lord's will, St. Peter and the other apostles constituted one apostolic college (Art. 22), the Constitution teaches that the bishops also constitute such a college.

> In it, the bishops, faithfully recognizing the primacy and pre-eminence of their head, exercise their own authority for the good of their own faithful, and indeed of the whole church. . . .
>
> The supreme authority with which this college is empowered over the whole Church is exercised in a solemn way through an ecumenical council (Art. 22).

Not the individual bishop, but the college of bishops together with its head, the Roman pontiff, "is the subject of supreme and full power over the universal Church" (Art. 22). "The infallibility promised to the Church resides also in the body of bishops when that body exercises supreme teaching authority with the successor of Peter" (Art. 25).[23]

In no sense, however, do these statements question what Vatican I said concerning the primatial authority of the pope. Over and over again it is emphasized that "the Roman Pontiff has full, supreme, and universal power over the Church. And he can always exercise this power freely" (Art. 22). The college of bishops, however, can use it only when the pope calls it to a collegial action or confirms such an action. Similarly, it is said of the infallibility of the pope that "his definitions, of themselves, and not from the consent of the Church, are justly styled irreformable. . . . Therefore they need no approval of others, nor do they allow an appeal to any other judgment" (Art. 25).[24] The college of bishops, however, can exercise the infallible supreme

---

[22] *Documents*, p. 47.

[23] *Documents*, pp. 42, 44, 43, 49.

[24] *Documents*, pp. 43, 49.

teaching office (Art. 25) only at the call of the pope and in agreement with him. The "Prefatory Note of Explanation," added to the constitution by the highest authority, makes abundantly clear that the distinction is not

> between the Roman Pontiff and the bishops taken collectively, but between the Roman Pontiff by himself and the Roman Pontiff together with the bishops. Since the Supreme Pontiff is the *head* of the College, he alone can perform certain acts which in no wise belong to the bishops, for example, convoking and directing the College . . . (Sec. 3).

> The Roman Pontiff proceeds according to his own discretion and in view of the welfare of the Church in structuring, promoting, and endorsing any exercise of collegiality (Sec. 3).[25]

A corresponding emphasis is found also in the *motu proprio, Apostolica Sollicitudo*, of September 15, 1965, in which the Pope published the directives for the college of bishops. The pope retains the exclusive right to decide whether, when, and where the college of bishops, consisting of elected representatives of the regional bishops' conferences, is to meet, what topics it is to consider, and whether the council is to be purely advisory or authorized to pass resolutions.

This definition of relationships between pope and bishops rests on the presupposition that they are the successors of Peter and the apostles and that the latter also governed the church as a college with corresponding degrees of coordination and subordination. Yet neither the discussion in the Council nor the constitution further pursued the historical situation or the problems presented in the New Testament texts. They did not discuss more precisely what Peter's predominant function among the apostles and in the first congregation was, nor did they take note of the fact that, already during Peter's lifetime, James assumed leadership in the Jerusalem church. They did not investigate the historical problem of the limits of the apostolic circle, nor did they provide sufficient historical support for transferring the concept

[25] *Documents*, pp. 98-100.

of a college to that circle. There is no historical clarification of the claim that the pope and the bishops are the successors of Peter and the apostles. Without a doubt, a much later concept of succession has here been read into the New Testament texts, and in the process some isolated suggestions were generalized in an unhistorical way.

(b) Bishops and Priests

The bishops, in turn, "have legitimately handed on to different individuals in the Church various degrees of participation in this ministry. . . . Although priests do not possess the highest degree of the priesthood, and although they are dependent on the bishops in the exercise of their power, they are nevertheless united with the bishops in sacerdotal dignity" (Art. 28). They share in the episcopal office on a lower level. They are the bishops' "helpers" (*adjutores*; Art. 20 *et al.*), "cooperators," "aids and instruments" (Art. 28), "assistants" (Art. 21).[26] The priests "make him [the bishop] present in a certain sense in the individual local congregations of the faithful, and take upon themselves, as far as they are able, his duties and concerns, discharging them with daily care" (Art. 28).[27] In the name of their bishop the priests "gather God's family together as a brotherhood of living unity."[28] In this way they can be said to represent the bishop in the individual parishes of his diocese.

"On their level of ministry" also the priests are "partakers of the function of Christ the sole Mediator" (Art. 28).[29] Their task, too, is unfolded as participation in the office of prophet, priest, and king. This presentation is made briefly in the Constitution on the Church and in detail in the Decrees on the Ministry and Life of Priests and on Priestly Formation. In a very prudent way these documents treat the different relationships of the priests' service to their parish and to the church at large, to the laity, to other

[26] *Documents*, pp. 53, 40, 54.
[27] *Documents*, p. 54.
[28] Decree on the Ministry and Life of Priests, Art. 6; *Documents*, p. 543.
[29] *Documents*, p. 53.

priests, to their bishop, and to the government of the universal church. These directives for the priestly life and training of priests are models of pastoral concern. Noteworthy in the Decree on Priestly Formation is the priority given to the study of the Bible and salvation history over the study of scholastic theology. In the midst of modern problems connected with theological education this decree deserves careful study in other churches as well.

"In virtue of their common sacred ordination and mission, all priests are bound together in an intimate brotherhood." "They constitute one priesthood with their bishop, although that priesthood is comprised of different functions" (Art. 28).[30] The bishop

> should gladly listen to them, indeed, consult them, and have discussions with them about those matters which concern the necessities of pastoral work and the welfare of the diocese.
>
> In order to put these ideals into effect, a group or senate of priests representing the presbytery should be established. . . . [It should] have a form and norms to be determined by law. By its counsel, this body will be able to give effective assistance to the bishop in his government of the diocese.[31]

There is no thought here of administrative authority over the diocese on the part of the presbytery or the senate of priests. In this respect the presbytery in association with its episcopal head does not correspond to the college of bishops in association with the pope, since the bishops, as a college together with the pope, besides being drawn in for consultation, have the same authority as he has by himself. The difference in grades of consecration between bishops and priests seems to be operating here.

While the Second Vatican Council elevated the episcopal office in its dignity, it enlarged the gulf between bishops and priests. This difference is now no longer understood primarily as a difference in jurisdictional authority but as a difference in consecration. Through this emphasis on the difference in consecration the Roman church has come closer to the Orthodox understanding of

---

[30] *Documents*, p. 54.

[31] Decree on the Ministry and Life of Priests, Art. 7; *Documents*, pp. 548 f.

episcopal consecration; but at the same time it has drawn further away from the churches of the Reformation in their understanding of the office. These view the difference between the office of pastor and bishop not as a basic difference of ordination, but rather as a difference of jurisdictional authority. Here the churches of the Reformation are closer to the predominant view of the scholastic theologians, including Thomas Aquinas, who rejected a sacramentality of episcopal ordination differing from priestly ordination. In other respects, however, the Constitution on the Church moved away from the Orthodox view of the episcopal office to the extent that the possibility of exercising the episcopal office without recognition of the pope is denied.[32]

This definition of relationships between bishops and priests is based on the installation of the bishops by the apostles, and the transmission of the office by the bishops to others by handing on "to different individuals in the Church various degrees of participation in this ministry" (Art. 28).[33] Here, too, the Council did not enter further into the historical situation and its problems. The priests are too easily equated with the New Testament presbyters. The New Testament writings contain a variety of terms for church government and a variety of structures for administering the congregation. Under no circumstances may the presence of a bishop everywhere be assumed. Nor can it be assumed that in the early days the congregation was provided with leaders only by transferring the office through the laying on of hands. Where the New Testament does speak of bishops, it presents them as leaders of a local congregation, and thus they correspond more closely to the priests than to the bishops in the constitution. The name "priest" is applied in the New Testament not to an individual incumbent of the office but only to the people of God as a whole. Again, the presbyters were the elders, the earliest believers, the mature members of the church. It cannot be shown from the New Testament that they were made presbyters by episcopal ordination.

[32] Cf. The Prefatory Note of Explanation, *Documents*, p. 101.
[33] *Documents*, p. 53.

Here, too, a later conception of offices and the transfer of office was read back into the beginning of the church.

(c) Priests and Deacons

Alongside the priests, the deacons are called "helpers" of the bishops. The Council made an important decision in opening the possibility of restoring the diaconate. This grade had been preserved as a step toward ordination to the priesthood, but now it is to be restored "as a proper and permanent rank of the hierarchy," entrusted with specific areas of service. This decision was made because of the shortage of priests in many areas and the impossibility of providing the parishes with pastoral care.

"It is the duty of the deacon, to the extent that he has been authorized by competent authority, to administer baptism solemnly, to be custodian and dispenser of the Eucharist, to assist at and bless marriages in the name of the Church, to bring Viaticum to the dying, to read the sacred Scripture to the faithful, to instruct and exhort the people, to preside at the worship and prayer of the faithful, to administer sacramentals, and to officiate at funeral and burial services." In addition he has "duties of charity and of administration" (Art. 29).[34] Hence the deacon may assume important priestly functions but is not permitted to offer the sacrifice of the Mass. He may, however, dispense the wafer consecrated by the priest.

Especially noteworthy is the following provision:

> With the consent of the Roman Pontiff, this diaconate will be able to be conferred upon men of more mature age, even upon those living in the married state. It may also be conferred upon suitable young men. For them, however, the law of celibacy must remain intact (Art. 29).[35]

On the basis of discussion in the Council, this provision appears to be more of a concession to the emergency created by the shortage of priests than a positive evaluation of the assistance which the pastor's wife can offer him in his ministry. In this matter the

---

[34] *Documents*, pp. 55 f.
[35] *Documents*, p. 56.

constitution therefore lags behind the rule prevailing in the Orthodox church (as well as in the Uniate churches) which permits priests, including *young* priests, to be married, provided that the marriage was made before ordination. The constitution lags altogether behind the order prevailing in the churches of the Reformation, which on the basis of New Testament tradition does not know of any objections to the marriage of their pastors and bishops.

(d) Hierarchy and Laity

"The term laity is here understood to mean all the faithful except those in holy orders and those in a religious state sanctioned by the Church. These faithful are by baptism made one body with Christ and are established among the People of God. They are in their own way made sharers in the priestly, prophetic, and kingly functions of Christ. They carry out their own part in the mission of the whole Christian people with respect to the Church and the world" (Art. 31).[36]

The task of the laity is called an apostolate. In the Constitution on the Church and especially in the Decree on the Apostolate of the Laity—but also in many other resolutions, such as, for example, the Decree on the Church's Missionary Activity and the Pastoral Constitution on the Church in the Modern World—the Council is intensively concerned that the general priesthood of all believers not remain an empty title but find expression in active apostolic service. Earnestly it sets forth how the layman is to be active in the prophetic, priestly, and royal office of this world.

> The laity, by their very vocation, seek the kingdom of God by engaging in temporal affairs and by ordering them according to the plan of God.
>
> It is therefore his special task to illumine and organize these affairs in such a way that they may always start out, develop, and persist according to Christ's mind, to the praise of the Creator and the Redeemer (Art. 31).

In addition, the laity are called to witness, to confess, and to bring the gospel to the world (Art. 35). By their activity they are to

[36] *Documents*, p. 56.

participate actively "in the saving mission of the Church itself" and "in a special way to make the Church present and operative in those places and circumstances where only through them can she become the salt of the earth" (Art. 33). "For the Lord wishes to spread His kingdom by means of the laity also" (Art. 36). In a comprehensive and exemplary way the duties of the laity are detailed in all directions. "Because the very plan of salvation requires it, the faithful should learn to distinguish carefully between those rights and duties which are theirs as members of the Church, and those which they have as members of human society" (Art. 36).[37]

In all directions the apostolate of the laity is associated with the services of the various ranks of the hierarchy.

> And if by the will of Christ some are made teachers, dispensers of mysteries, and shepherds on behalf of others, yet all share a true equality with regard to the dignity and to the activity common to all the faithful for the building up of the Body of Christ.
>
> For the distinction which the Lord made between sacred ministers and the rest of the People of God entails a unifying purpose. . . . Pastors of the Church, following the example of the Lord, should minister to one another and to the other faithful. The faithful in their turn should enthusiastically lend their cooperative assistance to their pastors and teachers (Art. 32).[38]

Within the area of such unified purpose and cooperation, however, the difference between laity and clergy consists not only in that the laity lacks the authority of ordination for offering the Mass, but also and especially in that for the exercise of its apostolate the laity is subordinated to the clergy and is expected to be obedient.

> Let sacred pastors recognize and promote the dignity as well as the responsibility of the layman in the Church. Let them willingly make use of his prudent advice. . . . Attentively in Christ, let them consider with fatherly love the projects, suggestions, and desires proposed by the laity (Art 37).
>
> The laity have the right . . . to receive in abundance from their

[37] *Documents*, pp. 57, 58, 62, 59, 62, 63.
[38] *Documents*, pp. 58 f.

> sacred pastors the spiritual goods of the Church. . . . Every layman should openly reveal to them his needs and desires. . . . [and] with ready Christian obedience . . . accept whatever their sacred pastors, as representatives of Christ, decree in their role as teachers and rulers in the Church (Art. 37).[39]

This obedience applies not only to their activity as members of the church but also to the recognition of their rights and duties in human society to the extent that the pastors interpret for them in the light of the gospel the natural law in force for human society.

As impressive as is the intensity with which the universal priesthood of all the faithful is emphasized, it is striking, in view of the line of demarcation drawn between clergy and laity, that the New Testament statements have not received their due attention. This is true especially of Paul's teaching about spiritual gifts. An excellent proposal by Cardinal Suenens had called attention to this teaching and there is an unmistakable intention to incorporate it (Art. 7).[40] Yet, on the basis of a more careful exegesis of I Corinthians 12:1-11, 27-31; 14; Romans 12:3 ff., and the historical reality of the Pauline congregations which is recognizable here, it is impossible to differentiate between the hierarchical offices and the charismata of the laity as it was done in the first two chapters of the Constitution on the Church and especially in chapters iii and iv. While fully recognizing the superior position of the apostles, the diversity of spiritual gifts and services in the New Testament is not caused by a corresponding diversity of assignments and missions from the apostles but by the freedom of the Holy Spirit who provides these gifts and services "as he wills" (I Cor. 12:11). In the list, the first place after the apostles is assigned to the kerygmatic gifts, especially the prophets (I Cor. 12:28). Administrators are listed later (I Cor. 12:28; Rom. 12:8), while the gift of discerning spirits constitutes yet another charisma (I Cor. 12:10). Thus, through the stimulation of mani-

[39] *Documents*, pp. 64 f.
[40] *Documents*, pp. 20 ff.

fold spiritual gifts the message concerning Christ comes to the world in a variety of forms. Through this operation of the Spirit new congregations are called into being. The order of the offices in the congregation, and above all their mutual coordination and subordination, is a topic for later historical developments. Even the Acts and the Pastoral Epistles offer nothing more than embryonic suggestions for this development.

(e) The Religious

Following the chapters on the hierarchical structure of the church (iii) and the laity (iv), a separate chapter treats the religious who have pledged themselves through their vows to chastity, poverty, and obedience. As in the teaching about the hierarchy, there is here the same significant trend toward drawing the religious orders more strongly into the totality of the church. Just as the chapter on the structure of the hierarchy is preceded by the chapter on the church as the people of God (ii), so the chapter on the religious is preceded by a chapter on the call of the whole church to holiness (v). After "all of Christ's followers . . . are invited and bound to pursue holiness and the perfect fulfillment of their proper state" (Art. 42)[41] the religious as being in a state of holiness are not viewed in isolation but as a form of the common holiness of all the baptized and "as a sign which can and ought to attract all the members of the Church to an effective and prompt fulfillment of the duties of their Christian vocation" (Art. 44). "The religious state of life is not an intermediate one between the clerical and lay states" (Art. 43)[42] but rather a gift, help, and stimulation for both. Here, too, the grouping of this estate and service with the other structures of the church has been thought through with great care and developed further in a separate decree.

If we summarize what the constitution says about the structures of the church, we can see clearly that every member receives his place in a pyramidal system of superiority and subordination, of

[41] *Documents*, p. 72.
[42] *Documents*, pp. 74 f.

comprehensive and limited authorities, and of corresponding obligations of obedience—in a system whose apex is the pope in the fullness of his governing authority.

Seen only from this side, however, an important purpose of the constitution would be misunderstood. Its interest lies not only in the existing superiority and subordination but also in the grouping of the several grades in the fellowship of the one people of God. All of them, each in his own way, participate in the threefold prophetic, priestly, and kingly office of Jesus Christ. In accordance with their specific tasks, all are to serve each other; not only is the laity to serve the hierarchy, but the hierarchy is also to serve the laity, and in the same reciprocity the several grades of the hierarchy are to serve each other. It is clear, furthermore, that everyone, within the context of his task, is encouraged and even obligated to use his own initiative. He is by no means expected only to obey his superior offices. It is this aim, to bring all members of the church to close cooperation and united endeavor and thus to loosen up the system of superiorities and subordinations in the direction of the fellowship structure of the church, that constitutes the new aspect in this doctrine of the structure of the church.

It is true, at the same time, that the sphere of autonomous activity, that is, the sphere of service for the spiritual gift bestowed on him, is granted and limited for everyone by the office above him. Already the bishops have no right to assemble as a college and pass resolutions; they must wait for the pope to grant them this possibility. Still less are the priests authorized to administer the diocese jointly with the bishop, and the laity have even less authorization to govern the parish in conjunction with the priest, or the diocese together with the bishop, or the whole church jointly with the college of bishops and the pope. They can only wait and see to what extent the hierarchy will seek their counsel and aid and entertain their wishes. Of course this does not exclude the possibility that the attitude of individual members of the hierarchy may in fact lead to a genuine synodal fellowship on various levels. However, in contrast to the hierarchical centralization, the structure of such fellowship is not legally guaranteed. Without doubt the Council in this respect lagged behind expectations that were widespread even in the Roman church herself.

It is therefore no accident that the constitution did not discuss more fully the New Testament statements concerning apostles, teachers, prophets, bishops, pastors, presbyters, etc., or the New Testament relationship between charisma and laying on of hands, and succession and tradition. It is true that one cannot derive from the New Testament a comprehensive and complete church order. There is too great a variety of approaches in the original congregations. Yet every church order will have to remain true to the historic apostolic foundation and the basic structures of life in the primitive Christian congregations. At this point, however, there are far-reaching differences between the Constitution on the Church and the New Testament writings. The New Testament testimonies concerning the freedom of the Holy Spirit who provides charismata and services where he wills, as well as the testimonies concerning the community of charismata and services, shatter the conception of hierarchical centralization.

The Boundaries of the Church

The draft of the Constitution on the Church presented to the Council during the second period of sessions contained an introduction which suggested the intention of making a solemn dogmatic definition. In addition it contained the statement that the one church, as a constituted and ordered community in this world, is "the Catholic Church, that is governed by the Roman Pontiff and the bishops in communion with him." Thus the one, holy, catholic church was identified with the Roman church. Now, an ecclesiological identification in itself need not be taken in an exclusive sense. In principle it is entirely possible for a church to confess her identity with the one holy church, and at the same time to reckon with the possibility that the one holy church is a reality in other churches also. In this form of the *schema,* however, the identification of the one holy church with the Roman church is intended to be exclusive, since the context did not speak of churches outside the Roman church. There was reference only to non-Catholic Christians, hence, non-Catholic individuals, but not non-Catholic churches. In conceding to such individual non-Catholic Christians that they are connected with the church, the document did not mean to say that as members of their non-Roman church they belong to the one, holy, apostolic church. It meant, rather, that such Christians are connected with the Roman church, which claims to be the one, holy, catholic, apostolic church. It was not stated whether this connection is intended to say that the non-Catholic Christians are members of the church, or whether they are only brought into relation with the church. This connection with the church was established by their baptism, which is identical with the baptism administered by the Roman church, even though they received it outside the Roman church. This connection was further based on the *votum ecclesiae*, that is, the longing for the one church. The yearning for unity, which moves the hearts of non-Roman Christendom, was thereby interpreted as a yearning for the Roman church governed by the pope. Because of this connection of non-Roman Christians with the Roman church, the possibility of salvation and the reception of grace was conceded to them.

The final form of the constitution shows considerable alteration. The statement that the one church in this world "is the Catholic Church [*est ecclesia catholica*] which is governed by the Roman Pontiff and the bishops in communion with him" was dropped and superseded by the formulation that the church "subsists in the Catholic Church [*subsistit in ecclesia catholica*], which is governed by the successor of Peter and by the bishops in union with that successor." This change permits thinking of an identity that is less exclusive. Occasionally, it is true, theologians of the Council were heard to say that this modification of the church's exclusiveness was merely taking into account the fact that the church is a reality not only on earth in the Roman church but also in the heavenly fellowship of the perfected saints. Yet it is clear from the context, as well as from the reasons for this textual revision stated in the Council, that the exclusiveness of identifying the one, holy, catholic, and apostolic church with the Roman church was to be relaxed within the realm of the church's earthly existence itself. The words added to the above-cited statement demonstrate, however, that the possibilities for openness toward others suggested by "subsists in" are to be pursued only with extreme caution: "Many elements of sanctification and of truth can be found outside of her visible structure. These elements, however, as gifts properly belonging to the Church of Christ, possess an inner dynamism toward Catholic unity" (Art. 8).[43] The reference is not to the church nor to the churches outside the boundaries of the Roman church but only to "elements of sanctification and of truth."

For a full understanding of "subsists in" it is necessary to draw in the explanations concerning the different ways in which believing Catholics, the believers in Christ, and ultimately all men who by God's grace have been called to salvation, belong together or are integrated with each other. In this context it is pointed out that there are many non-Catholics

> who honor sacred Scripture, taking it as a norm of belief and of action, and who show a true religious zeal. They lovingly believe in God the Father Almighty and in Christ, Son of God and Savior. They are consecrated by baptism, through which they are united with Christ. They also recognize and receive other sacraments within their own Churches or ecclesial communities. Many of them rejoice in the episcopate, celebrate the Holy Eucharist, and cultivate devotion toward the Virgin Mother of God. They also share with us in prayer and other spiritual benefits.
>
> Likewise, we can say that in some real way they are joined with us in the Holy Spirit, for to them also He gives His gifts and graces, and is thereby operative among them with His sanctifying power. Some indeed He has strengthened to the extent of the shedding of their blood (Art. 15).[44]

---

[43] *Documents*, p. 23.
[44] *Documents*, p. 34.

Although the concept "elements" is clarified in many respects, there are here no dogmatic affirmations concerning the churches outside the Roman church and references are made only to persons. The addition that they receive sacraments "within their own Churches or ecclesial communities" does not constitute a dogmatic statement concerning the ecclesiological status of these churches, but is simply a phenomenological way of fixing the place where they receive the sacraments. In general, here, too, the operation of the Spirit outside the Roman church is interpreted as arousing the desire for unity in the Roman church.

Further elucidations of the "elements" of the church beyond the boundaries of the Roman church are provided by the discussions concerning Jews and Moslems.

> Nor is God Himself far distant from those who in shadows and images seek the unknown God. . . .
>
> Those also can attain to everlasting salvation who through no fault of their own do not know the gospel of Christ or His Church, yet sincerely seek God and, moved by grace, strive by their deeds to do His will as it is known to them through the dictates of conscience (Art. 16).[45]

These statements have considerably weakened the original force of Cyprian's axiom that "there is no salvation outside the church." Yet the view on the church's boundaries has remained so narrow that the phenomenological recognition of the reality of other churches is prevented, and, above all, the mystery which is hidden in church history, that the body of Christ is indissolubly one in spite of schisms in the church, has been improperly rationalized and the inclusive breadth of the *Una Sancta* misunderstood. In its expressions concerning the earthly reality of the church, the Constitution on the Church makes a claim for the Roman church which all other churches reject.

The reasons for this narrow view of the church are to be found, on the one hand, in its temporal proximity to the encyclical *Mystici Corporis*, which in a strict sense had equated the bound-

---

[45] *Documents*, p. 35.

aries of Christ's mystical body with those of the legally constituted Roman church. Since, however, the Constitution on the Church in Vatican II goes beyond that encyclical in other essential points, the narrow concept of the church has other causes. Because of its weaknesses in method and in substance the constitution is itself responsible.

(a) The historical fact that there is a variety of witnesses, confessional statements, traditions, and church orders in the church of the New Testament and the early centuries is expressed neither in the different drafts of the *schema* for the Constitution on the Church nor in the discussions in the Council. Correspondingly, insufficient consideration was given to the understanding of church unity which prevails in the New Testament writings and which experienced extensive changes in the course of the first three centuries up to the establishment of the state church. The constitution did not derive its understanding of unity from the original juxtaposition of Jewish-Christian, Jewish-Hellenistic, and Hellenistic churches, nor from the structure of the ancient church which provided for a reciprocal acknowledgment of the offices and of the baptismal creeds which showed considerable variation from one area to another. Rather, this understanding is shaped by the unity existing today within the Roman church, whose understanding of unity in faith and of jurisdictional order differs markedly from the understanding which prevailed in the church in the New Testament and in the early centuries. A similar judgment may be made concerning the definition of relationships among pope, bishops, priests, and laity. In taking steps to loosen up uniformity in the direction of variety, and thus in the direction of seeing the unity as a fellowship, elements from the Bible and the ancient church were incorporated. Yet the understanding of unity and the structure of the Roman church were not confronted in the proper sense with the historical situation concerning the actual state of affairs in the church of the New Testament and the early centuries. Much less was that understanding critically evaluated by these criteria.

(b) In spite of clearly setting forth the ecclesiological significance of the worshiping community, as is done in the Constitution on the Liturgy, and in spite of the accented statements in the Constitution on the Church about elevating the baptized into the fellowship of the body of Christ through reception of the sacramental body (Art. 7; cf. Art. 11), the local parish plays only a subordinate role. From the start, the concern is directed to the universal church on earth and remains there. This creates the impression that the statements about particular churches and local parishes must be derived by deduction from what is said about the universal church. The New Testament writings designate as *ecclesia* and as the body of Christ both the local assembly for worship and the universal church, and they do this because one and the same Christ and one and the same Holy Spirit are present in the local assembly and in the universal church and impart themselves to them. Since this presence of the one Lord established the unity of the local churches in the universal church, both paths of ecclesiological thought must be pursued in a systematic-theological way—from what happens in the local worshiping community to the universal church and vice versa. If the latter path is one-sidedly preferred, the danger arises that in the understanding of unity, as distinct from the New Testament witness, priority is given to the jurisdictional-hierarchical order over the Lord who gives himself in the worshiping community. Furthermore, there is the danger of ecclesiologically disparaging the local congregation in favor of the cathedral churches of the hierarchy.

(c) From among the great variety of relationships between Christ and the church, the constitution one-sidedly favors the relationships of solidarity, fellowship, and unity, that is, those that are given in the designation of the church as the body of Christ. Yet the designation "people of God," already from the Old Testament witness, contains not only the relationship of communion but also the antithesis of the Lord as the judge of his people. The constitution mentions that those who do not preserve in love and do not respond to the grace of Christ in thought, word, and deed "will be the more severely judged" (Art. 14).[46] Yet the constitution does not speak of Christ as judge of the *church.* According to the New Testament witness his judgment will not be confined to individual persons who regarded themselves as his followers and even prophesied in his name and performed great deeds, to whom, nevertheless, the Lord will say, "I never knew you; depart from me" (Matt. 7:22 f.). On the contrary, Christ's judgment is announced to *entire churches*, as, for example, in the letter to the church in Laodicea: "So, because you are lukewarm, and neither cold nor hot, I will spew you out of my mouth" (Rev. 3:16; cf. also 2:5 and 16). The constitution did, indeed, incorporate the designation of the church as the people of God, and hence gave expression to the connection between Israel and the church. In spite of acknowledging the salvation-history identity of the Old Testament covenant people with the church as the true Israel, the constitution nowhere echoes the prophets' proclamation of judgment against the covenant people. God has indeed established a new covenant in Christ, achieved a new creation, and promised the church that it shall never be destroyed. Yet it must not be overlooked that the Old Testament covenant people had also received the promise of an abiding remnant, and that the difference in both covenants does not annul the identity of the people of God in the midst of the threats and temptations of this world and under the warnings of God. Thus the ancient fathers and the medieval theologians, in all earnestness and in an entirely proper manner, understood the prophetic preaching, for example, of Hosea and Ezekiel, as God's word to the church (cf. the extensive material in Hans Urs von Balthasar, *Wer ist die Kirche?* (1965), "Die heilige Hure," pp. 55 ff.).

(d) It has already been pointed out that the teaching about the hierarchical order of the church did not do full justice to the New Testament material on the sovereign freedom of the Holy Spirit, especially to the Pauline teaching on the community of spiritual gifts and services. Since the constitution in its under-

[46] *Documents*, p. 46.

standing of the church continues to be determined in a special way by the juridical structure of the hierarchy to which the free charismata are made subject, it is prevented from acknowledging the breadth of the operation of the Holy Spirit and his gifts, services, and offices outside the hierarchically governed Roman church.

(e) The narrowness of the constitution's concept of the church may also be accounted for by the fact that its assertions concerning the church proceed too one-sidedly from the substantive concepts and images which the New Testament uses to designate the church. Conversely, too little was said about the words of consolation and challenge with which the Lord and the apostles confronted the church and still confront her today. For example, attention must be paid to the fact that John's Gospel does not use the terms "church," "people of God," "body of Christ," and that the very significant ecclesiological statements in John 13-17 are expressed almost exclusively (with the exception of the Parable of the Vine) in terms of promise, encouragement, indicative, imperative, warning, threat, and intercession ("you are clean," "abide in me," "love one another," etc.). We must by no means fail to recognize that the constitution has gone beyond the older dogmatic texts in giving due expression to the variety of biblical concepts and images as well as to the comprehensive context of salvation history. Yet we dare not overlook one danger which otherwise, too, not infrequently appears in connection with a salvation-history oriented way of thinking, namely, that instead of listening to the Lord who confronts the church, a description of how the Lord and the church are related to each other is substituted. In this way the gathering, edifying, but also critical and judging activity of the Lord is crowded out by substantive and descriptive statements about the church's essence. In a similar way, the Council of Trent formulated its decree on justification in such a way that the doctrine is taught in an objectifying description rather than in existential involvement. The Constitution on the Church says too little about the *meeting* which takes place in divine worship between Christ and the assembly, too little about the Lord's speaking through the word, and too little about his offer of the sacrament. On the contrary, the constitution is too quick to subsume the event of worship as means to a universal process.

Thus in its doctrine concerning the hierarchical structure and the boundaries of the church, the constitution is apologetic, motivated by the need to justify the existing Roman church, rather than dogmatic, that is, determined by a critical evaluation of the present Roman church by the criterion of the historical apostolic and primitive Christian tradition. Nevertheless, we dare not overlook the forces which are here seeking to overcome a centralistic uniformity.

Mary and the Church

The Constitution on the Church closes with chapter viii, "The Role of the Blessed Virgin Mary, Mother of God, in the Mystery of Christ and the Church." The history of this chapter is among the most dramatic elements of the Council. Surprisingly, in November, 1962, the *schema* of an independent constitution, "On the Blessed Virgin Mary," was made public. This document aimed at a further development of Mariology by suggesting that Mariological statements from encyclicals of the most recent popes should be elevated to the rank of a dogmatic decision of the Council, and especially that the title "Mediatrix" should be explicitly acknowledged. In a comment it was stated that the title "Coredemptrix" was omitted out of deference to the Protestants, and yet the substance of the idea was included. On November 29, 1963, the Council by a narrow majority resolved not to treat the Mariological theme in an independent constitution but rather as a part of the Constitution on the Church. By September, 1964, the text on Mariology had become the closing chapter of the Constitution on the Church and the debate reached its climax. On the maximal side the demand was made to give dogmatic recognition to Mary as Mediatrix and Mother of the church, while the opposition rejected such a development of the Mariological dogma as theologically immature. The final formulation represents a compromise: Cautiously, the title "Mediatrix" was adopted, but the title "Mother of the church" was omitted. The closing chapter is therefore not maximal, since it defines no new Marian dogma, nor is it minimal, since it explicitly supports the dogmas of the Immaculate Conception (1854) and the Assumption (1950), and, in addition, recognizes Mary as Mediatrix.

Basic for defining the relationship between Mary and the church is the section entitled "The Role of the Blessed Virgin in the Economy of Salvation" (Arts. 55-59).[47] In line with the salvation-history approach in the doctrine of the church, this section treats first the Old Testament witness concerning Mary, then her earthly life, and finally her assumption into heavenly glory, as presupposition for her present activity on behalf of the church and her veneration by the church. In what follows we proceed from the New Testament material about Mary but cannot enter into a discussion of history-of-traditions and historical matters.

(a) On the basis of the Gospels all churches remember Mary, the mother of Jesus, as the elect member of God's people who was used by God in a unique way to execute his work of redemption, namely, to realize the incarnation of his Son, and who in the obedience of faith assented to this service. Beyond this, however, the Council thinks of Mary as "entirely holy and free from all stain of sin" "from the first instant of her conception," "fashioned by the Holy Spirit into a kind of new substance and new creature" (Art. 56).[48]

(b) According to the New Testament witness, Mary's yea of faith did not remain self-evident during the public ministry of Jesus. According to the Synoptics, Mary did not belong to the circle of disciples. Though she was a highly favored mother, she did not understand Jesus even as a twelve-year-old in the temple (Luke 2:50). Though she was his mother, Jesus let her stand

[47] *Documents*, pp. 87 ff.
[48] *Documents*, p. 88.

outside and, turning away from her, said to his disciples: "Here are my mother and my brothers! Whoever does the will of God is my brother, and sister, and mother" (Mark 3:34 f.). The same context reports that his friends regarded Jesus as "beside himself" (Mark 3:21). True, according to John, Mary accompanied Jesus to the wedding at Cana, but there she was rebuffed by him (John 2:4). Thus the Gospels present Mary as a woman who was assailed in her faith and who experienced grief, not only because of the suffering of her son but also because of her inability to understand his course. Apart from a formal reference to Luke 2:41-51, the Constitution on the Church ignores this peculiar lack of understanding on the part of Mary (Art. 57).[49]

(c) The New Testament accounts of the passion give no indication that Mary understood the death of Jesus as the redemptive act of the Christ and Son of God. She seems to have experienced the same shock as the disciples. The first confessions of faith are transmitted in the passion accounts as the words of the one malefactor on the cross and of the centurion. According to John's Gospel, Mary did not flee but remained beneath the cross. Yet even when the figures of Mary and John are taken symbolically, the words of Jesus (John 19:26 f.) are not an acknowledgment of her faith in him, but a loving provision and directive addressed to Mary and John or to the Jewish- and Gentile-Christian church for the future. The Constitution on the Church, however, teaches a participation of Mary in Jesus' sacrifice on the cross—in that she "lovingly consented to the immolation of this Victim which she herself had brought forth" (Art. 58).[50]

(d) As with the faith of the apostles, so with Mary it was the work of divine grace that in spite of these trials she was, with the other women and brethren after Jesus' resurrection, united in faith and in prayer with the apostles, and awaited the coming of the Holy Spirit (Acts 1:14). There is no indication in the New Testament that she occupied a special place in the first Christian

[49] *Documents*, pp. 89 f.
[50] *Documents*, pp. 89 f.

congregation. There is no record that the risen Jesus appeared to her (as he did to Peter, James, and others), nor that she had hurried to the disciples with the message of the empty grave or of Jesus' resurrection (as Mary Magdalene and others had done), nor that she proclaimed the message of God's saving deed in Jesus Christ to others, as the apostles did. Correspondingly, in the New Testament the apostles and prophets, not Mary, are named as the foundation of the church (Eph. 2:20; cf. Matt. 16:18 and Rev. 21:14). Nothing is said concerning the end of Mary's earthly life, even in those New Testament writings which came into being at the end of the first century or in the second century. Yet the Constitution on the Church teaches: "Finally, preserved free from all guilt of original sin, the Immaculate Virgin was taken up body and soul into heavenly glory upon the completion of her earthly sojourn. She was exalted by the Lord as Queen of all" (Art. 59).[51] This teaching is without historical foundation since neither the New Testament nor the church's tradition of the first five centuries provides any documentation for an assumption of Mary into heaven.

(e) It is said of Mary that "in an utterly singular way she cooperated by her obedience, faith, hope, and burning charity in the Savior's work of restoring supernatural life to souls. For this reason she is a mother to us in the order of grace" (Art. 61). Therefore she is "invoked by the Church under the titles of Advocate, Auxiliatrix, Adjutrix, and Mediatrix" (Art. 62).[52] The title of Mediator is used in the New Testament exclusively for the one who was sent by God to proclaim and execute the once-and-for-all historic act of salvation. Other titles of Jesus are in the New Testament transferred to members of the church, titles such as son of God, servant of God, holy one, shepherd, bishop, etc. Such transfers are called analogies and are explained in this way, that, for example, Jesus Christ alone is the Son of God by nature, while the believers are sons of God by adoption. The analogical

---

[51] *Documents*, p. 90.
[52] *Documents*, p. 91.

use of such honorific titles of Jesus remains lucid, however, only when the difference is perfectly clear. The New Testament safeguards the difference by refusing to transfer some titles as, for example, Christ, Lord, Mediator, Savior. Only when some titles are not transferred to members of the church can it be clearly maintained that the transfer of the other titles is intended to be merely an analogy. The New Testament witnesses decidedly to the exclusive character of the mediatorship of Jesus Christ. "There is one God, and there is one mediator between God and men, the man Christ Jesus" (I Tim. 2:5). The constitution cites this passage too (Art. 60) and goes on to say that the titles given to Mary, including Mediatrix, "neither take away from nor add anything to the dignity and efficacy of Christ the one Mediator" (Art. 62; cf. Art. 60).[53] Yet this statement is already largely refuted by the Catholic popular piety. There even the theological distinction between worship which belongs to God alone and veneration to which Mary is entitled is often not understood. In addition to the christological title of Mediator, the Constitution on the Church also transfers names to Mary which correspond to the New Testament statements concerning the activity of the Holy Spirit, such as, Advocate, Auxiliatrix, Adjutrix. Whereas the constitution's assertions about the Holy Spirit's activity are reduced, its Mariology has been exaggerated by the application of christological and pneumatological titles to Mary.

What is the significance of the mother of the Lord for an understanding of the church? It lies precisely in the fact that the New Testament documents witness to these two things: Mary as the physical mother of Jesus Christ and as the unpretentious member of the first Christian congregation, Mary as the one uniquely chosen for service and the one subject to trials—these make her remembrance precious and consoling. In just this way she is an example of faith and a type of the church. In both respects, in her choice to be the "Mother of God" and in the trials of the suffering mother, her life is an unforgettable doxology of divine grace.

---

[53] *Documents*, pp. 90 f.

The Constitution on the Church, however, presents Mary not so much as a member of the church but rather as the maternal counterpart to the members of the church. When she is presented as a member of the church it is in such a way as to distinguish her from all other members of the church, and she is distinguished by no means only through her conception of and giving birth to the Son of God. On the contrary, going beyond the New Testament statements, claims are made for her sinlessness, her cooperation in the sacrifice on the cross, her assumption, and her enduring mediatorship, and on the basis of these claims she is exalted above all believers and is to be venerated in a cultic way. In this sense she is a type of the church. The church, "contemplating Mary's mysterious sanctity, imitating her charity, and faithfully fulfilling the Father's will, becomes herself a mother by accepting God's word in faith. . . . The Church herself is a virgin" (Art. 64). While "the followers of Christ still strive to increase in holiness by conquering sin," in the "most holy Virgin the Church has already reached that perfection whereby she exists without spot or wrinkle (cf. Eph. 5:27)" (Art. 65).[54] In a similar way other privileges and titles of Mary may be transferred to the church. Thus the Constitution on the Church closes with a compromise in Mariology but at the same time ends with the church's glorification based on Mariology.

---

[54] *Documents*, pp. 92 f.

6

The Council and Non-Roman Churches

The Dogmatic Constitution on the Church provides the basis for the Council's pronouncements regarding the relationship of the Roman church to other churches, to non-Christian religions, and to mankind in general, that is to say, the relationship of the Roman church to the three concentric circles of which she considers herself the center. Among these pronouncements, the Decree on Ecumenism is especially significant for the rest of Christendom. This decree was adopted in the public closing session of the third period of the Council by an overwhelming majority of 2156 voting bishops to only 11; it was then proclaimed by Pope Paul VI. The significance of this decree becomes apparent as soon as one remembers the former negative attitude of the Roman church over against the ecumenical movement. In this chapter we shall first examine the content of this decree and then later, in Chapters 7 and 8, seek to determine the extent to which the provisions of the Decree on Ecumenism have influenced other decisions of the Council. It makes a difference whether the thoughts expressed in the Decree on Ecumenism merely stand beside other decisions of the Council, or whether the former permeate the latter.

The Approach to Non-Roman Churches

Originally, the *schema* of the Constitution on the Church had seen the problem of non-Roman churches only as a question concerning *individual* non-Catholic Christians who had a connection with the Roman church because of their baptism and their longing for that church. By way of contrast, the first form of the Decree on Ecumenism, treating in its first chapter the principles of ecumenism and thus also dealing with an understanding of the church, was far more open from the start. The statements about the one holy catholic church were initially made without mentioning the Roman church and without ever identifying the two in an exclusive way. Hence from the start there was here a great openness for the reality of the church, even beyond the boundaries of the Roman church. At the same time, there was a greater respect for the mystery of the church, a mystery we can witness correctly only if we know that it transcends human conceptuality and language. There was, furthermore, no explicit mention of the pope, but only of Peter whom the Lord had chosen from among the twelve to preside over the college of his brethren by strengthening each one in the faith and by shepherding the whole flock. To be sure, this statement was not meant to be purely historical. Yet in these treatments of the church's unity the primary emphasis was placed on the historical, apostolic basis and not so much on the form of the Roman primacy as it had developed in the course of Western church history. Undoubtedly, this approach made possible significant opportunities for ecumenical dialogue on this theme which is so controversial among the churches.

It was precisely this ecclesiological basis for the *schema* on ecumenism, however, that was sharply criticized in the assembly hall. Cardinal Frings demanded that clear expression be given to the idea that we need not look forward to the one church of Jesus Christ, but that this one church, founded by the Lord and built on Peter, was already in existence in the Roman Catholic Church. It is this one church, he claimed, that will be brought to consummation at the end of time. Other voices, too, asked for a clearer expression of what constitutes the unity of the church and oneness in faith and government, so that the separated brethren would not misunderstand. There was criticism of the fact that the *schema* did not maintain the complete identity of the mystical body of Christ with the Roman Catholic Church, as taught in the encyclical *Mystici Corporis Christi.* Love for the separated was said to call for the whole truth and the avoidance of all irenicism. By failing to mention the primacy of the *successors* of Peter in the *schema* on ecumenism in the interests of a false irenicism, the fundamental truths of the unity of the church were being suppressed. Bible passages must not be allowed by their indefiniteness to lead to inaccuracies in questions of controversy.

It is probably due to such objections that the official form of the Decree on Ecumenism emphatically and repeatedly states that the unity, fullness, and riches of the one, holy, catholic, and apostolic church are realized only in the Roman church and thus under the successor of Peter as the head. It is "through Christ's Catholic Church alone, which is the all-embracing means of salvation, that the fullness of the means of salvation can be obtained" (Art. 3).[1] Thus the final form of the Decree on Ecumenism has in some measure adapted its statements on the principles of ecumenism to the more cautious Constitution on the Church.

During the Council's discussion of the first form of the decree there were also those, to be sure, who desired to go even further. Many Council Fathers were especially dissatisfied with the designation of the churches of the Reformation as merely "communities." While one group of bishops insisted that "the associations that came into being in the sixteenth century" were being evaluated too favorably, and that the differences between the Orthodox and the Protestants was not stated plainly enough, another group (Cardinal König and others) emphatically demanded that these "associations" should in any case be called "ecclesiastical communions." Thirty Indonesian bishops went so far as to request that the name "church" be given not only to the Orthodox but also to the churches of the Reformation. Other bishops at the Council supported this request.

On this question the definitive text of the decree went beyond the first draft. It speaks explicitly of "Churches and Communities" alongside the Roman church. The text does not state in what sense non-Roman churches are called churches or churchly communities.

---

[1] *Documents*, p. 346.

On the one hand, it probably meant more than mere accommodation to the self-designation of these bodies and implied a certain ecclesiological recognition. On the other hand, however, it hardly meant what the Roman church understands herself to be as church, but is probably used only by analogy. It must not be regarded as a defect that the terms are not further clarified here. The ecumenical movement has created new ecclesiological problems for which all the churches of our day still lack adequate concepts. On the basis of the discussion in the Council, it seems clear that the changed designation for non-Roman churches is meant to grant them a larger ecclesiological significance, and these, in turn, should acknowledge this intent.

Thus on this point the decree goes beyond the assertions in the Constitution on the Church. This document in its final form speaks only of "elements" of the Catholic church outside of the boundaries of the Roman church. Hence the decree demonstrates a greater ecumenical openness toward non-Roman churches. Such a step beyond the Constitution on the Church was necessary if the ecumenical problem was to be tackled at all, for this problem is taken seriously only as a problem dealing with separated *churches*. To be sure, the more narrow Constitution on the Church continues to take precedence in rank and obligating significance over the more open Decree on Ecumenism, and the ecumenism of the Roman church will be able to cross the boundaries of the Constitution on the Church only to the extent that it can lend credence to the claim that in its statements about "elements" of the Catholic church in other churches, based on the communal character of some of these elements (such as Baptism and the Lord's Supper), the Constitution on the Church is already speaking implicitly about communions and even of churches outside the Roman church.

Directives for Ecumenical Attitudes

The second chapter of the Decree on Ecumenism bears the heading "The Practice of Ecumenism." In the impressive simplicity of its directives it contains the most ecumenically progressive sections of this decree. Since the first draft the material had been steadily improved. Newly added, for example, was the reference to the church on her pilgrim way as being summoned "to that continual reformation" (Art. 6). Also new was this paragraph:

> St. John has testified: "If we say that we have not sinned, we make him a liar, and his word is not in us" (I John 1:10). This holds good for sins against unity. Thus, in humble prayer, we beg pardon of God and of our separated brethren, just as we forgive those who trespass against us (Art 7).[2]

To be sure, the directives of this chapter are addressed to the members of the Roman church, yet in my opinion the other churches should also acknowledge them as valid in their essentials and take them to heart. They are in fact formulating the first requirement for intercourse among separated brethren—something that should be self-evident among Christians, but unfortunately is not everywhere so. If these basic principles of ecumenical behavior will be translated into practice, it is to be expected that many a tract of land which has long ago become hard and barren will be plowed anew on both sides of the churchly boundaries. In a special way, this chapter manifests the earnestness of the ecumenical desire that motivates the Secretariat for Christian Unity and many bishops besides. Every member of the Roman church is reminded of the prerequisites:[3]

(a) *The spiritual renewal of the heart* (Arts. 7 f.). Without conversion, without sanctification, without self-denial, humility, willing service, and an attitude of brotherly generosity toward the separated, without growth in love and a yearning for unity, there can be no ecumenism. In fact, a genuine ecumenical movement is always a movement of repentance. It does not begin by demanding that the separated repent but by one's own repentance; not by demanding that others change, but with one's own readiness to change.

(b) *The prayer for unity* (Art. 8), wherever possible even

---

[2] *Documents*, pp. 350 f.
[3] *Documents*, pp. 351 ff.

together with the separated brethren. In the discussions the objection was raised that a joint prayer for unity was a deception in that everyone prayed according to his own point of view. A Catholic could, however, pray only for the return of the separated brethren. To this Cardinal Bea replied (in the sense of Couturier, the French ecumenical pioneer) that it was enough if each person praying would leave it to God to decide when and how a unity fuller than that now recognized by the spirit of the prayers is to be achieved. Joint prayers, which are recommended, are distinguished from joint worship services, which may be permitted by the bishops only under certain circumstances.

(c) *A careful concern for learning the truth about the separated brethren,* their doctrine, their worship, their piety, as well as their historical and cultural presuppositions. To that end there is a demand for broadening theological education (Art. 10).

(d) *Dialogue with the separated brethren on the basis of equality* (Arts. 9 and 11). In this dialogue the Catholic doctrine is to be presented to the separated brethren clearly, adapted to their presuppositions, without diminution, (irenism), yet also without polemics. At this point the emphasis would seem to lie on the professional dialogue among theologians rather than on inter-church conversations. To be sure, the first draft of the *schema* on ecumenism did not specify in its statements on dialogue to what extent the dialogue was to be merely an explanation of Catholic truth with due regard for the presuppositions of the partners in the dialogue, or a common and joint wrestling for the truth. As a matter of fact, in every genuine dialogue every presentation is bound to lead to a joint seeking, questioning, and searching. It is not we men who possess the truth; rather, the truth lays hold on us. In the Council there were, in fact, voices which demanded such a joint quest with the separated brethren. In this sense Suffragan Bishop Elchinger of Strasbourg very emphatically called attention to the criteria for a genuine ecumenical dialogue. Consequently, the final form of the decree also explicitly speaks of "searching together with separated brethren into the divine mysteries," with the goal that "the way will be opened for this kind of fraternal rivalry to incite all to a deeper realization and a clearer expression of the unfathomable riches of Christ." Especially helpful in this connection is the directive: "When comparing doctrines, they should remember that in Catholic teaching there exists an order or 'hierarchy' of truths, since they vary in their relationship to the foundation of the Christian faith" (Art. 11).[4] According to Roman Catholic understanding of dogmatic validity, this hierarchy can, however, be understood as being merely *substantive-systematic*, and not in the sense of central and less central dogmas which have different *degrees of obligation.*

Let us pause a moment. In view of the extreme reserve of the Roman church that prevailed until recently over against other churches, these directives already imply more than may appear at first glance. They receive their special importance, however, from the fact that they are not simply words occupying space but words that must be heard in the context of the Council itself. They are not only demands but expressions of what has already begun to be realized in the Council's work and what we observers have experienced in numerous meetings with Council Fathers and theologians. There at the Council a new dialogue in mutual respect, love, and openness, and a united and genuine wrestling for the truth, had already begun.

(e) Further to be emphasized is the *call for cooperation with the separated brethren* (Art. 12),[5] especially in social questions, in problems of the technical evolution, and in relieving the afflictions of our times, such as famine and natural disasters, illiteracy, and poverty. These examples are from the confines of natural law. Yet the discussion in the Council made progress insofar as it pointed to the necessity of cooperation among the churches' relief programs in underprivileged countries, such as the cooperation of Catholics and Protestants in solving the problems of Christian

---

[4] *Documents*, p. 354.
[5] *Documents*, p. 355.

Africa. Moreover, an ecumenical collection, once proposed by Oscar Cullmann, was recommended. This collection is to be announced and gathered in the public services, by Evangelical churches for Catholic needs, and vice versa.

(f) Beyond all this the final form of the decree also explicitly mentioned *the united witness to the faith*:

> Before the whole world, let all Christians profess their faith in God, one and three, in the incarnate Son of God, our Redeemer and Lord. United in their efforts, and with mutual respect, let them bear witness to our common hope, which does not play us false (Art. 12).[6]

This readiness of the Council to bear witness to Christ conjointly with non-Roman Christendom is of extraordinary ecumenical significance.

(g) On many burning issues the decree says nothing. It makes no statements about the removal of particular frictions which make it difficult for separated Christians to live together, such as, for example, the refusal to recognize a mixed marriage performed by an Evangelical pastor, the conditional rebaptism of a proper baptism performed in an Evangelical church (under the condition of its invalidity), or the rivalry among churches on the mission field. The question will have to be raised later whether these problems are dealt with in other resolutions of the Council. Already at this point attention is called to the long and violently debated Declaration on Religious Freedom, which provides the presupposition for abolishing such distressing situations as exist, for example, for the Evangelical church in Spain and, far beyond Spain, seriously encumber the relationship between the Roman church and Evangelical Christendom. The reasons behind this delayed concern of the Roman church for religious freedom are undoubtedly quite varied. The Roman church herself today needs this freedom in areas where she is being suppressed. Yet the demand for religious freedom has also been made quite consciously by many for a new relationship to other churches, even in areas where the Roman church predominates. Many opinions expressly made the point that

---

[6] *Documents*, p. 354.

understanding of, and respect for, those of another faith, hence religious freedom, formed the necessary basis for ecumenism. To be sure, there was strong opposition in the Council to the Declaration on Religious Freedom, and attention was rightly called to the Roman church's tradition, including explicit rejection of religious freedom in the Syllabus of Pius IX (par. X). Against this opposition the declaration could prevail only by unilaterally going beyond the Decree on Ecumenism in its final form and assuming that the Roman church is the only true religion, by taking up the limitation of religious freedom by means of the imprecise concept of "the common welfare," and, in addition, by making special provision for countries where *one* religion predominates and where special legal recognition is given to one religious body (Art. 6).[7] Here, too, the demand is made that religious freedom be granted not only to the consciences of individual members of other religious communities but also to these communities themselves. Here, too, it is no longer simply a matter of toleration; it is also a matter of the right of religious fellowships to freedom of activity as detailed in the declaration (assembly for worship, religious education, election of officers, autonomy in managing their own affairs, etc., Art. 4).[8] Furthermore, it is the duty of the state to safeguard this right. Thus, in spite of its restrictions, the declaration represents a noteworthy step forward, a step designed to make possible the encounter between the separated churches on a new level.

At first, to be sure, the decree's directives concerning ecumenical behavior confine themselves to the initial steps. These directives are undoubtedly of great significance, indeed, for many Catholic theologians and laymen they are of revolutionary significance. Yet there is still a broad gulf between these initial steps and the desired union. The union of the separated churches cannot be expected without first removing the most serious hindrances to

---

[7] *Documents*, pp. 683 ff.
[8] *Documents*, pp. 681 ff.

living together, so that a common witness to Christ, which all the baptized owe God and the world, may become possible.

The Goal

The goal of Roman Catholic ecumenism is the union of the separated churches, more precisely their reunion with the Roman church. To be sure, this union is not the immediate goal of the Council—its objective is the renewal of the Roman church—yet it was kept in view at the Council, even though it is expected to follow upon the renewal. The church's renewal must take place so that the face of the Roman church may shine more convincingly on the separated brethren and so that a wider gate to this catholic house of the church may be opened to all. In this sense we must understand the hope of John XXIII, expressed also by his successor, that the Council become a "remarkable display of truth, unity and love, a display which those who are cut off from this Apostolic See will observe. We sincerely hope that they will receive it as a gentle invitation to seek and acquire that unity which Jesus Christ prayed for so ardently to His heavenly Father."[9] The goal of ecumenism consists, therefore, of a succession of integrated goals. That the Council fixed on the renewal of the Roman church herself as the first goal is quite in line with what other churches in their union endeavors found to be necessary. One can only have the highest respect for the earnestness and the humility with which so many Council Fathers attacked this problem of renewal.

(a) The Renewal of the Roman Church

The demand for inner renewal expressed in the Decree on Ecumenism is addressed not only to the individual members of the Roman church but also to the Roman church as a whole (Arts. 4 and 6).

> Christ summons the Church, as she goes her pilgrim way, to that continual reformation of which she always has need, insofar as she

[9] Opening encyclical of John XXIII, *Ad Petri Cathedram*, Part 3 in Anne Freemantle (ed.), *The Papal Encyclicals* (see above, p. 19, n. 2), p. 320.

is an institution of men here on earth. Therefore, if the influence of events or of the times has led to deficiencies in conduct, in Church discipline, or even in the formulation of doctrine (which must be carefully distinguished from the deposit itself of faith), these should be appropriately rectified at the proper moment (Art. 6).[10]

The demand for churchly renewal was discussed in a great number of formal opinions; it was expressly affirmed and made concrete in a variety of ways, even going so far as to demand a new theological vocabulary, a new churchly structure, and a renunciation of the display of churchly representation. All of this compels one to see in these words not only a set of postulates but also clear indications that the renewal has already begun. A new attitude was manifested in deeply moving expressions which spoke, without consideration for church history, of what they had neglected in their duty to the world and their separated fellow Christians. A number of opinions expressly took over the words from Pope Paul's opening address concerning the necessity of mutual forgiveness. Most emphatically, the Council rejected the objection that statements which involved the Catholic church in guilt for the splits in the church created displeasure in the Council, and that those who cannot rid themselves of a guilt complex should go to their father confessor (Bishop Muldoon, Sydney). It was stressed that a public and truthful admission of guilt is the first step in all endeavors at restoring unity (Presiding Abbot Butler, England). It is unmistakable that in the Council a movement toward renewal manifested itself in spite of all retarding factors.

The renewal in attitude had its effect in a special way on the struggle concerning the structure of the church's order. Thus the Council was vigorously engaged in relaxing the centralization of the church by promoting collegiality and permitting the diversity of the church to be featured instead of uniformity. Remembering also the struggle for a collegial understanding of church government, one notices in the area of the church's liturgical and can-

[10] *Documents*, p. 350.

onical order the outlines of a renewal in the direction of the communal character of the church. There is, in addition, the noteworthy intensity with which former ideas and forms of behavior were critically reviewed and a new dialogue with the surrounding world undertaken.

The church's dogma, of course, sets the limits for this renewal. As already indicated, the liturgical reform in no sense signifies a change in the teaching of Trent concerning the sacrifice of the Mass. The Marian dogmas of 1854 and 1950 also remain unchanged. The bishops in their conciliar oath committed themselves explicitly to all dogmatic decisions of Roman church history and hence also to all existing anathemas against the teachings of non-Roman churches. Yet these very antitheses in statements on the faith that are contained in the dogma, together with the respective anathemas, constitute the most serious hindrance to union. As far as doctrinal differences among the churches are concerned, the Council repealed none of the existing anathemas to pave the way for union. To be sure, in Evangelical and Roman theology today we see the task of translating dogmatic statements from the approach and thought patterns of their historical origin, as well as their specific thought and language structures, into contexts, concepts, and structures of our time that are in part radically different. In this we see the possibilities of reinterpreting dogmatic statements and opening them in the direction of a consensus among separated churches. Yet it seems to me that the Council made hardly any use of this insight into the historically conditioned character of the dogmas and of this possibility of reinterpreting them. Nor was there an attempt to distinguish between the greater or lesser obligation of the various dogmatic decisions from the perspective of the confession of Christ.

(b) Unfolding the Catholicity of the Roman Church

Unfolding the catholicity of the church also serves to promote the goal of union and it is given priority. It is intimately connected with renewal.

The demand for this development signifies, first of all, the task of granting the broadest kind of freedom to the diverse forms of Roman Catholic spiritual life, theological endeavor, etc. Beyond this, however, it points to the necessity of recognizing "the riches of Christ and virtuous works" in the lives of the separated brethren (Art. 4).[11] As long as the Roman church regards herself exclusively as the catholic church, she can acknowledge as means and operation of grace in other churches only what she recognizes as elements of the Roman church still present in them. Increasingly, however, there is recognition of spiritual realities in other churches that were not developed in the Roman church but that nevertheless belong to a fully developed catholicity. Increasingly it is recognized that the divinely created catholicity is greater than that which has come to realization in an individual church, even in the Roman church. Because of splits in the church, the Roman church "finds it more difficult to express in actual life her full catholicity in all its aspects" (Art. 4).[12]

Thus there is growing awareness of the obligation to open up and to grant a place and naturalization rights within the Roman church to all that has been discovered in other churches to be a true expression of spiritual life, an aid to biblical insight, an experience in social concern, etc. Even before the ecumenical theme was officially dealt with, chorales of Reformation churches were in past years taken over into Catholic hymnbooks, and methods and results of Evangelical biblical scholarship, as well as their approaches to systematic and ecumenical theology, were adopted (for example, the question of lay activity). Much the same has long been true of the liturgy, the patristic theology, and the mysticism of the Orthodox church. These approaches to others are now to be deliberately actualized. The potential catholicity of the Roman church is now to be developed as comprehensively as possible in actual catholicity. In this connection there was sharp criticism of, for example, the practice of standardizing and Latinizing earlier resorted to in the treatment of Uniate churches.

---

[11] *Documents*, p. 349.
[12] *Ibid.*

It is true that the possibilities of this expansion are limited for the canonistic and especially the dogmatic structure of the Roman church. But perhaps in this area there will be larger expansions than may be logically deduced from existing dogmatic and canonistic presuppositions.

(c) The Union of the Separated Churches

In spite of differences in evaluating the churches separated from Rome, the Council Fathers shared the common conviction that the unity of the church is a reality in the Roman church and that union must be achieved by bringing about a full fellowship of the non-Roman Christians with the Roman Catholic Church. This is the goal of ecumenism that "all Christians will be gathered, in a common celebration of the Eucharist, into that unity of the one and only Church. . . . This unity, we believe, dwells in the Catholic Church as something she can never lose" (Art. 4).[13]

Prerequisites for full fellowship are the confession of the one faith, the common celebration of the divine cultus (hence the fellowship of the sacramental life), and agreement in government, that is to say, in acknowledging the full primatial authority of the bishop of Rome in matters of faith and discipline, in accordance with Vatican I.

This is not a new goal, and yet one does not do justice to the Decree on Ecumenism if one sees in it nothing more than the invitation to return to the Roman church, an invitation simply repeated by different methods and under a different name. It dare not be overlooked that this ultimate goal of ecumenism admits of quite different interpretations. The approach to the unity existing in the Roman church is not the same if it is a matter of the present situation or of a renewed Roman church of the future—if the primacy is administered only in the sense of Vatican I or in fraternal fellowship with the leaders of other churches—if it is a matter of return to the Roman church or a mutual reconciliation between the Roman church and other churches—if according

[13] *Documents*, p. 348.

to the Roman church's understanding non-Roman churches attain the status of true churches only by a return—or if churches which mutually acknowledge each other establish full fellowship. To be sure, the concept "return" has thus far not disappeared either from the formal opinions expressed in the Council or from papal pronouncements. The fact that prominent Council Fathers and theologians consciously avoid using the term must, however, not lead us to look only for tactical reasons, but rather to presuppose the insight that the idea of return is not an adequate term for the desired union, either on historical or on ecclesiological grounds.

Hence the goal of union presents itself in various ways, depending upon the degree of renewal and the extent of the development of catholicity regarded as necessary. This situation will depend, in turn, on whether the renewal and the Catholic advance toward others is thought to be already realized in the Council or only a task begun by the Council but still to be accomplished in the future:

(1) The stronger the conviction that the Roman church has through the Council already renewed herself in her present state and has already unfolded her catholicity, the more the union will be understood as a return. Already in possession of unity and catholicity, the Roman church awaits the return of the others and is ready to take from her own wealth and give them what they lack. The possibility must be reckoned with that many Council Fathers voted for the decree because they thought they could interpret it in this way. In such a stance, however, there is the danger of believing that the renewed invitation to return, as expressed in the decree of the Council, is all that is necessary. In that case the inevitable disappointment can only deepen the sense of separation once more.

(2) On the other hand, the more the people within the Roman church look upon the events of the Council as a beginning, but not yet the required realization of renewal and catholic development, the more they will expect unification as the result of change on both sides, of a mutual turning to each other—not as a return

but as a reconciliation, not as a submission but as mutual acceptance of fellowship, not as a one-sided bestowal, but as reciprocal giving and receiving. When reunion is understood in this manner there will be room for growing in mutual intellectual discovery, in drawing closer to each other and in working together. The length of this way cannot be determined in advance, nor can the individual steps be fixed in advance, but it will be a way on which both sides must entrust themselves to the guidance of the Holy Spirit. Here, too, the Roman dogma and the papal primacy remain untouchable, but that does not exclude a reinterpretation by means of a changed form of ecclesiastical teaching and activity.

(3) Within the Roman church there are also theologians and laymen who regard the future shape of unified Christendom as far less automatically certain than is the case in the Decree on Ecumenism and, still more, in the Constitution on the Church. Such people keep themselves consciously open, not only in view of the goal, to an act of the unifying Holy Spirit which cannot be calculated in advance and which cannot be circumscribed by canonistic thinking. In this view also, changes in dogmatic understanding and in the centralized order are considered possible, changes that would in fact be a correction of existing dogmas rather than simply reinterpretation. In this refusal to insist on a predetermined dogmatic and canonistic conception of union, the way is open most freely and immediately for the dimension of fellowship among the separated churches in mutual giving and receiving—a fellowship which in its essence also presses on toward realizing the unity in confession, in the sacraments, and in offices, and in this pressing prays for the God-pleasing order.

The Decree on Ecumenism permits various possibilities in understanding the union that is to be achieved. The text, however, points above all in the second direction just indicated, without entirely excluding the first one mentioned. In the decree, and especially in the constitution, the last named conception has the least support, even though on the basis of the presuppositions of the decree its advocates may be tolerated for a part of the way toward unification. It is consistent with these various possibilities that from the documents of the Council no full clarity can be gained on precisely what the difference is between ecumenism and the work of gaining converts, which is also affirmed in the same decree (Art. 4).[14]

There is no reason to give up hope for a future enlargement of the possibilities of understanding the issue of unification. For the time being, however, non-Roman churches can only deal with the present reality of the Roman church, and in all sobriety they must see that the Roman *conditio sine qua non* for unification is the acceptance of *all* Roman Catholic dogmas, including the dogma of *papal primacy* in the *full* significance of the infallibility declared by Vatican I.

Possibilities and Limits of Ecumenism

The ecumenism of Vatican II springs from an elementary urge for fellowship with the separated brethren—an urge which gripped more and more bishops in the course of the Council. The directives for ecumenical behavior, which are an excellent clarification of what has priority, provide guidance for the steps that should be taken toward the separated churches as a result of this urge for fellowship.

At the same time, the decree also indicates the limits which the Council in its understanding of ecumenism feels it is its duty to observe.

(a) The goal of ecumenism is limited by the dogmatic and canonistic decisions which were already in force at the time of the Council. Dogmas are regarded as incorrigible, as are also the provisions of canon law to the extent that they are regarded as divine law. These boundaries remain comparatively narrow, not only because the Roman church feels very strictly obligated to her dogma and her understanding of the divine law—this is true also of other churches—but also because in her dogmas and in her canon law this church has fixed her position so comprehensively,

[14] *Documents*, p. 348.

and by her numerous anathemas has so decidedly segregated herself from other churches as no other church has done. Consequently, this church has less maneuverability for ecumenical activity than other churches.

There are, furthermore, the limits which this Council itself added to the already existing limitations by means of the Dogmatic Constitution on the Church. Although this constitution is not regarded as a dogma in the strict sense of a solemn dogmatic definition, it nevertheless occupies a highly authoritative rank as a decision of the Council. In view of the fact that the doctrine of the church—except for the papal primacy—had not hitherto been fixed by a conciliar decision, the statements of the Constitution on the Church concerning the borders of the church, for example, as well as the ascription of the title of Mediatrix to Mary, constitute an additional restriction to the Roman church's freedom of movement in ecumenical dialogue. Hence the ecumenical openness of the Roman church is limited not only by the dogmas already in operation before the Council but also by the dogmatic pronouncements of the Council itself. This raises questions: Was it necessary to decide and proclaim a definition of the church's essence at this time? Did not the ecumenical movement bring to light many new problems and dimensions of ecclesiology, even in the Roman church, for which there are as yet no adequate concepts? Did it not constitute a hope for ecumenical dialogue that in the questions surrounding ecclesiology in all churches there were far fewer fixed dogmatic positions than, for example, in the doctrines of justification or the sacraments? Was it not possible to wait and see what would come out of the possibilities created by the Decree on Ecumenism for theological cooperation among the separated churches in providing *common* answers to the new ecclesiological questions that have arisen? It makes some sense, in view of this Council's temporal proximity to the pre-ecumenical and narrow encyclical on the church, *Mystici Corporis*, by Pius XII, that it could not now say much more about the other churches than was said in the Constitution on the Church. Nevertheless, was it necessary for that document to restrict the ecumenical dialogue at the very moment that the constitution made it possible?

(b) These presuppositions determine the understanding and evaluation of the various non-Roman churches which are dealt with in the third chapter of the Decree on Ecumenism under the title "Churches and Ecclesial Communities Separated from the Roman Apostolic See." For the moment, our concern is not with the concrete statements of the decree concerning these churches but rather with the criterion by which they are measured. What is of primary importance in the encounter between separated churches is not so much the concrete judgment that one church makes about the other but the criterion by which they evaluate each other. What, then, is the yardstick applied to the rest of Christendom in the various forms of the decree and the pertinent discussions?

Corresponding to the self-understanding of the Roman church as being the one, holy, catholic, apostolic church, the first criterion is the Roman church herself, and, to be sure, in her present reality as it developed in history and as it has been dogmatically and canonistically determined. The yardstick is not the early church, nor the church of the first centuries as such, except to the extent that the early church is identical with the present Roman church, that is, as the former becomes manifest in the latter. In a certain sense this criterion corresponds to the rule that the first source of Roman Catholic dogmatics is not Holy Scripture, but the church, specifically the church's teaching office. As the ecclesiological reality of the non-Roman churches is thus measured by the reality of the Roman church, a peculiarly quantified judgment results. These churches are judged according to the quantity of those elements that are constitutive of the Roman church and are also present in the other churches, that is to say, according to the quantity of dogmas, sacraments, and offices which they possess in common with the Roman church. This quantified thinking determines the order of precedence of non-Roman churches. In this connection the presence of a hierarchical order in the apostolic succession of ordinations plays a special role. In line with this approach, when individual bishops called for union discussions with others, only the Orthodox church was mentioned. Subsequently, in view of the Anglican church, it was recommended that, first of all, the question of the validity of Anglican consecrations, which Pope Leo XIII had answered in the negative, be re-examined. Naturally such quantified thinking makes it exceedingly difficult to understand other churches from the center of their life, and it was evident that this kind of thinking was unable to fathom the peculiar spirituality of the Orthodox church.

At the same time there are statements, in the Decree on Ecumenism and in the formal opinions offered in the discussion, that break through this kind of quantified thinking. These are statements determined by the immediate impression of witness to Christ, of prayer, of the worship life and sacramental piety, of service to the world, and of martyrdom in the areas of the separated churches. Much more directly, the yardstick here is the christological and pneumatological one, that is, the biblical yardstick common to all churches. These statements speak from the perspective of the experience of the mystery of a oneness in Christ, something that cannot be grasped by means of traditional ecclesiological concepts. Here the hearts meet in the certainty of the same faith, even though the forms of the creedal statements and of the churchly life differ. A further breakthrough of quantified thinking occurs when operations of grace are discovered and acknowledged in non-Roman churches, manifestations not developed in the Roman church and yet regarded as necessary for the full realization of the mystery of Christ in the church and hence for the full realization of the church's catholicity. Individuals were explicitly critical of the quantified thinking in the *schema* since Jesus Christ himself is the center of all elements of the church. Accordingly, the American Cardinal Ritter (St. Louis) demanded that all thought about unity must proceed much more strongly from Christ.

On the basis of the very animated discussion it is difficult to say which basic attitude predominates. The majority of opinions suggests that it is the first one mentioned, namely, that the separated churches are understood primarily not as churches that have grown on apostolic ground and live by the present power of Christ and the Holy Spirit but rather as churches that have split off from the Roman church. In this situation the intrusive question regarding their evaluation is concerned with determining what these churches still have in common with the Roman church since their separation. Quite apart from the historical question which seems not to have been considered here—that the Roman church itself has experienced further dogmatic and canonistic development both since her separation from the Orthodox church and since her own exclusion of the Reformation churches—it must be borne in mind that, in accord with all other ecumenical experiences, a deeper mutual understanding can begin only when the start is made with the common historical apostolic foundation of the church, and when the separated churches meet each other anew in jointly listening to the witness of the Holy Scriptures, by which each church permits herself to be judged and its view of the others to be determined. This is possible even without a prior definitive clarification of the relationship between Scripture and tradition, since *in fact* Holy Scripture has remained the heritage of all the separated churches.

(c) Chapter three of the Decree on Ecumenism directs its attention to the historically developed multiplicity of non-Roman churches and concretely evaluates them. The first part deals with "the Eastern Churches," while the second part deals with "the Separated Churches and Ecclesial Communities in the West."

Highly significant and new is the consistent tendency to seek and accentuate what is positive in the separated churches. Undoubtedly this represents a new note over against earlier official pronouncements of the Roman church regarding other churches. Above all, attention is called to what the Roman church and the other churches have in common, and the effort to avoid offensive expressions is unmistakable. Thus this chapter avoids the terms "schismatics" and "heretics," and left undecided is the question whether the Orthodox churches may still be labeled schismatic, or whether, in view of their rejection of papal primacy as dogmatically defined by Vatican I, they have become heretical. Meanwhile the classic distinction between schismatics and heretics does not seem to have been abandoned but, without use of the terms, appears to live on in the distinction between churches and ecclesiastical communities. At the same time there was no attempt to specify which non-Roman churches, with exception of the Orthodox, are labeled "churches" and which only "ecclesial communities."

Coupled with the positive statements concerning the non-Roman churches are references in every section to the differences between them and the Roman church. In characterizing the Eastern churches, these differences are viewed almost exclusively from the point of view of a permissible and mutually complementary diversity. In characterizing the churches of the Reformation, on the other hand, the differences are presented more strongly as anthitheses. Fixing the differences leads to the development of themes to be discussed in future dialogues. Here, too, the other churches can only approve. A fruitful ecumenical dialogue can begin only when the participating churches are made aware not only of what they have in common but also of existing differences, or, more precisely, "the similarities in the differences" and "the differences in the similarities" (Karl Barth), and then proceed on this basis to formulate the questions that must be painstakingly and jointly clarified from the perspective of each side. This method has proved effective in other ecumenical endeavors.

Nevertheless, observers at the Council from the most diverse churches—in part even some Council Fathers and theologians—have felt that precisely this chapter iii contributes very little to the cause, mainly for two reasons:

In the first place, many felt that the groupings and characterizations which were imposed on them showed no real understanding of them. To mention only a few examples, while the preamble (Art. 13)[15] alludes briefly to the rise of non-Chalcedonian churches (Copts, Nestorians, etc.), the first main section of this chapter speaks, in fact, only of the Eastern Orthodox churches. This was all the more surprising since the heterodox Eastern churches were more strongly represented at the Council than the Orthodox. Yet the Orthodox were also irritated because they could not consider the Decree on Ecumenism in isolation from the "Decree on Eastern Catholic [e.g., Uniate] Churches," a decree simultaneously discussed, adopted, and proclaimed by the Council. That decree also made very plain to them the difference between the juridical Roman understanding of Orthodoxy and the latter's pneumatic self-understanding. The second main section ignores the medieval schisms in the West, of which, indeed, only the Waldensians and the Bohemian Brethren escaped annihilation. The characterization of the Reformation churches remains colorless and appears to be controlled by a general concept of Protestantism that may be handy but does not do justice to the real situation. It is as if there were no church bodies in Protestantism with dogmatic obligations and canonically ordered offices. If the situation were turned around, would the Roman church have felt herself correctly understood if she had been characterized on the basis of a general concept of catholicism which would include more or less common marks of the Roman, the Old Catholic, the Orthodox, the Monophysite, and the Nestorian churches, plus perhaps the original apostolic church?

In the second place, many thought it strange that the characterization of non-Roman churches was still linked, even before the beginning of the ecumenical dialogue, with judgments concerning the divine activity in their midst. These judgments are difficult to reconcile with a demanding ecumenical readiness to be open to the spiritual reality of another church, if indeed such judgments should not be removed from human manipulation entirely and

[15] *Documents*, pp. 355 f.

left in God's hands. What can the praise accorded the Orthodox church mean to her when the same decree decidedly asserts that fullness is to be found only and exclusively in the Roman church? What is the church of the Lutheran Reformation to make of the courtesies in statements concerning Reformation churches when at the same time it is denied that the body and blood of Christ are received in the Lutheran communion? What right has the Council to judge that the Reformation churches "have not preserved the genuine and total reality [*substantia*] of the Eucharistic mystery" (Art. 22),[16] even though the Evangelical Lutheran Church affirms the true and substantial presence of the body and blood of Christ in the Lord's Supper? What right had the Pope to delete a statement already adopted by the Council concerning the use of Scripture in the Reformation churches, namely, that "moved by the Holy Spirit, they *find* God who speaks through Christ in the Holy Scriptures," and to substitute the weakened form, "They call on the Holy Spirit and *seek* God in the Holy Scriptures"? Would it not be more appropriate for people about to begin an ecumenical dialogue to be first of all open to God's activity in other churches before passing judgment on them? It goes without saying that the churches subjected to such judgments will repudiate them.

(d) It is surprising, furthermore, that in characterizing the Eastern and Western churches separated from Rome there is no mention at all of their membership in the World Council of Churches. Oddly enough, there is no mention in the entire decree of this association which was canonically constituted in Amsterdam in 1948 and which now embraces more than two hundred churches from all non-Roman denominations. The decree speaks only of the ecumenical *movement* and its confession of the triune God. However, it is impossible today to do justice to the reality of the Eastern and non-Roman Western churches if they are looked upon as isolated groups, and if the fact is ignored that these churches, as member churches of the World Council, live together in a

[16] *Documents*, p. 364.

fellowship which in many ways has proved worthwhile and is steadily growing, a fellowship of giving and receiving which results in new opportunities and new influences.

This silence concerning the World Council of Churches is all the more surprising since the Secretariat for Unity maintains contacts with the World Council and made use of its offices in the process of inviting observers from non-Roman churches. This unusual silence of the decree may perhaps be accounted for by the fact that the World Council is something new in church history, something that in a peculiar way escapes measurement by the yardstick the Roman church applies to other churches. The World Council cannot in any way be understood as a splinter off the Roman Church. If it were, one could measure what elements of the Roman church it had retained since the split. The World Council is rather the instrument of a movement seeking to overcome the separation by means of cooperation among the separated churches. Membership is open also to the Roman church. Moreover, the failure to mention the World Council in the Decree on Ecumenism may perhaps rest on the claim of the Roman church that unity is already a reality in that church and therefore need not first be looked for. Accordingly, no one rose in the Council's discussions to propose that the Roman church participate in the fellowship existing in the World Council among the various Orthodox, Evangelical-Lutheran, Reformed, Angelican, Methodist, and other churches.

Roman Ecumenism

The net result of these analyses is that the ecumenism of the decree is a specifically Roman ecumenism. It represents the attempt at a peculiar synthesis between the canonically exclusive concept inherent in the Roman church's practice of calling her own general synods ecumenical councils, and the broader concept as it is employed today in the ecumenical movement to designate the union endeavors and the growing fellowship among the separated churches. The Roman church calls her councils ecumenical because she believes herself already to be the one, holy, catholic, apostolic church, and she therefore uses this title regardless of whether such a council is dealing with the problem of reunion or not. Without giving up this narrow concept of ecumenism the Roman church has taken up another very different one, namely, the one which has universally established itself in the course of union endeavors among non-Roman churches, and she has sought to combine the two concepts. Even Council Fathers have often observed that the new concept of ecumenism requires further clarification, both in its relation to the exclusive idea in canon law and in its relation to the ecumenical movement of the non-Roman churches of the East and of the Reformation.

7

The Council and Non-Christian Religions

The Council also subjected the relationship to non-Christian religions to review. Here, too, an attempt was made to resume the conversation in a new way. This second concentric circle, by which the Roman church sees herself surrounded together with the rest of Christendom, forms the subject of the Declaration on the Relationship of the Church to Non-Christian Religions and the Decree on the Church's Missionary Activity. It is noteworthy that one and the same subject matter is treated in two separate resolutions. Of these, the first named teaches a positive evaluation of the religions and a due respect for them, while the second stresses the need for missionary proclamation on the basis of their inadequacies. Even though the two decisions of the Council present different accents they do not contradict each other. It is surprising, furthermore, that the Declaration on the Relationship of the Church to Non-Christian Religions does not refer to the Decree on the Church's Missionary Activity, and that the latter does not refer to the former. In their subject matter, however, they belong so close together that the one document cannot be isolated from the other and that neither can be correctly understood apart from the other. A misleading picture could easily be drawn if the adherents of non-Christian religions would note only the declaration and if Catholics would note only the decree. Both documents aim at giving members of the Roman church instructions for their behavior over against their non-Christian religious environment. The juxtaposition of these two decisions of the Council is perhaps best understood in the light of the declaration's genesis. This declaration was originally planned specifically as the Council's message to the Jews, and then, because of the objections of the Arab world and the bishops from Arab countries, the document was gradually enlarged and developed into a declaration concerning non-Christian religions in general. Besides, the statements about the attitudes toward non-Christian religions are imbedded in general statements about the unity of the human race and the necessity of meeting every human being with a brotherly attitude. Thus the Declaration on the Relationship of the Church to Non-Christian Religions flows into the thoughts expressed in the Declaration on Religious Freedom and the Pastoral Constitution on the Church in the Modern World.

> The ground is therefore removed from every theory or practice which leads to a distinction between men or peoples in the matter of human dignity and the rights which flow from it.
>
> As a consequence, the Church rejects, as foreign to the mind of Christ, any discrimination against men or harassment of them because of their race, color, condition of life, or religion (Art 5).[1]

The Opening Toward Non-Christian Religions

As the Council had made an approach to non-Roman churches, so it also approached non-Christian religions. The systematic perspective for this, too, is provided in the Dogmatic Constitution on the Church, particularly in its remarks about "many elements of sanctification and of truth" that can be found outside the Roman church (Art. 8).[2] The presence of such "elements" is taken into account not only in the case of non-Catholic Christians but also of non-Christian religions. Even non-Christians "are related in various ways" to the Roman church—the Jewish people, first of all, but also "those who acknowledge the Creator. In the first place among these there are the Moslems, who, professing to hold the faith of Abraham, along with us adore the one and merciful God, who on the last day will judge mankind"—and even "those who in shadows and images seek the unknown God" (Art. 16).[3]

---

[1] *Documents*, pp. 667 f.
[2] *Documents*, p. 23.
[3] *Documents*, pp. 34 f.

On this basis the declaration and the decree issue their directives for behavior toward non-Christian religions.

Religions are understood as

> answers to those profound mysteries of the human condition which, today even as in olden times, deeply stir the human heart: What is a man? What is the meaning and the purpose of our life? What is goodness and what is sin? What gives rise to our sorrows and to what intent? Where lies the path to true happiness? What is the truth about death, judgment, and retribution beyond the grave? What, finally, is that ultimate and unutterable mystery which engulfs our being, and whence we take our rise, and whither our journey lead us? (Declaration, Art. 1)[4]

While the Decree on the Church's Missionary Activity speaks of the religions only in a general way, the declaration refers to several historical religions: to Hinduism, in which "men contemplate the divine mystery and express it through an unspent fruitfulness of myths and through searching philosophical inquiry"; to Buddhism, which acknowledges the radical insufficiency of this shifting world and teaches a path by which men can either reach a state of freedom or obtain supreme enlightenment (Art. 2); and above all to Islam, where mention is made of characteristics it has in common with the Christian faith, such as adoration of one God, the creator, association with Abraham, reverence for Jesus, certainly not as God but as a prophet, honor for the Virgin Mary, and expectation of the day of judgment (Art. 3).[5] Thus far, all of this is limited to describing the existing state of affairs.

The declaration does not stop there, however. It acknowledges that those religions, "though differing in many particulars" from what the church holds and sets forth, "nevertheless often reflect a ray of that Truth which enlightens all men" (Art. 2). It acknowledges what is "true and holy in these religions," "the spiritual and moral goods found among these men, as well as the

---

[4] *Documents*, p. 661.

[5] *Documents*, pp. 661 ff.

values in their society and culture" (Art. 2).[6] It looks on them, especially on Islam, "with esteem" (Art. 3). Also, the Decree on the Church's Missionary Activity acknowledges that "truth and grace are to be found among the nations" (Art. 9) and that there are "seeds of the Word" lying hidden in their traditions (Art. 11).[7] To that extent the religions are not only witnesses of searching but also possessers of valid answers.

The declaration accentuates above all what the non-Christian religions have in common with the Christian faith and refers only in passing to the differences. The religions are evaluated positively, and the descriptive observations and theological statements concerning the truth they possess are blended together. What St. Paul says about the pagans' consistent perversion of the knowledge of God revealed in creation (Rom. 1:18-32; 3:8-20) is not taken into account by the declaration. Furthermore, there seems to be no consideration of the fact that the advanced monotheistic religions especially, in spite of what they have in common with Christianity, have in a special way opposed the gospel. Again, the declaration does not enter on the upsurge of these religions and their missionary activity in our time. The question must be raised whether the "grace and truth" in the non-Christian religions has not been too optimistically appraised, indeed, whether on the basis of a phenomenological comparison such judgments concerning the truth there can be made at all. Does not the truth hidden in the religions become perceptible only when the gospel confronts them and when their adherents again recognize the truth of the message concerning Christ as the truth that puts them under obligation? In any case, the two documents of the Council remain cautious over against theories of "anonymous Christianity" among non-Christians and the "cosmic Christ" active in their midst. Such theories make the dialogue with non-Christian re-

[6] *Ibid.*

[7] *Documents*, pp. 595-98.

ligions more difficult to the extent that they do not take the self-understanding of these religions seriously. The Council is right, however, in not limiting the freedom of God's saving activity that is concealed from us.

Israel

From the beginning, the Council had planned to say something about the relationship of the Roman church to the Jews. In this statement the Council desired to highlight the unique position of the Jews, which has no parallel in any other non-Christian religion, and to exhort the members of the Roman church to adopt a brotherly attitude toward the Jews. Cardinal Bea's *relatio* (presentation), in which he supported the first draft of this text which was initially transmitted to the bishops as an appendix to the Decree on Ecumenism, constitutes one of the most impressive and most thoroughly biblical formal opinions presented to the Council. The document was based on Romans 9–11 and the Pauline theology was given its due.

At that time the presentation was opposed, not only by bishops from Islamic countries, who had reason to fear reprisals from their respective governments (because of their enmity toward the state of Israel), but also by a conservative minority from Italy and other countries independent of Islam, who objected to any mitigation of the collective guilt of the Jewish people. Out of deference for these two kinds of opposition, several statements in the final form were toned down so that many of the former opponents were able to vote affirmatively in the final balloting. Thus the declaration was separated from the Decree on Ecumenism and the Jews are no longer mentioned in the title by name. In addition, assertions about other religions, especially Islam, were strengthened, so that the remarks about the Jews now appear simply as remarks about one religion among others, and the whole discussion is circumscribed by statements about the universal brotherhood of all men. In contrast, some expressed the opinion that the Constitution on the Church was a more appropriate place for a word about the Jews than the Declaration on Non-Christian Religions.

The substance of the section was retained, however, and the statements were further refined and represent an excellent, biblically well-based stance and directive. The most important paragraphs follow.

> The Church of Christ acknowledges that, according to the mystery of God's saving design, the beginnings of her faith and her election are already found among the patriarchs, Moses, and the prophets. She professes that all who believe in Christ, Abraham's sons according to faith (cf. Gal. 3:7), are included in the same patriarch's call, and likewise that the salvation of the Church was mystically foreshadowed by the chosen people's exodus from the land of bondage.
>
> The Church, therefore, cannot forget that she received the revelation of the Old Testament through the people with whom God in his inexpressible mercy deigned to establish the Ancient Covenant. Nor can she forget that she draws sustenance from the root of that good olive tree onto which have been grafted the wild olive branches of the Gentiles (cf. Rom. 11:17-24). Indeed, the Church believes that by His cross Christ, our Peace, reconciled Jew and Gentile, making them both one in Himself (cf. Eph. 2:14-16).
>
> Also, the Church ever keeps in mind the words of the Apostle about his kinsmen, "who have the adoption as sons, and the glory and the covenant and the legislation and the worship and the promises; who have the fathers, and from whom is Christ according to the flesh" (Rom. 9:4-5). . . . The Church recalls too that from the Jewish people sprang the apostles, her foundation stones and pillars, as well as most of the early disciples who proclaimed Christ to the world. . . .
>
> True, authorities of the Jews and those who followed their lead pressed for the death of Christ (cf. John 19:6); still, what happened in His passion cannot be blamed upon all the Jews then living, without distinction, nor upon the Jews of today. Although the Church is the new people of God, the Jews should not be presented as repudiated or cursed by God, as if such views followed from the holy Scriptures. All should take pains, then, lest in catechetical instruction and in the preaching of God's Word they teach anything out of harmony with the truth of the gospel and the spirit of Christ.
>
> The Church repudiates all persecutions against any man. Moreover, mindful of her common patrimony with the Jews, and motivated by the gospel's spiritual love and by no political considerations, she deplores the hatred, persecutions, and displays of anti-Semitism directed against the Jews at any time and from any source (Art. 4).[8]

[8] *Documents*, pp. 664 ff.

Directives for Attitudes Toward Non-Christian Religions

The declaration admonishes the members of the Roman church above all to acknowledge, preserve, and promote "the spiritual and moral goods found among these men" (Art. 2), to hold other religions, especially Islam, in esteem (Art. 3), to "act in a brotherly way" and to "keep peace" (Art. 5).[9] The Decree on Missionary Activity contains similar directives.

At the same time every Christian's attitude toward non-Christian religions must be shaped by the missionary obligation. Though only alluded to in the declaration, this constitutes the theme of the Decree on Missionary Activity. The endeavors of the non-Christian religions "need to be enlightened and purified." "The sainted Fathers of the Church firmly proclaim that what was not taken up by Christ was not healed" (Art. 3). As "words of judgment and of grace, of death and of life," the words of Christ must be proclaimed to all religions. "For it is only by putting to death what is old that we are able to come to a newness of life" (Art. 8).[10] Here, too, Paul is quoted: " 'All have sinned and have need of the glory of God' (Rom. 3:23)." The Christian message liberates

> whatever truth and grace are to be found among the nations, as a sort of secret presence of God, . . . from all taint of evil and restores to Christ its maker, who overthrows the devil's domain and wards off the manifold malice of vice (Art. 9).
>
> [Christians should try] to illumine [the "treasures a bountiful God has distributed among the nations of the earth"] with the light of the gospel, to set them free, and to bring them under the dominion of God their Savior (Art. 11).[11]

It is by no means a matter only of supplementing a partial truth by the fullness of Christian truth but also of the necessity of conversion. As the Constitution on the Church had already taught, this missionary activity among the religions grows out of the essence of the church, and in this activity God's plan of salvation

[9] *Documents*, pp. 663, 667 f.
[10] *Documents*, pp. 586, 595.
[11] *Documents*, pp. 595 f., 598.

for mankind, which Jesus served, becomes a reality. This missionary command "was inherited from the apostles by the order of bishops, assisted by priests and united with the successor of Peter and supreme shepherd of the Church" (Art. 5)[12] and, beyond that, also concerns the laity. There is a circumspect presentation of the missionaries' tasks (chap. iv), of the direction of missionary work, where provision is made for a reorganization of the curial Congregation for the Propagation of the Faith by involving bishops from all over the world, the directors of missionary institutes, and the papal mission endeavor (chap. v), and the cooperation of the whole church in the missionary enterprise (chap. vi).

This grandly conceived missionary thrust appears to contradict the admonition to live peaceably with other religions. Yet a form of missionary activity is called for that differs from many a practice known from history. For one thing, the Declaration on Religious Freedom forbids the use of political power. Secondly, members of the church are admonished "gladly and reverently" to lay bare "the seeds of the Word which lie hidden" in the religions and "by sincere and patient dialogue" to look for the "treasures" which God has given the nations (Art. 11).[13] Finally, it is demanded again and again that there be a loving adaptation to the special forms of thought and action among the people to be evangelized, including even a relevant reshaping of the church's rites. On the basis of one and the same love, Christians are to live at peace with the non-Christian religions and to proclaim to them the one and only salvation in Christ.

The Goal

On the one hand, the goal of such behavior is to be peace between the church and non-Christian religions. Perhaps in the background there is the thought of an eventual cooperation in a common defense against atheism.

---

[12] *Documents*, p. 589.
[13] *Documents*, p. 598.

At the same time, the goal includes the expansion of the Roman church, not indeed by imposing something foreign on the nations but by liberating the truths and values contained in their religions, philosophies, and ceremonies so that these truths and values may develop independently. Thus the idea is to establish particular churches with native bishops, priests, and deacons. This kind of church, "endowed with the riches of its own nation's culture, should be deeply rooted in the people," and its members "should practice true and effective patriotism" (Art. 15).[14] In the training of the clergy, special value shall be placed "on the points of contact between the traditions and religion of their homeland and the Christian religion" (Art. 16). "From the customs and traditions of their people, from their wisdom and their learning, from their arts and sciences, these Churches borrow all those things which can contribute to the glory of their Creator, the revelation of the Savior's grace, or the proper arrangement of Christian life" (Art. 22).[15] This "goal of adaptation" is constantly and emphatically kept in view. The limits of such adaptation, however, are the dogmas of the Roman church and the papal primacy, together with canon law to the extent that it is taught as divine law. Accordingly, every young church, in spite of all her independent development, is to be a faithful replica of the Roman church.

We dare not, of course, overlook an important factor. The tension which in essence exists between the goal of peace with other religions and the goal of expanding the Roman church among the religions cannot be removed, no matter how far-reaching the adaptation is, if it is not to lead to syncretism and particularism. Such a result is explicitly rejected by the Council (Art. 22).[16] The goal of expanding the Roman church has priority. Yet in Christian missions the non-Christian religions see a threat to their continued existence in the future.

---

[14] *Documents*, pp. 602 f.

[15] *Documents*, pp. 604, 612.

[16] *Documents*, pp. 612 f.

Missions and Ecumenism

In a comparison of the ecumenical and missionary programs of the Council many analogies may be noted: There is an opening toward non-Roman churches as well as toward non-Christian religions. In both, "elements" of truth and grace are acknowledged. Over against both, the axiom of Cyprian, "Outside the church there is no salvation," is not maintained in its original vigor. Over against both, the members of the Roman church are exhorted to display a loving, new understanding and engage in a dialogue in which they should present Catholic teaching unabridged. In both cases the goal is peaceful coexistence and unity, as it already exists in the Roman church. For this purpose provision is made for an unfolding of the Roman church's catholicity by incorporating the special gifts peculiar to the non-Roman churches and the non-Christian religions. Neither the non-Christian religions nor the non-Roman churches are supposed to remain what they are. By analogy there is also the tension between the goal of peaceful coexistence and the goal of the expansion of the Roman church. Is there perhaps in the background the widespread traditional view, according to which the separated Christians are as far removed as non-Christians, indeed, even further removed than a pious pagan, since, as distinct from the pagan, the Christians knowingly separated themselves from the Roman church?

In spite of these analogies it would be a mistake to interpret the decisions of the Council as if ecumenism were only a specific aspect of missionary activity. The Decree on Missionary Activity clearly sets forth what all Christians have in common over against non-Christian religions, and it repeatedly calls on the church's members to strive for cooperation with non-Roman churches in missionary activity. "Thus, missionary activity among the nations differs from pastoral activity exercised among the faithful, as well as from undertakings aimed at restoring unity among Christians" (Art. 6). Missionary activity and ecumenism are indeed "most closely connected" because the separation among Christians harms the missionary proclamation and hinders its credibility. For that reason missionary activity urgently demands the ecumenical task of reuniting all the faithful in one flock (Art. 6).[17] Even before this reunion, however, the directive stands:

> In coordination with the Secretariat for Promoting Christian Unity, [the Congregation for the Propagation of the Faith] should search out ways and means for bringing about and directing fraternal cooperation as well as harmonious living with the missionary undertakings of other Christian communities. Thus, as far as possible, the scandal of division can be removed (Art. 29).

> This living testimony will more easily achieve its effect if it is given in unison with other Christian communities, according to the norms of the Decree on Ecumenism (Art. 36).[18]

To be sure, the document is not speaking here of a partition of mission fields among the churches, yet the Decree on Missionary Activity prohibits the Roman church from doing mission work among the young churches of other Christian denominations.

---

[17] *Documents*, p. 592.
[18] *Documents*, pp. 620, 623.

8

The Council and the World

Beyond the circles of non-Roman Christendom and the non-Christian religions encompassing the Roman church, the Council also turned its attention to the outermost of the concentric circles, which embraces all humanity, and entered upon problems which face mankind as such in the world of today. These problems are treated comprehensively in the Pastoral Constitution on the Church in the Modern World.

In attacking this heavy task the Council took a courageous step which has no precedent in conciliar history. The concern here was not, as in customary decisions of councils, about fixing the church's doctrine and order in delimitation against heresy and schism, nor about removing internal ambiguities and contradictions; the concern was, rather, an approach to mankind as a whole and an attempt to clarify the problems which today press so hard on human society. The concern is not for a decision which the Council expects to be binding for all time like a dogmatic definition, but rather for clarification and guidance for the present situation which in many respects will have changed in ten years and will then require further reflection and guidance. Aware of the menacing situation of our time, the Council has attempted to speak to this concrete situation of what faith in Christ can offer by way of assistance.

In line with the significance which the Council attached to this task, the Constitution on the Church in the Modern World addresses itself directly to all men. The Council here desires to address itself "not only to the sons of the Church and to all who invoke the name of Christ, but to the whole of humanity. For the

Council yearns to explain to everyone how it conceives of the presence and activity of the Church in the world of today" (Art. 2 *et al.*).[1] This special approach is all the more noteworthy since the Decree on Ecumenism although dealing with non-Christian religions does not address them directly but speaks to the members of the Roman church. Similarly, the Decree on Missionary Activity and the Declaration on the Relationship of the Church to Non-Christian Religions do not speak directly to the adherents of these religions but aim to instruct the members of the Roman church. While these documents concern non-Catholics and non-Christians to a high degree as far as their contents are concerned, those contents are brought only indirectly to the attention of those people. The Pastoral Constitution on the Church in the Modern World, however, wants to speak directly to those people whose "rescue" and social "renewal" are the concern of the constitution (Art. 3). For that purpose the constitution desires to engage in immediate dialogue with them (Art. 3 *et al.*).[2]

This double task of clarifying the current human situation and addressing all men naturally creates various difficulties. The obvious presupposition for this document also is the Dogmatic Constitution on the Church (Art. 2).[3] One difficulty is that the Constitution on the Church speaks of the church in general and timeless categories, while the declaration is to deal with a very specific historical situation confronting the church in the world, a situation which is new and which hence existed neither at the time the New Testament was written nor when the early dogmatic decisions were formulated. If it is already no small problem to grasp the exceedingly complex world situation of today, it is altogether a difficult task to arrive at concrete answers for today's problems by way of fixed general dogmatic statements which largely came into being in completely different historical circumstances. A second difficulty lies in the task of speaking to non-

---

[1] *Documents*, p. 200.
[2] *Documents*, p. 201.
[3] *Documents*, p. 200.

Christians. From what common presuppositions can they be addressed and which arguments will satisfy them? In addition, there was the technical difficulty that, as distinct from all other texts before the Council, this text had not been prepared in advance by a pre-conciliar commission but had to be worked out during the Council, even though it could make use of some pre-conciliar elements. Thus there was little time to permit this document to reach full maturity and to allow for systematic and stylistic adjustments in the individual sections prepared by different commissions. For the rest, there were so many historical, sociological, sex-ethical, political, and other problems that there was hardly a bishop or theologian who would feel competent in all these areas at once. Accordingly, it was necessary to consult more extensively than otherwise with competent laymen, who, however, were not entitled to voice or vote in the Council.

Until shortly before the final vote the newness of this procedure induced in many Council Fathers a feeling of uncertainty about whether the matter under consideration had really matured sufficiently and was ready for action, or whether it might not be better to confine themselves to general principles or to a declaration on the question of world peace and turn the remaining questions or the whole matter over to a post-conciliar synod of bishops to be authorized by the pope. There was further question about what title to give to such a new-fangled document, which in ten years would probably have to be considerably revised in view of further changes in the world situation. The term "constitution" suggested itself because of the bulk and substantive importance, but on the other hand that title seemed too imposing for an undertaking which in many of its statements could not from the start lay claim to the abiding significance given to presentations dealing with fundamental principles. Consequently, consideration was given to less assuming titles, such as "conciliar letter," or "declaration," or "exposition." For these titles, however, the document appeared to be too significant and too large in scope. Thus in the end the newly devised title of "pastoral constitution" was chosen, and the word "pastoral" was designed to give expression to the church's concrete approach to the man of today.

It cannot be said that the Council surmounted all of the methodological and substantive difficulties surrounding this task. Most of the bishops and theologians of the Council were themselves aware of this when they prepared the document, and it is therefore no disparagement of their achievement to point to some of the remaining unanswered questions. It is certainly obvious that not all of these new problems could be solved during the few years the Council was in session, nor have they been solved in other churches; they remain in a constant state of flux and review. It is all the more to the Council's credit that in spite of these difficulties it undertook to deal in the broadest scope with the theme, "the church in the modern world," and addressed itself directly to all men. The fact that for the sake of the many urgent problems they were willing to take some unresolved textual inadequacies into the bargain is not only an impressive indication of the Council's sense of responsibility toward today's human situation, but also a proof that it was ready to take seriously the dogmatic statements in the Constitution on the Church concerning God's pilgrim people. The church in this world is in fact on a pilgrimage, in which it must constantly reconsider its next concrete steps as it puts its faith in the saving act which was performed once and for always. In this conscious tentativeness and openendedness which characterizes the pastoral constitution, the Council came quite close to the dialogue method of work that is customary in the World Council of Churches and, in a fuller measure than is explicit in this document, has become a partner in the churches' common striving, from which no church can stand aloof in the midst of this rapidly changing world.

After a preface concerning its aim, the constitution treats the following topics: "The Situation of Men in the Modern World" (Introduction); "The Church and Man's Calling" (Part One); and "Some Problems of Special Urgency" (Part Two).

> In the first part, the Church develops her teaching on man, on the world which is the enveloping context of man's existence, and on man's relations to his fellow men. In part two, the Church gives closer consideration to various aspects of modern life and human society; special consideration is given to those questions and problems which, in this general area, seem to have a greater urgency in our day. As a result, in part two the subject matter which is viewed in the light of doctrinal principles is made up of diverse elements. Some elements have a permanent value; others, only a transitory one.[4]

Hence, the first part offers above all the abiding dogmatic presuppositions while the second part deals above all with the actual consequences.

It is therefore difficult and often impossible to determine in individual cases which of the constitution's statements claim permanent basic significance and which are to be interpreted as transitory adaptations to the current situation. This question is all the more important since the document goes beyond, and even contradicts, earlier decisions of the Roman church in such matters as, for example, the freedom of science, the freedom of religion, the distinction between church and state, and the autonomy of secular areas. Do these statements have permanent validity as basic decisions for the future as such, or could older decisions against religious freedom, against the autonomy of the state, etc., be reactivated as binding in a changed situation? Such questions no doubt also cause difficulties for the Catholic interpreters. There is, moreover, the difficulty of interpretation caused by the document's dramatic genesis out of heterogeneous stimuli and proposals which did not receive full systematic adjustment in the official formulation. The history of this text is perhaps the most interesting of all, and with the publication of all preparatory and preliminary drafts it should become evident with what intensity the Council wrestled here not only for new individual insights but also for a new basic orientation. It is particularly praiseworthy that the Council avoided the danger of gathering a collection of condemnations of erroneous opinions in the areas of sexual ethics, science, and politics, in other

[4] Explanatory note appended to the title, *Documents*, p. 199.

words, the danger of a new syllabus, and instead gave expression to what needed to be said in the totally different, dialogically determined form of positive statements.

The Opening Toward the Modern World

Following the preface, the constitution begins with a description of the situation of modern men in the world. This discussion is continued and itemized in the two main chapters which follow, for example, Articles 19–20 of Part One, where atheism is considered, and consistently at the beginning of the chapters in Part Two. These chapters in turn proceed from the current situation in the light of special thematic points of view. We must "recognize and understand the world in which we live, its expectations, its longings, and its often dramatic characteristics" (Art. 4).[5]

"Today, the human race is passing through a new stage of its history. Profound and rapid changes are spreading by degrees around the whole world." These changes are "triggered by the intelligence and creative energies of man" and they recoil upon him. This social and cultural transformation "has repercussions on man's religious life as well" (Art. 4). In this connection, special attention is directed to the development of the natural sciences, to anthropology, and sociology, which make possible a technology now transforming the face of the earth and already trying to master outer space, and which make possible a regulation of population growth (Art. 5).[6] In addition, attention is directed to the development of an industrial society with its impact on rural populations and the growth of metropolitan areas.

Attention is circumspectly called to the manifold problems raised by these developments, problems not only between individuals or professional groups but also, for example, between technically advanced nations and developing nations, between nations that possess atomic weapons and those that do not, and between economic and political systems and power blocs that encroach

[5] *Documents*, p. 202.
[6] *Documents*, pp. 202 f.

upon each other. The document points up both the general problems involved in population density and the quite specific problems, such as, for example, the structure of leisure time. Special note is then taken of the effects of the indicated changes on religious life, and the various forms of atheism currently active are pointed out. Included in the causes of atheism is also the failure of Christians who "neglect their own training in the faith, or teach erroneous doctrine, or are deficient in their religious, moral, or social life." To that extent "they must be said to conceal rather than reveal the authentic face of God and religion" (Art. 19).[7]

When the Roman church engaged in dialogue with non-Roman churches and non-Christian religions, a *positive* approach resulted. This is true also in regard to the world of today. To be sure, there is reference to a variety of "tensions," "contradictions," "imbalances," "unresolved issues," "antitheses," "conflicts," and "dangers" in today's world. Nor are the decline of religious commitment and the growth of atheism in any way overlooked. Yet the Constitution on the Church in the Modern World is free from every mood of catastrophe and holds to the line adopted by John XXIII in his address at the opening of the Council when he warned against those who "can see nothing but prevarication and ruin" in our time, and added: "We feel we must disagree with those prophets of gloom, who are always forecasting disaster, as though the end of the world were at hand."[8] Without ignoring the difficulties and dangers of the current world situation, the constitution affirms the present world and, if anything, sees in the "difficulties," "contradictions," and "antitheses" a transition to a better life for mankind. The positive acceptance of the idea of progress is especially typical. Without ignoring the difficulties associated with cultural, technical, and economic progress, such progress is expressly affirmed in all these areas and its promotion is made a matter of duty. The Decree on the Instruments of Social

---

[7] *Documents*, p. 217.
[8] *Documents*, p. 712.

Communication has similar accents. There, too, remarkably little is made of the dangers connected with the mass media over against the opportunities these give the church. The document looks upon advances in the sciences and technology above all as a divinely sanctioned unfolding of the creative abilities which God has given man, and in this context it understands the political and economic difficulties on the international level as a growing awareness of the unity of mankind. Thus a comprehensive and hopeful view provides the setting for the severity of the conflict between the ideologies of atheism and freedom and between the political power blocs committed to these ideologies, as also for the strength of the new nationalism manifested by the former colonial nations, and the contrasts between the races. In conformity with this approach, the constitution with equal emphasis specifies as influences on the religious life brought about by changes in the world "on the one hand," the cleansing of the religious life and the intensification of a more personal and explicit adherence to faith, and, "on the other hand," the growing abandonment of religion and denial of God (Art. 7),[9] without letting the steadily growing spread of atheism and the feeling of God's remoteness, which destroy religious commitment, assert themselves in their strangeness and epochal force. It is striking, moreover, that the discussion of atheism is separated from the discussion of communism (which discussion is carried through almost in an oblique way). Nevertheless, though fully acknowledging the circumspect manner of presentation and the absence of picturing things only in black and white, the question arises whether the attempt to engage all men in dialogue has not led to a weakening of hard reality. Even some of the Council Fathers raised this question, and not only those whose dioceses are directly involved and who regard a dialogue with the rulers as impossible.

Hence the pastoral constitution does not begin with a biblical or dogmatic understanding of the world, something which only Christians could understand, but rather with the empirical reality

---

[9] *Documents*, p. 205.

of this world as it is for all to see. The concern is less for an analysis of the more basic historical causes of the present world situation than for a cataloging of the phenomena. To be sure, reference is made to modern natural science as a cause of the technical and social changes, but there is no further probing of the complex reciprocal effects of the various factors or of the intellectual roots of modern science. This would in fact have transcended the possibilities of this constitution. It does, however, pursue the reactions of these phenomena on mankind: the perplexity, anxiety, and questions that arise in men in view of the present world situation. These questions are, first of all, concrete inquiries after the relation of the sexes, a just social order, the elimination of the danger of war, etc. Yet they are not only penultimate questions concerning ways to overcome external difficulties. In his troubles, perplexities, and anxieties man has become a question to himself.

> In the face of modern development of the world, an ever-increasing number of people are raising the most basic questions or recognizing them with a new sharpness: what is man? What is this sense of sorrow, of evil, of death, which continues to exist despite so much progress? What is the purpose of these victories, purchased at so high a cost? What can man offer to society, what can he expect from it? What follows this earthly life? (Art. 10).[10]

Perhaps this overrates the extent to which the last question is a live issue for modern man. Perhaps this question has been crowded out of man's consciousness more strongly than the constitution assumes. To be sure, faith is able to recognize this last question again as the motivating force of atheism and as the pathos of nihilism in our time. Yet for the consciousness of such men it is generally no longer an open question.

The constitution, therefore, does not begin with the questions which God through his revelation addresses to mankind today but rather with the current world situation and the questions which this situation suggests to man.

---

[10] *Documents*, p. 208.

The Approach to Dialogue with the World

The pastoral constitution addresses all men. It desires to engage them all in dialogue—whether they are members of the Roman church or other Christians, followers of non-Christian religions or skeptics or atheists. For all of them the constitution wants to answer the penultimate and ultimate questions that have arisen in the world situation of our time. What arguments does the document employ and on what universally human presuppositions does it base these arguments?

(a) The common point of departure is the empirical reality of our time, since it is plain for all to see in cultural, economic, social, and political phenomena.

(b) Furthermore, the fears, longings, and questions which today's situation suggests to man are presupposed as common to all—that is, concrete questions about ultimate meaning.

(c) Additional presuppositions are a "godlike seed" (Art. 3), an "eternal seed" (Art. 18) in every man, God's "voice . . . in his depths," God's "law" in the depths of his conscience (Art. 16),[11] the natural law which God has given to all men and which reason can recognize as a demand (*passim*), as well as the self-attestation of God through creation that confronts all men.

(d) Contact is also established with what man knows, however pervertedly, about values—"permanent values" (Art. 4), "accepted values" (Art. 7), "positive values" (Art. 57). "For insofar as they stem from endowments conferred by God on man, these values are exceedingly good" (Art. 11). Also the adoption of ideas concerning "truth, goodness, and beauty" (Art. 57) and "the wisdom of the ancestors"[12] would seem to belong in this context.

(e) In addition to the possibilities given to all men for knowing God and his law as well as for knowing about values, the constitution presupposes that grace is active not only in Christians but invisibly in all men of good will, and that the Holy Spirit

---

[11] *Documents*, pp. 201, 215, 213.
[12] *Documents*, pp. 203, 205, 263, 209.

offers not only Christians but all men the possibility of being associated with Christ "in a manner known only to God" (Art. 22).[13]

(f) Finally, the biblical statements about creation, about God's saving deed in Jesus Christ, about the church and eschatological consummation are offered as arguments, and frequently the christological and eschatological statements are placed at the end of individual lines of thought.

Thus the arguments employed by the pastoral constitution in addressing modern man are quite varied, quite different in their philosophical and theological origins, and often imprecise in their understanding of concepts (e.g., values). Concepts involving phenomena, natural law, philosophical values, and salvation history are used side by side without having been integrated into a systematic whole. It is clear that the constitution attempts to attach itself as broadly as possible to the presuppositions of the addressees in order to begin the dialogue. It is also clear, however, that the Council did not confine itself to those presuppositions which all men have in common. Rather, by employing arguments that are by no means apparent for everybody, the Council passes from dialogue to teaching. This is true especially of the biblical-redemptive statements (f), but also of the assertion that all men of good will are spiritually associated with Christ in a hidden way (e). Even where the argument revolves around God's voice in every conscience and the natural law given to all men (c), it is not presupposed that this demand of God is actually recognized by all men in truth. Repeated reference is made to the erring conscience. Likewise the values (d) "are often wrenched from their rightful function by the taint in man's heart, and hence stand in need of purification" (Art. 11).[14] Man's questions will accordingly be revealed in truth only in the light of the revelation of Christ. The natural law must be interpreted in the light of the gospel (*passim*), and only thus are the "principles of justice and

[13] *Documents*, p. 222.
[14] *Documents*, p. 209.

equity," "as right reason demanded," recognized in truth (Art. 63). Values must be judged in the light of the Christian faith and referred to their divine source (Art. 11).[15]

The variety of arguments is encompassed by the idea of the agreement between revelation and man's experience, especially his self-experience (Art. 13), and the idea of the correspondence between the church's message and the "most secret desires of the human heart" (Art. 21).[16] However, these questions and the most secret desires of the human heart will ultimately be laid bare only in the revelation of Christ. Thus in the pastoral constitution the church confronts mankind in the act of teaching not only in the statements concerning Christ, but also in the argumentation involving conscience and natural law which all have in common, etc. The question arises whether it is enough for the constitution to use the saving deed of God in Christ as one argument among others in its dialogue with mankind. How are non-Christians to understand this argument? Since faith alone is able to comprehend the foolish word of the cross as the revelation of God's wisdom, should not the constitution as an address to all men be more strongly oriented to awakening faith? Should it not proceed to the proclamation of Christ?

In substance, the answers to the questions of today begin with the doctrine of man. The "pivotal point of our total presentation will be man himself, whole and entire, body and soul, heart and conscience, mind and will" (Art. 3).[17] By starting with the doctrine of man rather than the doctrine of God, the constitution has its point of contact in the fact that in modern man's consciousness the question about God has largely been replaced by the question "What is man?" The first major part deals in chapter i with the dignity of the human person, in chapter ii with the community of mankind, and in chapter iii with man's activity throughout the world. Accordingly, Part One answers, first of all, the ultimate

[15] *Documents*, pp. 272, 209.
[16] *Documents*, pp. 211, 220.
[17] *Documents*, p. 201.

questions concerning the meaning of human existence, and on this basis Part Two offers answers to the concrete penultimate questions of our time.

The doctrine of man as developed here contains many familiar components of philosophical anthropology which the Roman church has taken over from the ancient heritage and the new philosophy and has incorporated in her fundamental theology and dogmatics. This is true, for example, of the statements concerning reason, conscience, freedom, man's personal worth, as well as the equality of all men and their personal fellowship.

At the same time the doctrine of man is developed in a biblical-redemptive way. The doctrine does not begin with a philosophical statement but with man's creation "in the image of God." As such, man is "capable of knowing and loving his Creator, and was appointed by Him as master of all earthly creatures that he might subdue them and use them to God's glory" (Art. 12). Also, man's being destined for interpersonal communion is derived from creation as "male and female" (Art. 12). At the instigation of the personified Evil, man "set himself against God and sought to find fulfillment apart from God," and thus "became out of harmony with himself" and came to grief (Art. 13). "He who is 'the image of the invisible God' (Col. 1:15), is Himself the perfect man. To the sons of Adam He restores the divine likeness which had been disfigured from the first sin onward." He "merited life for us by the free shedding of His own blood" (Art. 22). Through his Spirit he has consummated man's created destiny of interpersonal relations in the fellowship of the church, which he will one day bring to perfection (Art. 32).[18] As the understanding of the church in the Constitution on the Church is oriented to salvation history in a special way, so also the understanding of man in the pastoral constitution.

The philosophical and redemptive understandings of man (here again oriented more directly to creation and a christocentric ap-

---

[18] *Documents*, pp. 210 f., 220 f., 231.

proach) have not been reduced to a full systematic unity. All in all, however, the accents appear in many respects more biblical than is often the case in Roman Catholic theology. Over against the widespread conception of man as a "rational being" (*animal rationale*), consisting of body and immortal spirit-soul, the emphasis points more strongly to man as a unit, and his dignity is based not only on his spirituality but also on his corporeality. In this way the relationship between man and woman is drawn into a new light, and the significance of the physical in interpersonal relationships is elsewhere clearly stressed. Over against the widespread attempt to differentiate between nature and supernature in man, and to interpret the succession of original state, fall, and redemption as the possession, loss, and restored reception of supernatural grace, while in an unhistorical way man's "pure nature" remains identical, the constitution in the framework of a salvation-history view of man looks more definitely to his historicality. In this way the changes in the orders of human communal life and human dominion over nature are more clearly seen.

Directives for Service in the World of Today

Under the heading "Some Problems of Special Urgency" the five chapters of Part Two draw concrete conclusions from theological anthropology and furnish guidelines for practical behavior. Each chapter is so interesting that it deserves to be thoroughly analyzed by experts in the sexual, cultural, social, and economic sciences, as well as in political science. In such a study it would be especially interesting to see a careful comparison with former positions of the Roman church and with the answers given nowadays outside the Roman church. Space limitations compel us to confine ourselves to calling attention to those statements of special significance for human social life today. We shall follow the sequence of the five chapters.

(a) Marriage and Family

After presenting the present situation, the document continues with the following basic statements:

> The intimate partnership of married life and love has been established by the Creator and qualified by His laws. It is rooted in the conjugal covenant of irrevocable personal consent. Hence, by that human act whereby spouses mutually bestow and accept each other, a relationship arises which by divine will and in the eyes of society too is a lasting one. For the good of the spouses and their offspring as well as of society, the existence of this sacred bond no longer depends on human decisions alone. For God Himself is the author of matrimony, endowed as it is with various benefits and purposes (Art. 48).[19]

It is consistent with the view of marriage in the Catholic tradition when it is pointed out in this connection that Christ meets Christian spouses through the sacrament of marriage. At the same time there has been a significant shift in accent. The traditional moral theology taught that the primary purpose of marriage is progeny and the second mutual assistance, and that marriage is a cure for sexual desire. This desire was understood as rebellion against the spiritual powers. By contrast, the constitution sets as the first goal of marriage the union of the spouses in personal love (Art. 49) and only then the procreation of children (Art. 50). Conjugal love "is uniquely expressed and perfected through the marital act" (Art. 49) with the aim "to cooperate with the love of the Creator and the Savior, who through them will enlarge and enrich His own family day by day" (Art. 50). Thus matrimony is a union in personal bestowal and is crowned by the procreation and education of children (Art. 48).[20]

Without injuring the essence of marriage and its own conjugal covenant given to it by God (Art. 48), this shift in accent makes it possible to face up to the problem of responsible parenthood (Art. 50) and to recognize that there are situations in which "at least temporarily the size of their families should not be increased" and in which "the faithful exercise of love and the full intimacy of their lives are hard to maintain" (Art. 51). Where "the intimacy of married life is broken off, it is not rare for its faith-

[19] *Documents*, p. 250.
[20] *Documents*, pp. 252 ff., 250.

fulness to be imperiled and its quality of fruitfulness ruined. For then the upbringing of the children and the courage to accept new ones are both endangered" (Art. 51). It is highly significant that this problem is recognized, even though the constitution suggests no concrete ways of legitimately preventing conception. It demands only that no methods of regulating procreation be undertaken "which are found blameworthy by the teaching authority of the Church in its unfolding of the divine law" (Art. 51). The document calls attention to current studies undertaken by a papal commission.[21] Abortion is condemned as an unspeakable crime. Hence the problem of the population explosion in some areas of the world has not been solved. Yet through the Council the dialogue on this problem has received an altered presupposition on the part of the Roman church.

(b) The Proper Development of Culture

Following marriage and family, man "can come to an authentic and full humanity only through culture, that is, through the cultivation of natural goods and values." The word "culture" is used to designate

> all those factors by which man refines and unfolds his manifold spiritual and bodily qualities. It means his effort to bring the world itself under his control by his knowledge and his labor. It includes the fact that by improving customs and institutions he renders social life more human both within the family and in the civic community. Finally, it is a feature of culture that throughout the course of time man expresses, communicates, and conserves in his works great spiritual experiences and desires, so that these may be of advantage to the progress of many, even of the whole human family (Art. 53).[22]

Here, too, the current situation is the point of departure, and then the cultural task is defined in its basic principles. In his cultural work man

> carries out the design of God. Manifested at the beginning of time, the divine plan is that man should subdue the earth, bring creation to perfection, and develop himself. When a man so acts he simul-

---

[21] *Documents*, pp. 250, 254 ff., and note 173.
[22] *Documents*, p. 259.

> taneously obeys the great Christian commandment that he place himself at the service of his brother men (Art. 57).

Men are willing to assume this obligation because they are confident that "the mystery of the Christian faith furnishes them with excellent incentives and helps toward discharging this duty more energetically and especially toward uncovering the full meaning of this activity, a meaning which gives human culture its eminent place in the integral vocation of man" (Art. 57).[23] In contrast to earlier authoritarian claims of the Roman church, it is striking to what high degree the constitution acknowledges the "independence" of culture, the consciousness of modern men "that they themselves are the artisans and the authors of the culture of their community" (Art. 55), and the importance of culture for the maturity of the human race. In spite of the danger of "a humanism which is merely earthbound, and even contrary to religion itself" (Art. 56), the autonomy of culture is expressly affirmed. Furthermore, the freedom which culture needs to develop is demanded, as well as the "legitimate possibility of exercising its independence according to its own principles" (Art. 59). This recognition of "the legitimate autonomy of human culture and especially of the sciences" (Art. 59) is expressed in spite of the difficulties it may provide for the relationship of culture and Christian education.

> These difficulties do not necessarily harm the life of faith. Indeed they can stimulate the mind to a more accurate and penetrating grasp of faith. For recent studies and findings of science, history, and philosophy raise new questions which influence life and demand new theological investigations. . . . The deposit of faith or revealed truths are one thing; the manner in which they are formulated without violence to their meaning and significance is another (Art. 62).

For such tasks "all the faithful, clerical and lay, possess a lawful freedom of inquiry and of thought, and the freedom to express their minds" (Art. 62). It is striking that, in contrast to the well-known tendency of the Roman church toward a cultural monism bearing the church's stamp, a plurality of cultures is affirmed

---

[23] *Documents*, p. 262.

(Art. 53). Moreover, there is approval of a "universal form of human culture," embracing Christians and non-Christians, "one which will promote and express the unity of the human race to the degree that it preserves the particular features of the different cultures" (Art. 54).[24]

The Council teaches that the autonomous progress of culture is limited by "morality" and may proceed "as long as the rights of the individual and of the community, whether particular or universal, are preserved within the context of the common good" (Art. 59).[25] Furthermore, it is impossible without the church to know the "full meaning" of culture or "the intimate meaning of things" since the methods of empirical science are inadequate for this purpose (Art. 57).[26] The freedom of theological inquiry is limited by the teaching office of the church. Thus both the affirmation and the restriction of culture are expressed side by side. The beneficial connection between Christian faith and the sciences is asserted but not really clarified, as little as is the historical fact that the natural sciences frequently had to fight for their advances in opposition to the church. Some opinions in the Council chambers went much further and called, for example, for a rehabilitation of Galileo. Nevertheless, the constitution furnishes new presuppositions for a dialogue on these questions.

(c) The Socio-Economic Life

After presenting the current state of "anxiety" and insisting that "numerous reforms are needed at the socio-economic level, along with universal changes in ideas and attitudes" (Art. 63), chapter iii proceeds to speak of the "principles of justice and equity" as "right reason demanded" and as the church has worked them out "in the course of the centuries and with the light of the gospel" and has enlarged upon them in "modern times especially" (Art. 63). Hence, the expositions in this chapter refer particularly to the social encyclicals of the popes since Leo XIII, above all the

---

[24] *Documents*, pp. 259-70.
[25] *Documents*, p. 265.
[26] *Documents*, pp. 262 f.

encyclical *Mater et Magistra* (1961) of John XXIII; but the material goes even further. We cannot here go into the very interesting comparison between the encyclicals and the constitution but must confine ourselves to the most important instructions of the text adopted by the Council. The whole is determined by the strong endorsement of economic progress expressed at the beginning:

> Today, more than ever before, progress in the production of agricultural and industrial goods and in the rendering of services is rightly aimed at making provision for the growth of a people and at meeting the rising expectations of the human race. Therefore, technical progress must be fostered, along with a spirit of initiative, an eagerness to create and expand enterprises, the adaptation of methods of production, and the strenuous efforts of all who engage in production—in a word, all the elements making for such development (Art. 64).

All men are to share in this progress. It is, therefore, not only "every man's duty to labor faithfully" but also "his right to work" under circumstances that respect human dignity (Art. 67). Furthermore, the worker is entitled to a wage that enables him to cultivate his life worthily and to "have a share of earthly goods sufficient" for himself and his family (Art. 69). Private property is regarded "as an extension of human freedom" and "constitutes a kind of prerequisite for civil liberties" (Art. 71). To safeguard these rights "the active participation of everyone in the running of an enterprise should be promoted" and the workers' right to strike as a "necessary, though ultimate, means" is acknowledged (Art. 68). Everyone has the right, "in extreme necessity," "to take from the riches of others what he himself needs" (Art. 69). "In that case, the old principle holds true: 'In extreme necessity all goods are common, that is, all goods are to be shared' " (n. 224). Expropriation in the interests of the common welfare, as long as there is fair compensation, is considered. Corresponding demands for the participation of all in economic progress are also made for the coexistence of nations. The immense economic inequalities which now exist between nations, and which are often still increasing and coupled with discrimination, must be removed "as quickly as possible" (Art.

66). Emphatically, people are put under obligation to join the common war on starvation and to give aid to underdeveloped areas (Art. 69 *et al.*).

In this way socio-economic progress is affirmed as a service to humanity, "viewed in terms of his material needs and the demands of his intellectual, moral, spiritual, and religious life" (Art. 64). Individual and political abuse of economic development in the name of "a false liberty" must be repudiated (Art. 65). In their support of the socio-economic development Christians should take the lead in promoting justice and charity and let their lives "in faithfulness to Christ and His gospel" be permeated "with the spirit of the beatitudes, notably with the spirit of poverty" (Art. 72).[27]

(d) The Life of the Political Community

Also, in evaluating opposing systems of political order the constitution upholds the rights of the human person. Protecting the person is the necessary condition for active participation of citizens in the political community. The political community is derived not from power but from the common good.

> Individuals, families, and various groups which compose the civic community are aware of their own insufficiency in the matter of establishing a fully human condition of life. They see the need for that wider community in which each would daily contribute his energies toward the ever better attainment of the common good. . . .
>
> Hence the political community exists for that common good in which the community finds its full justification and meaning, and from which it derives its pristine and proper right (Art. 74).

The divinely ordained authority of the state, "primarily as a moral force," must dispose the energies of the whole citizenry toward the common good. "At the same time the choice of government and the method of selecting leaders is left to the free will of citizens" (Art. 74). When governmental authority oversteps its bounds, the citizens have the right, within the "limits imposed by natural law and the gospel" (Art. 74), to resist for the sake of

---

[27] *Documents*, pp. 271-82.

the common welfare. It "harms humanity when government takes on totalitarian or dictatorial forms injurious to the rights of persons or social groups" (Art. 75). The form of political order to be aspired to gives all citizens the freedom "to participate freely and actively in establishing the constitutional bases of a political community, governing the state, determining the purpose and scope of various institutions, and choosing leaders" (Art. 75).[28] A division of governmental roles and institutions should be rooted in law.

In contrast to the history of the Roman church and her former claim to both spiritual and temporal swords, the constitution expressly concedes that in "their proper spheres, the political community and the Church are mutually independent and self-governing." (It is true, however, that there is no reference to the problems involved in the papal state, where the secular sovereign is at the same time the head of the Roman church.) In line with this independence on the part of both,

> the faithful will be able to make a clear distinction between what a Christian conscience leads them to do in their own name as citizens, whether as individuals or in association, and what they do in the name of the Church and in union with her shepherds (Art. 76).

Yet church and state must cooperate. The church must foster the political freedom and responsibility of citizens by "preaching the truth of the gospel and shedding light on all areas of human activity through her teaching and the example of the faithful" (Art. 76). The church performs her role, furthermore, by interpreting the universally binding natural law in the light of the gospel and by standing ready "to renounce the exercise of certain legitimately acquired rights if it becomes clear that their use raises doubt about the sincerity of her witness or that new conditions of life demand some other arrangement" (Art. 76). The government, on the other hand, is obligated to grant the church freedom to preach the gospel and the social teachings of the

---

[28] *Documents*, pp. 283-86.

church, and "to pass moral judgments, even on matters touching the political order, whenever basic personal rights or the salvation of souls make such judgments necessary" (Art. 76).[29] The Declaration on Religious Freedom also corresponds to these statements concerning the differentiation and the coordination of the political and ecclesiastical spheres of activity.

(e) Peace and the Community of Nations

Here the Council wishes to point out "the authentic and most noble meaning of peace" and to condemn "the frightfulness of war" (Art. 77). Peace is "not merely the absence of war" but rather "an enterprise of justice," the result of "that harmony built into human society by its divine Founder, and actualized by men as they thirst after ever greater justice." Indeed, peace is "the fruit of love, which goes beyond what justice can provide" and it "symbolizes and results from the peace of Christ who comes forth from God the Father." In the last analysis, peace is rooted in the reconciliation of man with God through the incarnate Son of God (Art. 78). Because of man's sins the danger of war threatens until the return of Christ. In a traditional manner aggressive war is condemned, while the right of legitimate defense is acknowledged, without, however, conceding that all means are permitted in time of war. The observance of the natural law of nations and of international conventions aimed at humanizing military activity are recommended, as are humane provisions for the conscientious objectors who should, however, be encouraged to accept some other form of service to the human community (Art. 79). But beyond this, in view of the danger of atomic war, the Council feels compelled to discuss total war, which indiscriminately destroys entire cities or extensive areas along with their population, and to condemn it as a crime against God and man (Art. 80). It finds no comfort in the stalemate of the reciprocal atomic threat as a guarantee of peace but demands that the nations begin disarmament, "not indeed a unilateral disarmament, but one proceeding

---

[29] *Documents*, pp. 287-89.

at an equal pace according to agreement." The goal must be that all war be "completely outlawed by international consent. This goal undoubtedly requires the establishment of some universal public authority acknowledged as such by all, and endowed with effective power to safeguard, on the behalf of all, security, regard for justice, and respect for rights" (Art. 82).[30]

The Council urgently exhorts men to eradicate enmity and dissension (Art. 83) and to establish cooperation among the international agencies in various fields of social life, such as food, health, education, and employment, as well as care for refugees and promoting the growth of developing nations (Art. 84). If there is to be an economic order "which is genuine and universal, there must be an abolition of excessive desire for profit, nationalistic pretensions," etc. (Art. 85). There must be responsibility for achieving a progressive social settlement, and in this way the causes of military conflicts will be removed at the roots. Also, the problems involved in the population explosion must be attacked through international cooperation. On this point the Council grants the decision on the size of the family exclusively to the parents, not to the state. There can be no violation of the moral law. There is, however, no indication of the methods of birth control that conform to the moral law (Art. 87).[31]

In its answers to the diverse cultural, economic, social, and political problems of our time—apart from the accented peculiarity of the Catholic view of marriage and its restraint regarding contraceptives—the Council has brought about an extensive adaptation to what many consider to be necessary today. The Council has given up some traditional positions taken by the Roman church, for example, over against the natural sciences, progress, the sovereignty of the state, conscientious objection, labor strikes, etc. Against these traditional positions the modern development could in part be realized only by severe struggle. There is now, on the contrary, an extensive affirmation of the autonomy of the

[30] *Documents*, pp. 290-95.
[31] *Documents*, pp. 297-302.

sciences, the fundamental principles of social business management, of democratic government, and the principles and goals of the United Nations. To be sure, the Council offers a basis (namely, theological) different from what is customary today in, for example, scientific research and the United Nations, but the concrete directives themselves come quite close to what is accepted today and contain little that is new. Naturally, this extensive agreement does not subtract from the value of the Council's instructions. Their value, however, consists less in their suggestion of newfangled and special ways than in their support and strengthening of the imperiled forces for order in this world. Reflecting the makeup of the pertinent commissions of the Council, these chapters of the constitution to a high degree bear the stamp of Western, specifically European, thinking. Accordingly, their suggestions are more in line with the practical possibilities of people in the Western world than in the Oriental and African worlds.

Since the constitution is addressed not only to Christians but to all people, the question arises whether non-Christians are able to understand it. Certainly many of them could understand the concrete directives. These, however, are based on a theological doctrine of man which, in turn, rests ultimately in the doctrine of Christ. Jesus Christ, however, can only be known by faith. Hence questions again arise: Is it enough to address non-Christians with repeated citations of biblical passages? Should there not be a much more relevant interpretation of the Scriptures? Is it enough to cite Jesus Christ again and again as one argument among others for being involved with the world? Should not the constitution proclaim Christ to non-Christians far more directly, since "faith comes from what is heard" (Rom. 10:7)? What, then, are non-Christians to think of Jesus Christ, if the constitution appeals to him and yet has hardly anything concrete to offer for the present world situation that is different from what many reasonable men today regard as necessary, even though they do not have this faith? Does the pastoral constitution, the text of the Council which addresses itself expressly to the non-Christians, really confront them with Jesus Christ as Lord?

Christ and the World

The pastoral constitution, as indicated, begins by considering the world of today, by identifying the current questions, and by answering these questions, first of all, on the basis of the doctrine of man and then by concretely dealing with the most acute individual problems. This structure corresponds to a widespread apologetic method. The danger in this procedure, however, is admittedly that the participants in the dialogue too obviously presuppose the questions for which they already have a ready answer, and the opposite danger is that the answers are so accommodated to the questions of the partners in dialogue that the Christian witness is weakened. Both things can, of course, happen simultaneously.

For this reason I propose to reverse the procedure in the following two sections by beginning with the witness of the New Testament revelation and then asking to what extent the statements of the pastoral constitution concerning the relationship between Christ and the world and between the church and the world correspond to the New Testament. We must confine ourselves to a set of theses.

(a) According to the witness of Paul's letters and John's Gospel, the world, especially mankind, is God's creation which, through rebellion against God, has come under the dominion of the powers of destruction and is subject to God's judgment. This judgment will come upon the world and signal its end. "The form of this world is passing away" (I Cor. 7:31), "the world passes away, and the lust of it" (I John 2:17). The fact that the world still continues to exist in spite of being subject to God's judgment is due to the patience of God the preserver and the love of the Redeemer.

(b) Out of love for the world God sent his Son and delivered him to death. In Jesus Christ God's deliverance has burst upon this lost world. By his message of the coming of God's kingdom, by his beatitudes and his woes, Jesus has placed men before the decision, and in being confronted with his person man's future salvation and judgment are decided. In his death on the cross Jesus took the sins of the world upon himself. Yet deliverance from the judgment of divine wrath is given to man not simply by the fact of Christ's death but by faith in the Crucified.

(c) Having been raised from the dead and exalted to the right hand of God, Jesus is Lord. All things have been made subject to him that he might make them all subject to God. In the New Testament, however, Christ is not called "Lord of the world." Christ is Lord of the church, of the community of those whom he has called to be not of this world and whom he has delivered from the fetters and the decay of this world by faith. He is the head of the new creation. "He who believes in the Son has eternal life; he who does not obey the Son shall not see life, but the wrath of God rests upon him" (John 3:36).

(d) Christ will come as judge of the world—of the living and the dead. "We must all appear before the judgment seat of Christ, so that each one may receive good or evil, according to what he has done in the body" (II Cor. 5:10). Then Christ will receive some and reject the others. Then all will confess Christ as Lord. His coming will constitute the end of the world and the consummation of the new creation, which began with his resurrection and grows in the church in a hidden manner. The New Testament, however, does not speak of a "new world," but of a "new creation," "a new heaven and a new earth."

These biblical statements are also the basis for the pastoral constitution. Nevertheless, there have been some shifts which must not be overlooked.

The world is looked upon above all as the creation and as the object of God's love in Christ, while the rule of sin and the forces of corruption and the world's condemnation to judgment appear peculiarly palliated, and there is no mention of God's wrath against the world. We should ask, furthermore, whether, in the framework of the New Testament assessment of the world, the constitution ought to have spoken more modestly of human dignity and freedom and the autonomy of culture.

The constitution presents Jesus Christ less as the deliverer from this world than the preserver of this world. His saving work is claimed above all for the task of overcoming the world's cultural, economic, and political difficulties of our time. There is not always a sufficiently clear distinction between deliverance from the world's difficulties and deliverance in God's judgment, between justice in the life of the human community and the divine righteousness of believing sinners, between the peace in this world and the peace that comes to the believers through God's reconciling act in Christ, as well as between human freedom in a mundane sense and the freedom of God's children.

The imminent return of Christ is viewed less as the end than as the consummation of this world. Nothing is said about the sufferings and catastrophes which, according to the New Testament, must precede his coming. Nor is there any mention of Antichrist, in whom the world's revolt against Christ will concentrate. The "signs of the times" (Art. 4)[32] are not brought to bear as omens of the end and the coming Christ. Because of the ideas of development and progress, the conflict between the world and Christ and the nearness of his sudden appearance is made to fade, and the progress of this world is coupled with the coming of the kingdom of God in a way that indeed does not equate them but that nevertheless assigns to this earthly progress a role of "vital concern to the kingdom of God" (Art. 39)[33] in a manner foreign to the New Testament.

As strange as the New Testament assessment of the world may appear at first glance, the question should be raised whether the constitution would not have viewed the current world situation in its peril more realistically if it had avoided weakening the New Testament statements because of its desire to accommodate itself to

[32] *Documents*, p. 201.
[33] *Documents*, p. 237.

modern ideas of development. This would seem to reflect not so much an American as a French influence, that is to say, the impression of the evolutionistic-cosmic conception of Teilhard de Chardin.

The Church and the World

(a) The church is the people of God called to be not of the world and consists of those who believe in Jesus Christ, who were given into his death through baptism and who are built up as his body through the Lord's Supper. They are in the world but have through Christ been set free from the fetters of this world and are now admonished, "Do not be conformed to this world" (Rom. 12:2), "Do not love the world or the things in the world" (I John 2:15). Rather, faith is the victory that overcomes the world (I John 5:4).

(b) The church, as God's people called to be not of the world, is sent by God into the world in order to proclaim salvation in Christ alone to all men. This word of the cross is a foolish and offensive message for the world, a message that contradicts the wisdom of this world and demands faith. Hence, wherever the gospel is authoritatively proclaimed, it brings men either to life or to death. Just as Jesus came "not to bring peace, but a sword" (Matt. 10:34), so the gospel occasions contradiction and conflict, for the world resists the lordship of Christ. In the midst of the conflict, however, the peace of God is given to those who by faith commit themselves to Christ as their Lord, glorify him, and go to meet him at his return. Thus the church as Christ's witness is the instrument of the approaching reign of God.

(c) Faith in Christ knows that God is preserving the world in spite of its being subject to judgment, so that the gospel may be proclaimed to it and many saved by faith. Hence the church is not only sent to proclaim the message of Christ but also to take responsibility for the world's preservation. This responsibility is expressed in the New Testament admonitions to obey political powers and to disobey them when obedience to God demands it, in admonitions to slaves and masters, and in other statements in the virtue and vice catalogs and the "tables of duties." In these admonitions the church has rightly seen the systematic stimulus for pledging herself to the establishment of a just and peaceful order of communal life which embraces believers and non-believers alike.

(d) It is necessary to differentiate between the two tasks of the church, spreading the saving message of Christ and contributing to the preservation of this world. They do belong together, for one and the same God is the preserver of this world and the deliverer from its fetters, and the expectation of the coming kingdom clothes everything men do for their fellow men with an ultimate urgency. Yet the proper and primary assignment given to the church is the message of Christ, not the order of this world. Jesus himself had been sent to proclaim the reign of God, not to be a "judge or divider" over quarreling men (Luke 12:13 f.). Through the message of Christ the reign of Christ comes to the world. The church must above all serve the world as the instrument for establishing the reign of Christ.

(e) The church is, therefore, a stranger in this world. "Here we have no lasting city, but we seek the city which is to come" (Heb. 13:14). The church in this world is on a pilgrimage, and her way leads to glory in the train of Jesus through misunderstanding, persecution, and suffering. By the same divine necessity as the way of Jesus, this is the church's way. In this insecurity and weakness, which the church experiences in this world, the power of the risen Lord seeks to manifest itself. "Do not be surprised at the fiery ordeal which comes upon you to prove you, as though something strange were happening to you. But rejoice in so far as you share Christ's sufferings" (I Pet. 4:12 f.).

Such New Testament statements are indeed given their due in the Constitution on the Church and in the Decree on the Church's Missionary Activity. In the Pastoral Constitution on the Church in the Modern World, however, this biblical material is peculiarly toned down.

"Christ, to be sure, gave His Church no proper mission in the political, economic, or social order. The purpose which He set before her is a religious one" (Art. 42).[34] Yet this is followed mainly by a treatment of questions concerning the secular order. The New Testament relationship between the two tasks appears to be shifted out of focus. The foreground is occupied not by the scandal of the word of the cross, the message concerning the deliverance of believers from this world, but rather by a concern for the preservation and progress of the world. Christ is appealed to principally in this context, and he appears here more as an argument than in the interest of bringing his saving deed and his judgment in direct address to all men.

Correspondingly, the New Testament understanding of the church has also undergone a change here. Though the title is "The Church in the Modern World," little is said in the document concerning the church's real situation. Instead, in a peculiar sort of timelessness, the church seems to be placing herself over against the changing world and instructing it. The church's freedom under governmental guarantees appears to be her normal existence, while a lack of security or even persecution is regarded as something abnormal. But does it really help when those who are oppressed and deprived of their liberty are given directives for the social and political order which they cannot possibly realize? Does the church owe them nothing more than guidelines for an ordered human society? Does it not above all owe them the consolation of Jesus: "Blessed are you when men revile you and persecute you and utter all kinds of evil against you falsely on my account. Rejoice and be glad" (Matt. 5:11 f.); "Count it all joy, my brethren, when you meet various trials" (Jas. 1:2); "Rejoice in so far as you share Christ's sufferings" (I Pet. 4:13)? The first word of the church must not be a complaint about injustice experienced but the recognition of the privilege of being permitted to suffer with Christ. It is in the brothers who suffer with him that the risen Christ manifests his glory in the midst of the

[34] *Documents*, p. 241.

world. The pastoral constitution refers only incidentally to those great areas of Christendom whose commitment and faithfulness today constitute the church's glory.

These criticisms would be less important if the constitution's title read, "The Church and the Present World Order" or "The Church's Contribution to the Preservation of the Present World." However, the title "The Church in the Modern World," or as originally formulated, "The Presence of the Church in the Modern World," imposes a far more comprehensive task. We must not overlook, of course, the fact that much of what is missing here is given expression in the Constitution on the Church and the Decree on Missionary Activity. Those documents, however, offer direct instruction only to the members of the Roman church. Even though the Constitution on the Church "wishes to set forth more precisely to the faithful and to the entire world the nature and encompassing mission of the Church" (Art. 1)[35] it does not, in fact, address non-Christians directly and explicitly. Thus the Council has remained strangely reticent about a direct witness concerning Christ to the world—unless the way the Roman church presented herself at the Council be understood as such a witness to Christ. While fully appreciating the courageous advance which the Council has undertaken by means of its pastoral constitution, one would have to say, in the language of Reformation theology, that Law and Gospel have here not been properly distinguished.

Service to the World and Ecumenism

The pastoral constitution has attacked problems which likewise confront the rest of Christendom and for which the World Council of Churches since Amsterdam (1948) has offered similar and, in part, identical answers. It must also be admitted that in many respects the World Council has not sufficiently clarified the theological bases for the church's involvement with the world order (problems of natural law, the two kingdoms, Christ's cosmic rule, etc.). The pastoral constitution makes no explicit reference to the

[35] *Documents*, p. 15.

concrete proposals of other churches or of the World Council. It simply confines itself to this general remark: "The Catholic Church gladly holds in high esteem the things which other Christian Churches or ecclesial communities have done or are doing co-operatively by way of achieving the same goal" (Art. 40).[36] Looking to the future, the Council "desires that by way of fulfilling their role properly in the international community, Catholics should seek to cooperate actively and in a positive manner both with their separated brothers, who together with them profess the gospel of love, and with all men thirsting for true peace" (Art. 90; cf. Art. 92).[37] It would seem that the connection between this constitution and the Decree on Ecumenism remains rather general, and that what the Decree on Ecumenism says about cooperation in the social area has not led to further concrete proposals in the constitution.

To what extent is the Decree on Ecumenism reflected in the other resolutions of the Council? Does it simply stand beside them, or do its thoughts permeate the other resolutions? The Decree on the Instruments of Social Communication makes no mention of ecumenical cooperation, though that would seem natural. Otherwise, the ecumenical obligation is mentioned in numerous texts, such as the Decrees on the Bishops, on the Priests, and on the Laity. Hence the ecumenical idea is introduced into various areas of the church's life. Yet most of the references are purely formal; they do not go beyond the Decree on Ecumenism, and they fall short of the urgency of the directives given in that decree. The Decree on Ecumenism is most strongly echoed in the Decree on Missionary Activity.

---

[36] *Documents*, p. 239.
[37] *Documents*, p. 304.

9

Scripture, Tradition, Teaching Office

At the beginning of every session of the Council there was a solemn procession in which the gospel in the form of a priceless manuscript was carried into the assembly down the center aisle of St. Peter's and enthroned on a golden throne atop the altar where Mass had just been celebrated. During the procession the Council Fathers sang the hymn, "*Christus vincit, Christus regnat.*" This chant, together with this symbolic acknowledgment of the gospel as Lord and judge of the deliberations and resolutions of the Council, conforms to the ancient and the Reformation understanding of Christ as the center of Holy Scripture and as present in the word of Scripture.

This impressive ritual acknowledgment of the dominant function of the biblical word of God was echoed in numerous biblically based expressions during the Council's deliberations and in the course of the sessions biblical arguments were increasingly emphasized. This fact was also reflected in the resolutions of the Council, not only in important details but beyond that in a general preference for biblical concepts over against those of scholastic dogmatics. It was reflected further in the decision to employ a biblically based salvation-history concept as the foundation asserted again and again in the treatment of the various Council themes.

On the other hand, in spite of enthroning the gospel manuscript, it is noteworthy that throughout the Council no sermon was preached in which a previously read biblical text was expounded. The papal addresses did incorporate biblical words and ideas, but the themes and structures of these addresses were determined not by a biblical text but by the situation prevailing in the Council at the moment. It was equally remarkable that the biblically based speeches in the Council were circumscribed by the official dogmas of the Roman church. The biblical lines of argument were developed only in what could be said theologically in the area not fixed by dogma.

This gives rise to the question of what kind of authority was accorded the Holy Scriptures by the Council. The answer can be gained not only indirectly, from the actual use which the Council made of Scripture, but also directly and fundamentally, in the Dogmatic Constitution on Divine Revelation. One must ask what the relationship is between the basic coordination of Scripture and tradition and the actual appeal to Scripture and tradition in the opinions expressed by the Council Fathers and in the resolutions of the Council.

The most important reasons for this basic reflection were, on the one hand, the unrest that had crept into a part of the Roman church as a result of the new Catholic biblical scholarship, and, on the other hand, the discussion set in motion above all by the Tübingen theologian Geiselmann on the interpretation of the statements of the Council of Trent concerning the relationship between Scripture and tradition. Formerly, the Tridentine decision had been generally understood as saying that the apostolic teaching was contained partly in Holy Scripture and partly in oral tradition. Now Geiselmann had shown that it was possible to hold that the sum total of apostolic teaching may be found both in Holy Scripture and in oral tradition. This was a possibility which broadened the base for ecumenical dialogue. It is evident also in the various formulations of the Dogmatic Constitution on Divine Revelation that the Council was engaged in a genuine struggle in the course of which the initial rejection of the new biblical scholarship and of Geiselmann's thesis was overcome.

The Revelation of God in Jesus Christ

If the Constitution on the Church can be properly evaluated only by comparison with the *schema* on the church in the First Vatican

Council, the significance of the Constitution on Revelation emerges only by comparison with the Dogmatic Constitution of Vatican I on the Catholic Faith (especially chapter ii). Compared with the Vatican I text, the new document on revelation is in a striking way shaped by the Holy Scriptures.

The statements of Vatican I on revelation were governed by the relationship between the natural knowability of God and supernatural revelation, and they held to this distinction between nature and supernature so rigidly that (apart from a reference to Hebrews 1:1 f.) the historical act of salvation of God in Jesus Christ was not discussed. By way of contrast, God's saving deed stands in the center of the Constitution on Revelation of Vatican II. The preface begins with the prologue of the First Epistle of John: " 'We announce to you the eternal life which was with the Father, and has appeared to us' " (I John 1:2 f.). The first chapter begins with these words:

> In His goodness and wisdom, God chose to reveal Himself and to make known to us the hidden purpose of His will (cf. Eph. 1:9) by which through Christ, the Word made flesh, man has access to the Father in the Holy Spirit and comes to share in the divine nature (cf. Eph. 2:18; II Pet. 1:4).

The same paragraph closes with this sentence: "By this revelation then, the deepest truth about God and the salvation of man is made clear to us in Christ, who is the Mediator and at the same time the fullness of all revelation" (Art. 2).[1]

This revelation of God in Christ is not placed unilaterally over against natural revelation, as was done in Vatican I, but is understood as the consummation of God's entire activity of revelation in history. This revelation is prepared through God's enduring witness in creation, through opening the supernatural salvation to our first parents and, after their fall, to God's people, through the promise of redemption, the call of Abraham, and the ministry of Moses and the prophets. All of this pointed to the goal of

---

[1] *Documents*, p. 112.

God's revelation in Christ (Arts. 3 and 4). The salvation-history approach of the Constitution on the Church is repeated here.

"This plan of revelation is realized by deeds and words having an inner unity: the deeds wrought by God in the history of salvation manifest and confirm the teaching and realities signified by the words, while the words proclaim the deeds and clarify the mystery contained in them" (Art. 2). While the statements of Vatican I placed in the foreground an understanding of revelation as a disclosure of things to be known, revelation is now presented much more emphatically as God's saving activity toward man.

Such salvation-history and christocentric shifts in accent lead to fruitful approaches to a new dialogue between the Reformation churches and the Roman church.

In common with all churches the Council teaches the finality of God's revelation in Jesus Christ. He has manifested himself

> through His words and deeds, His signs and wonders, but especially through His death and glorious resurrection from the dead and final sending of the Spirit of truth. Moreover, He confirmed with divine testimony what revelation proclaimed.
>
> The Christian dispensation, therefore, as the new and definitive covenant, will never pass away, and we now await no further new public revelation before the glorious manifestation of our Lord Jesus Christ (Art. 4).[2]

Scripture and Tradition

The completion of revelation in Jesus Christ insures the permanently fundamental significance of the proclamation of the apostles as the eyewitnesses commissioned by Christ. It also points up the necessity for the church constantly to preserve the apostolic message intact (Arts. 7 and 8). The preaching commission which Jesus gave the apostles

> was faithfully fulfilled by the apostles who, by their oral preaching, by example, and by ordinances, handed on what they had received from the lips of Christ, from living with Him, and from what He

[2] *Documents*, pp. 112 f.

> did, or what they had learned through the prompting of the Holy Spirit. The commission was fulfilled, too, by those apostles and apostolic men who under the inspiration of the same Holy Spirit committed the message of salvation to writing.
>
> But in order to keep the gospel forever whole and alive within the Church, the apostles left bishops as their successors, "handing over their own teaching role" to them (Art. 7).

The constitution failed to take note of the important fact that Paul addressed all believers as his successors (I Cor. 4:16; I Thess. 1:6). "This sacred tradition, therefore, and sacred Scripture of both the Old and the New Testament are like a mirror in which the pilgrim Church on earth looks at God . . ." (Art. 7).[3]

The statements concerning the Holy Scriptures and their inspiration, the fact that God as the author chose men to write the biblical books while making use of their powers and abilities—these are traditional. It is important for historical research that no blanket inerrancy is asserted for Holy Scripture; rather, "the books of Scripture must be acknowledged as teaching firmly, faithfully, and without error that truth which God wanted put into the sacred writings *for the sake of our salvation*" (Art. 11; italics added). Thus it is explicitly said that the Old Testament books "also contain some things which are incomplete and temporary" (Art. 15). The historical reliability of the four Gospels is emphatically affirmed. Yet here, too, it is conceded that the writers made a selection from the oral and written traditions available to them, that they synthesized some things and explicated others "in view of the situation of their churches" (Art. 19).[4] It is surprising that there is no reference to the historical motives behind the formation of the canon, motives so important for the understanding of tradition.

Alongside the New Testament writings preserved in the canon there is the apostolic preaching preserved in oral tradition. In the Constitution on Revelation the concept of this tradition is very

---

[3] *Documents*, pp. 115 f.

[4] *Documents*, pp. 119, 122, 124.

broad. Nothing is said about the concrete substance of oral tradition.

> [It] includes everything which contributes to the holiness of life, and the increase in faith of the People of God; and so the Church, in her teaching, life, and worship, perpetuates and hands on to all generations all that she herself is, all that she believes.
>
> The words of the holy Fathers witness to the living presence of this tradition, whose wealth is poured into the practice and life of the believing and praying Church (Art. 8).[5]

There is also no mention of criteria that might assist in establishing the apostolic tradition in the midst of other existing expressions of the church's life, as, for example, the age and spread of certain doctrines or regulations. The constitution does not help us to take hold of the specific content of oral revelation. But since the "practice and life of the church" and its "doctrine, life, and worship" are perceptible, it might be inferred that tradition, which "bears" the life of the church and "flows into" this life, is to be identified with the life of the church. In any case, however the theological schools may give more definition to the content of oral tradition, all dogmas of the Roman church claim to be the valid definition of apostolic teaching. Special difficulties are here created by the dogma of the bodily assumption of Mary, since this is attested neither by the New Testament nor by the tradition of the first centuries. This dogma called into question the formerly held view of tradition as the uninterrupted historical transmission of apostolic teaching, and the attempt was made to base this dogma on the present faith-consciousness of the Roman church. The concept of tradition presented by the Constitution on Revelation is so broad that it embraces the faith-consciousness of later periods in the church even when the content of that consciousness can be demonstrated neither from the Scriptures nor from the tradition of the first centuries.

How does the constitution define the relationship between Scripture and tradition? When the third version of the text was

---

[5] *Documents*, p. 116.

presented, it was explicitly stated that left open was the debated question whether revelation is transmitted only in part by Holy Scripture and in part by oral tradition, or whether it is transmitted as a whole both by the Holy Scriptures and by oral tradition. If the former is true, then Holy Scripture is not enough for a full knowledge of revelation, but if the latter is true, then tradition may be viewed as the history of the biblical interpretation. This understanding approaches that of the Reformation churches. To be sure, here, too, the Tridentine demand is maintained, namely, that "both sacred tradition and sacred scripture are to be accepted and venerated with the same sense of devotion and reverence" (Art. 9).[6] Since oral tradition is presupposed as the correct interpretation of Scripture, even this second view of the relationship does not permit Holy Scripture to confront tradition as the critical norm in the strict sense. The difficulty with the first answer ("in part—in part") lies in the fact that the anti-Gnostic church fathers and even the medieval scholastic theologians emphatically regarded themselves as biblical theologians. The difficulty with the second answer ("as a whole") lies in the fact that some dogmas of the Roman church cannot be documented on a historical reading of Holy Scripture. For that reason there are today Catholic biblical scholars whose historical integrity causes them to reject the biblical-exegetical burden of proof for the whole of dogmatic tradition. In spite of the intensity and productivity of their biblical-theological work, they prefer the first answer.

At the Pope's request the final form of the text included the following sentence: "Consequently, it is not from sacred Scripture alone that the Church draws her certainty about everything which has been revealed" (Art. 9).[7] Accordingly, the conservative view ("in part—in part") seems to have won out in the end. However, this sentence is meaningful even when tradition is understood as the normative interpretation of Scripture which is necessary for the understanding of Scripture. Nevertheless, this sentence runs

[6] *Documents*, p. 117.
[7] *Documents*, p. 117.

counter to the Scripture principle of the Reformation. An effort could be made to deny this by pointing out that the Evangelical faith also does not live by Scripture alone but by the proclaimed gospel. Yet the constitution does not accord the living, proclaimed gospel the primary significance it had, for example, with Paul.

Otherwise it is noteworthy that, in contrast to the formulations of Trent, the Constitution on Revelation in many statements inverts the Tridentine order of Scripture-tradition and mentions tradition first (Arts. 7-10). Beyond this, the constitution employs "tradition" as the principal term under which the oral and written transmissions are subsumed (Art. 8). To this extent the idea of tradition has become more important as compared with the Tridentine expressions.

The Interpretation of Holy Scripture

Whether the one or the other view of the relationship between Scripture and tradition is taught, the principles governing the interpretation of Scripture are in any case highly significant.

The constitution emphatically demands that the interpreter carefully investigate "what meaning the sacred writers really intended." "The interpreter must investigate what meaning the sacred writer intended to express and actually expressed in particular circumstances as he used contemporary literary forms in accordance with the situation of his own time and culture" (Art. 12). The interpreter must distinguish the different "literary forms" which the biblical authors employed (Art. 12). In addition, he must distinguish between the oral and written traditions which were available to the authors and the way they reworked them (Art. 19).[8] In this way the methods involving the history of forms and traditions are approved. This concern of exegesis with the historical sense of the text is of the greatest significance. In the results of this historical endeavor far-reaching agreement has come to light in a way that cuts diametrically across denominational lines.

---

[8] *Documents*, pp. 120, 124.

To uncover the true meaning of the biblical text, "serious attention must be given to the content and unity of the whole of Scripture" (Art. 12). This demand, too, must be met, since the same God has revealed himself in historical sequence, and since his definitive revelation in Jesus Christ was proclaimed in its essence by a multitude of human witnesses. To be sure, laying hold of the unity of Holy Scripture is already a systematic task and is possible in more than one way. At this point the constitution emphasizes that the "living tradition of the whole Church must be taken into account along with the harmony which exists between elements of the faith" (Art. 12).[9]

"According to these rules" exegetes must work "toward a better understanding and explanation of the meaning of sacred Scripture, so that through preparatory study the judgment of the Church may mature" (Art. 12).[10] This would seem to indicate a sense of Scripture that goes beyond what the authors intended to say, and to suggest that historical research is not adequate for grasping that sense. Such a going beyond the intended sense is often found in New Testament interpretations of Old Testament texts. This is justified there to the extent that the saving activity of God in the Old Covenant is fully disclosed only in Christ. Such a method is questionable, however, when the interpretation even goes beyond the historical sense of the New Testament witness concerning the definitive revelation in Jesus Christ. Although the church is hastening to meet the coming revelation of Christ, she does await the same Christ who as the risen one has already revealed himself in glory. Even though the "tradition which comes from the apostles develops in the Church with the help of the Holy Spirit" (Art. 8),[11] the activity of the Holy Spirit consists essentially in "bringing to remembrance" all that Christ has said (John 14:26). Hence the Spirit points back to the historically original witness and makes it contemporary. The constitution offers no criteria for grasping

---

[9] *Documents*, p. 120.
[10] *Documents*, pp. 120 f.
[11] *Documents*, p. 116.

the deeper sense of Holy Scripture. Thus, for example, the possibility remains of appealing to Genesis 3:15, Romans 5 and 6, I Corinthians 15:21-26, 54-57 (as the apostolic constitution *Munificentissimus Deus* [1950] of Pius XII actually does) to teach that Mary was assumed body and soul into heavenly glory, even though these texts do not speak of Mary.

The Teaching Office of the Church

In view of the undefined broadness of the concept of tradition and the undefined possibility of going beyond the historical sense of Holy Scripture, the necessity of safeguarding the unity of faith arises. The constitution assigns this responsibility to the church's teaching office. "The task of authentically interpreting the word of God, whether written or handed on, has been entrusted exclusively to the living teaching office of the Church, whose authority is exercised in the name of Jesus Christ" (Art. 10). To be sure, it is expressly added that the teaching office is not above the word of God (as transmitted through tradition and Holy Scripture) but serves it, "teaching only what has been handed on, listening to it devoutly, guarding it scrupulously, and explaining it faithfully by divine commission and with the help of the Holy Spirit; it draws from this one deposit of faith everything which it presents for belief as divinely revealed" (Art. 10).[12] Nevertheless, the teaching office in fact infallibly defines what counts as apostolic tradition and as the deeper sense of Scripture in the midst of the church's life, and the members of the Roman church are not permitted to call this into question on the basis of the historical sense of Scripture and the historically demonstrable tradition of the ancient church.

To the non-Catholic, therefore, the basic definition of relationships among Scripture, tradition, and teaching office appears in some respects to be more an apologetic presentation than a dogmatic one. This is so because the presentation defends the way the Roman church is constituted and upholds her possibilities for

[12] *Documents*, pp. 117 f.

development in the future. However, it does not clearly and distinctly subject this church and her teaching office to a norm that confronts them, that is, the norm of the historic apostolic tradition.

Instruction for the Use of the Holy Scriptures

The Constitution on Revelation closes with a chapter on "Sacred Scripture in the Life of the Church." Here, too, it is stated that the church has always regarded Scripture together with sacred tradition as the supreme rule of faith. In fact, however, the exhortations of this chapter assign to the Scriptures an importance that goes beyond the basic definition of the relationship between Scripture and tradition.

Not only are there urgent admonitions that there should be new translations of the original text ("in cooperation with the separated brethren as well"), diligent Bible study (the study of the fathers is not mentioned as something independent of Scripture but as serving the interpretation of Scripture), preaching and every form of instruction (especially in the liturgical homily), as well as regular and prayerful reading of the Scriptures, etc. (Arts. 22-25).[13] There are, furthermore, highly significant principles in support of these admonitions. Thus the Scripture is mentioned alongside the Lord's body as an object of the church's veneration. "From the table of both the word of God and of the body of Christ" the church "unceasingly receives and offers to the faithful the bread of life" (Art. 21).[14] Here the meaning of the ancient designation of the word as "audible sacrament" comes alive again. The word of Holy Scripture is a present and active word: The sacred writings "impart the word of God Himself without change, and make the voice of the Holy Spirit resound in the words of the prophets and apostles." Through the word of Scripture God acts here and now: "For in the sacred books, the Father who is in heaven meets His children with great love and speaks with them; and the force and power in the word of God is so great that it

[13] *Documents*, pp. 125-28.
[14] *Documents*, p. 125.

remains the support and energy of the Church, the strength of faith for her sons. . . ." Consequently, "like the Christian religion itself, all the preaching of the Church must be nourished and ruled by sacred Scripture" (Art. 21).[15] These impressive statements about the power of the divine word go beyond the weak statements of Trent, where the gospel had been given a mere preparatory role in the reception of justification. These statements do fall short of Paul's teaching since they are not thinking primarily of the living voice of the proclaimed word of God but rather of the written word. Here, too, a difference over against Reformation theology remains.

The recognition, far surpassing oral tradition, which this chapter actually gives the Holy Scriptures is extremely important. If these exhortations are followed the word of Scripture will in fact be able to exert itself in the Roman church as a norm and power to a far greater degree than the basic definition in chapter ii concerning the relationship between tradition and Scripture leads us to expect.

Looking back from these statements in the Dogmatic Constitution on Revelation over what happened in the Council as a whole, we may note a far-reaching correspondence between both.

In line with the dogmatic definition of the relationship between Scripture and tradition is the fact that among the theologians of the Council the dogmaticians, canonists, and liturgists were by far in the majority, while experts in the biblical sciences were consulted surprisingly little. It is further in line with this definition of relationships that the statements of Scripture could be unfolded only in the space not taken up by dogma, while Scripture was elsewhere utilized only to support and clarify dogmatically defined statements. But the latter were not subjected to the critical norm of Holy Scripture and amended on the basis of new insights gained through historical exegesis. The special position of the

---

[15] *Ibid.*

church's teaching office made its impact not only in the papal interference in the proceedings of the Council, as mentioned earlier, but also in the fact that the notes added to the *schemata* to furnish documentation quite often contained more citations from the encyclicals of recent popes than Scripture proof. Even some of the Council Fathers criticized this state of affairs. This weakening of biblical authority in favor of the teaching office may also account for the fact that in the Pastoral Constitution on the Church in the Modern World the New Testament understanding of the world and the expectation of judgment were noticeably weakened in the process of making adjustments to the world of today as demanded by the papal program of *aggiornamento.*

However, the overbalancing aspect of the statements in chapter vi of the Dogmatic Constitution on Divine Revelation, that is, the statements concerning Holy Scripture in the life of the church, also has its counterpart in the events of the Council. There was an increasing variety of lections in the conciliar masses, there was the growing importance given to biblical proof over against a mere appeal to tradition as the Council Fathers voiced their opinions, and, beyond this, the increasing preference for biblical concepts over neo-scholastic ones. In addition, corresponding to the directives given in the Constitution on Revelation, there were emphatic exhortations to Bible study, biblical instruction, and preaching in numerous other resolutions of the Council, for example, in the Decree on Priestly Formation.

The Ecumenical Significance

The Dogmatic Constitution on Revelation has been evaluated by the other churches in a generally restrained manner. They recognized its considerable significance for intra-Catholic discussion and welcomed the possibilities which this document guaranteed Catholic theologians. Its significance was seen less in its bringing about clarifications going beyond the traditional teaching than in its resisting the attacks of the conservative forces on the new biblical scholarship and on a new discussion of the problems involved with Scripture and tradition. On the other hand, there was generally a low estimate of the document's significance for the ecumenical dialogue.

It must not be overlooked, however, that the understanding of revelation in this constitution is already of considerable ecumenical significance. If one continues along the line of thought about revelation as God's saving activity in the word, one is bound to discover new aspects of the disputed understanding of dogmas as "revealed truths" and that a more careful distinction between revealed truth and its attestation in the church is needed. There is also a positive ecumenical significance in the peculiar vagueness in the concept of tradition and in the definition of the relationship between Scripture and tradition. Not only in the Roman church, but also in the churches of the Reformation, the problem of tradition has been set in motion again. Both the tradition-historical study of the Old and New Testaments and the discussion of the hermeneutical questions involved in exegesis, together with studies in the history of exegesis, have raised points of view which the older controversy among the churches had not yet recognized in their significance in this way. Thus the vagueness of the constitution's statements allows room for a new ecumenical conversation on these questions which are so much disputed among the churches. Especially welcome, however, are the impressive directives for the use of Holy Scripture. For the Bible—aside from certain not very important differences in the limits of the biblical canon—is the basis common to all churches for their dialogue. There is hope that, as these directives are followed, the Holy Scriptures will *in fact* count for considerably more in the general consciousness of Catholic theologians and laymen than the theoretical definition of the relationship between Scripture and tradition leads us to expect. There is hope, furthermore, that on this basis many of the traditional doctrinal differences among the churches may be discussed and clarified in a new way. None of these possibilities must in any way be underestimated.

SCRIPTURE, TRADITION, TEACHING OFFICE

What ultimately decides the issue in every ecumenical dialogue is, of course, a common norm acknowledged by the participating churches as the court of judgment to which all will submit. However, even though all churches have the Holy Scriptures in common, the Dogmatic Constitution on Revelation presents them so enveloped by tradition—and not just the tradition of the ancient church but also the special tradition and even the present life of the Roman church—as well as by the church's teaching office, that the authority of the Scriptures is sharply reduced. The authentically transmitted historical witness of the apostles and the primitive church in the Holy Scriptures is not clearly given its due in its superior normative and hence also critical role over against the present Roman church and the pope. As long as this is not done, the agreed and jointly acknowledged basis for dialogue between the Roman church and others will be quite narrow, even though all have the Bible in common.

10

Post-Conciliar Possibilities for the Roman Church

Not all questions with which the Council dealt could be treated in the preceding chapters. We had to confine ourselves to those answers of the Council which are especially significant for the rest of Christendom. Now an attempt will be made to understand the resolutions of the Council as a whole.

Opening Up and Introspection

No matter how one arranges the sixteen resolutions of the Council, it will become clear in any case that the Council brought about a noteworthy opening up as well as an introspection of the Roman church.

(a) First of all, we must emphasize the Roman church's opening up toward the outside, beyond its own boundaries. The Council has in many ways corrected the Roman church's past attitude toward non-Roman churches, toward Jews, and toward other non-Christian religions, as well as toward the problems of man's social life. These corrections were not made in the Council's resolutions in explicit criticism of former behavior; they do, in fact, go far beyond that behavior. In all areas of the surrounding world, which we distinguished by the pattern of concentric circles, the Council strove in a positive way to become aware of what the members of the Roman church have in common with other people in their various Christian, non-Christian-religious, and politico-social areas of life.

At the same time, in the Dogmatic Constitution on Revelation and especially also in the Dogmatic Constitution on the Church, the Council brought about an introspection which in many respects constitutes a narrowing. Before this, the Roman church had no comprehensive conciliar doctrine of the church, and various possibilities for the understanding of the church were open. Now, however, the possibilities have been narrowed down. This is true particularly in the doctrine of the hierarchy, which has now been spelled out in detail. The systematic rigor of this presentation has, if anything, increased the gap between the Roman church and the churches of the Reformation. A further narrowing is contained in a supplement to Mariology which acknowledges Mary as Mediatrix.

(b) The Council's openness was directed not only toward the outside but also toward the inside, if we may put it that way; that is, toward the realities which had been crowded out or isolated in the Roman church. Following a long era of increasing centralizing uniformity in the liturgical rites and in the provisions of canon law, the Council consciously turned to remnants of ancient non-Roman liturgies which had been preserved in the West within the Roman church in a few places, and especially gave due recognition to the variety of liturgies of the Eastern churches united with Rome, churches which can look back on a long and hard fight against the encroachments of uniformity. The explanations of the Constitution on the Church concerning particular churches and their separate traditions also demonstrate the tendency to relax the uniformity of the Roman church and move in the direction of variety within this church. The prominence given the patriarchs of the Uniate churches in the Council's seating arrangements, by assigning them to choice seats opposite the cardinals and in front of the bishops' gallery, points in the same direction.

Yet this introspection, too, must not be seen in isolation from the simultaneous introspection and delimitation which the Council accomplished dogmatically and canonically. Along with all established dogmas, the unlimited power of the pope over the church has been explicitly confirmed, and the actualization of the bishops' exercise of their authority to rule and teach is made to depend entirely on the pope. Thus the limits of possible variety are clearly set.

(c) Beyond this, there is also an opening up toward the past, namely, a new concern for the historical foundations of the church, as witnessed by the Bible and the ancient church. Many important details demonstrate this, such as, for instance, the use of the manifold New Testament concepts and images of the church, the salvation-history understanding of the church as the people of God, the emphasis on the universal priesthood of all believers (Constitution on the Church), the understanding of revelation (Constitution on Revelation), and the incorporation of statements from the New and Old Testaments concerning man's divine image (Pastoral Constitution). And even though arguments from the ancient church succeeded only in part, they did play a role in the struggle to define the relationship between Scripture and tradition and between the pope and the college of bishops. It is clear, in any case, that a stronger preference for biblical terms created a greater freedom of possibilities for theological formulation.

Yet this opening, too, could extend only to areas left open by dogmas which could not be touched and by components of tradition which could not be given up. Even the papal encyclicals of the last century have narrowed this opening up in a number of conciliar texts.

Aggiornamento

The threefold opening and introspection must be summed up in the concept of *aggiornamento*. It means more than a mere adjustment to a changed environment. It means at the same time a renewal in seeking to determine what God commands today. In this sense, *aggiornamento* means not only an adaptation but a starting out. To be sure, this renewal cannot be termed "reformation" in the sense of the Reformation upheaval of the church in the sixteenth century. For, in contrast to that reformation, the Roman church at Vatican II did not subject itself to a comprehensive critique by means of the historical apostolic message, as authentically transmitted in the Holy Scriptures. On the contrary, the Roman church has essentially excepted its dogmatic, canonical, and other traditions from such a critique. Thus, the plea of Pope Paul VI, which was connected with the renewal and which asked the separated brethren for forgiveness, would be misunderstood if construed as a repeal of the condemnations of the teachings of non-Roman churches through which the abyss between the Roman church and other churches had been deepened. A change in the dogmas of the Roman church was never contemplated throughout the Council. The Reformation principle, *ecclesia semper reformanda*, taken over by the Council, has a different meaning there than in the Reformation churches. These follow the principle of constantly resubmitting even their confessional writings together with their dogmatic formulations to the judgment of Holy Scripture.

Nevertheless, to speak only of individual reforms achieved by the Council would be to underestimate the Council. There came into being a movement of renewal which reaches further than the individual resolutions—a movement which has taken hold of many hearts in the Roman church so that they yearn to serve God and their fellow men with greater faithfulness, devotion, openness, and love.

The Dialectics of the Council Resolutions

When a church desires to cling decidedly to her traditions and at the same time to attack new problems and tasks, there will inevitably be unresolved aspects and tensions in her pronouncements—tensions not only in the terminology but also in content. This is also true regarding some expressions in the resolutions of Vatican II.

Among such tensions between the new and the old—where the new is often what is old in church history, and the old is often what goes back only to the Counter-Reformation—the following are noteworthy:

On the one hand, a strong new emphasis on Holy Scripture—on the other hand, the classification of Scripture in the tradition and the subordination of Scripture interpretation to the papal teaching office;

on the one hand, a strong basic emphasis on the church's unity as a unity in diversity—on the other hand, a clinging to the uniformity of dogmatic formulas and the fundamental hierarchical structure;

on the one hand, a strong emphasis on the structure of fellowship and a new understanding of the church's unity as a fellowship of particular churches—on the other hand, a renewed dogmatic and canonical guarantee of papal primacy in the sense of Vatican I;

on the one hand, the positive statements in the Decree on Ecumenism concerning the non-Roman churches and communities—on the other hand, the bare recognition in the Constitution on the Church of "elements of sanctification and truth" beyond the boundaries of the Roman church;

on the one hand, an understanding of church union as reciprocal reconciliation—on the other hand, elements of the concept of return and submission;

on the one hand, recognition of efficacious grace far beyond the number of the baptized—on the other hand, clinging to the axiom "outside the church there is no salvation";

on the one hand, a call for religious liberty and its governmental guarantee—on the other hand, limitation of this freedom by means of the general moral law as interpreted by the Roman church, and by means of consideration for the common welfare and for those nations in which a specific religion predominates;

on the one hand, the emphatic acknowledgment of the autonomy of the sciences and of culture, etc.—on the other hand, the claim of the church's teaching office to a theocratic responsibility for these areas;

on the one hand, a clear distinction between the spheres of the church and the state—on the other hand, continued resort to the political possibilities at the pope's disposal as sovereign of Vatican City.

Further comparisons could be made.

If we remember the various forms of the texts, the diverging opinions expressed by the Fathers in the Council, and the reasons their proposed amendments were in part accepted and in part rejected by the respective commissions, it becomes clear that such tensions within the resolutions of the Council are largely involved with compromises which were supposed to make it possible for the conservative minority to accept the proposals. At the same time one gets the impression that these tensions have their source not only in such tactical necessities and that they were by no means regarded only as a burden. On the contrary, they were affirmed as an appropriate expression of the catholicity of the Roman church. By combining various possibilities by means of a both-and, the door was left open for further concerted development on the part of the various forces that wrestled with each other in the Council. While the "conservatives" believe they have salvaged for the future many an item about which they had been anxious, many of the "progressives" view such disagreements and tensions as the dialectic of an historical progress which the Council has made possible. Indeed, many see precisely these unresolved aspects as giving expression to the Council's dynamics which point to the future. Hence these tensions must be evaluated not only as a weakness inhering in the resolutions of the Council, but also as symptoms of the awakening of the Roman church. Everything will, of course, depend on how these unresolved aspects are overcome in future advances.

Possibilities for Post-Conciliar Activity

On the basis of such unsettled situations it is to be expected that different interpretations of some texts will be offered to the extent that specific authoritative interpretations are not supplied. Not everyone will observe and hold fast to the dialectic of the statements. Some will understand the one or the other interpretation as expressing what the Council actually meant to say and will try to gain acceptance for that view. Such differences in interpretation had manifested themselves in the opinions, conversations, and essays during the Council. The partner in the ecumenical dialogue will have to look with great care at the whole of the Council's statements and ponder the full breadth of variation possible in their interpretation. Otherwise the ecumenical dialogue will lose the ground of reality under its feet.

This breadth of possible interpretations in some points cannot remain without effect on theological thought. Already at the Council, Roman Catholic theology was far from being a monolithic block. There were supporters of neo-scholastic theology, supporters of an ontology loosened up by existential philosophy and salvation history, and also theologians whose thought was so strongly controlled by biblical theology that they could in many ways be called evangelical. It was remarkable that these diverging theological trends were not represented by specific religious orders (in contrast to earlier councils, the theological fronts were generally not drawn between the orders) but ran diagonally through the orders. This variety in Catholic theology will continue to grow after the Council. Already during the Council it was not easy to recognize in the expressions of many bishops and theologians the formerly well-known Catholic theology. For example, one could encounter specific problems and approaches of neo-Protestantism which have now arisen within Catholicism as a result of the attempt to adjust to modern thought. Karl Barth's thesis concerning the kinship between Catholicism and neo-Protestantism was often corroborated. We shall have to expect further surprises in the future, and it will become more difficult than before to state what is characteristic of Catholic theology.

Because the resolutions of the Council contain many tensions, the post-conciliar activity of the Roman church has not been fixed in every respect. The resolutions leave elbowroom in which quite different methods of action are possible, depending upon which side of the resolutions is accented. Thus the Constitution on the Church makes it possible for the bishops' co-responsibility in governing the whole church to be activated to a high degree; but the traditional centralized form of government can also be maintained. The Council's statements on the laity can make it possible for them to participate spontaneously in the church's life on the various levels of the parish, the diocese, and the church as a whole; but such lay activity can also be hindered and kept from being responsibly exercised by insistence on the laity's obligation to obey the clergy. From the pastoral constitution's emphasis on the autonomy of secular areas it follows that the church's proclamation should confine itself to the principles of political and social ethics; but the same constitution could also be appealed to in support of a political Catholicism. The Decrees on Ecumenism and on Religious Freedom likewise permit a variety of practical application.

Which forces will prevail in the future? No one will be able at this point to make a sure prognosis. This is impossible because the "conservatives" and the "progressives" do not constitute solid blocs, and because even at the Council it became evident that, depending on the topic, many a person considered to be a conservative could vote progressively and vice versa.

There is much in favor of an initial period of deceleration. The bishops are now faced with the difficult task of implementing in their dioceses the reforms decided upon. It is well known what difficulties among the people the liturgical reforms encountered in some places—for example, in France. The new ecumenical program will appear even stranger to some areas of the church, as will the recognition of religious freedom. Back in their home dioceses the bishops are no longer borne up directly by the *élan* of the elite of the Roman church assembled in Rome, and the different situations prevailing at the Council and in the home diocese will have their impact for many a bishop. At the same time, greater possibilities for influence will present themselves to the conservative forces in the Roman Curia after the adjournment of the Council, and the possibility must be reckoned with that these forces, in the process of administration, will attempt to apply the brakes to, or even to reverse, some of the things set in motion by the Council.

It should indeed be out of the question that the dynamic that erupted in the Council can be permanently held in check, especially since the theological youth has largely been captured by it. Even a temporary standstill can be nothing more than a transition. Doors have in fact been opened which cannot be closed again. A return to the state of affairs before the Council is inconceivable.

11

Pope and Curia

One may have expectations about the possibilities sketched in the resolutions of the Council and wonder which of them will be realized and which of the forces manifested in the Council will establish themselves in the future. Yet one must not forget that in the Roman church, less than in any other, the decisions will not result from a free interplay of the forces at work in the church but rather will ultimately be made by the pope.

The Post-Conciliar Position of the Pope

From the discussions during the first period of sessions one could occasionally get the impression that the concentration of power to govern the whole church and the concentration of the infallible teaching office in the pope, as declared by Vatican I, might be weakened, and that the concern of the minority, then suppressed, might still be recognized. That such trends were present at the Council, or at least were feared, may be inferred from the startlingly emphatic way in which Pope Paul VI presented himself to the world, for example, in the addresses during his audiences, as the Vicar of Christ and the successor of Peter. This trend may further be inferred from the unusual bulk of references in the Constitution on the Church to the definition of the primacy offered by Vatican I. Has Vatican II amended the decisions of Vatican I? Has the pope's position been weakened?

A look at the resolutions of the Council, especially chapter iii of the Constitution on the Church (see above, pp. 73 ff.), makes it unambiguously clear that the Council did indeed supplement but did not amend the definition of primacy as given by Vatican I.

Nor did the pronouncements concerning the college of bishops weaken the pope's position. Many even assume that his position has been further enhanced, since now the *freedom* of the exercise of papal power is taught. "For in virtue of his office, that is, as Vicar of Christ and pastor of the whole Church, the Roman Pontiff has full, supreme, and universal power over the Church. And he can always exercise this power freely" (Art. 22).[1] In substance, however, this statement was already contained in the dogmatic constitution of Vatican I.

Many hope that, as a result of the dogmatic statements concerning the college of bishops and the prescriptions concerning the synod of bishops, the weight will shift in practice, and that the former centralized government of the church will be supplanted by a government which the pope exercises in conjunction with the bishops. There is good reason for this hope. Yet the statements of the Constitution on the Church have guaranteed in a dogmatically and canonically unambiguous way that it rests exclusively with the free decision of the pope whether and to what extent he will allow the bishops to participate in the exercise of the universal power to rule the church. He can rule the church alone as well as provide room for a synodal government of the church. In the succession of pontificates the one or the other form of government may predominate at different times.

Many also expect that the doctrine of the Roman church will in the future be more strongly determined by the Holy Scriptures. There is in fact some ground for the hope that the importance of the historical meaning of Scripture will increase in the Roman church. However, apart from the fact that it is up to the pope's free decision whether he wants to discharge his infallible teaching office alone or together with the bishops, it is also up to him whether he wants to base the decisions of his teaching office on biblical statements and their historical meaning, on the historically verifiable tradition of the ancient church, or on the present faith-

[1] *Documents*, p. 43.

consciousness of the Roman church. He has the authority to give obligatory definition also to such contents of this consciousness as cannot be demonstrated by means of historical research into what the authors of the biblical writings intended to say, nor by means of the tradition of the ancient church. The pope can do this by insisting that his definitions are implicitly contained in the Bible and are a part of the oral apostolic tradition. Pius XII made use of this authority in proclaiming the dogmatic definition of Mary's bodily assumption into heaven. Without doubt, the pope retains this authority after the Council also.

In the preceding chapters repeated use was made of the picture of the three concentric circles which surround the Roman church as the center, namely, non-Roman Christendom, non-Christian religions, and finally all mankind. To this picture we must now add the precise detail that the pope is the center of these three circles insofar as he is the center of the Roman church. He sees himself surrounded by four circles. The innermost one was manifested at the Council. Pope Paul addressed himself to the second circle when he met with the patriarch of Constantinople and the leaders of other churches; to the third during his experiences in Bombay; and to the fourth in his address to the United Nations in New York. In line with this conception, Paul VI addressed the United Nations not only in his own name and the name "of the great Catholic family, but also in the name of the Christians who share the feelings we express here."

In view of all of this it is clear that the pope is of decisive significance for the interpretation and execution of the Council's resolutions. To be sure, every pope will feel obligated to carry out these decisions; yet in the end it is up to him to determine which of the possibilities for doctrine and action contained in the tensions and unresolved aspects of the resolutions are to be realized, and which of the forces now alive in the Roman church will be permitted to exert themselves. In what direction will Pope Paul VI determine the interpretation and execution of the Council's resolutions?

By interfering in the procedure of the Council during the third period, the Pope supported the conservative forces, and through the changes he brought about in the text of the Decree on Ecumenism, this document's openness toward the churches of the Reformation has been toned down. His proposals for changes in the Constitution on Revelation during the fourth period likewise represented a reduction in the conservative sense. In his encyclical *Mysterium Fidei*, which appeared just before the fourth period of sessions, the Pope, in contrast to the Constitution on Liturgy, again laid greater stress on low masses and votive masses without Communion as well as the adoration of the elevated sacrament. Furthermore, he rejected the attempt of Dutch theologians to reinterpret the doctrine of transubstantiation, which rests on outmoded philosophical presuppositions, and their attempt to give expression to the presence of Christ in the Lord's Supper in more contemporary thought forms (transfinalization). This encyclical elicited deep consternation in the circles of the Council Fathers and theologians since the distinction between the unchangeable substance and the changeable form of the church's doctrine had been part of the program of John XXIII for the Council and had opened up new possibilities for conversation with other churches. Also the apostolic constitution, *Mirificus Eventus*, which on December 7, 1965, announced a council jubilee, remained altogether conservative in its directives regarding indulgences. Furthermore, in this document, as in no document of the Council, non-Catholic Christians are again called heretics and schismatics and mentioned in the same breath with apostates, atheists, and freemasons. These incidents would seem to suggest that after the Council the Pope will quell the "progressive" forces. It is difficult to say, however, to what extent these statements gave expression to the Pope's own theological conviction or to the voice of his theological advisers and of the Holy Office, or whether they reflected tactical points of view for the purpose of reconciling opposing views.

There was nothing conservative, on the contrary, about the intensity with which Pope Paul VI personally addressed himself to the non-Roman churches. His meeting with the Ecumenical Patriarch in Jerusalem, his reception of the same patriarch's delegation at the last session of the Council and the paper he presented to them, in which he expressed regret for the excommunication of Cerularius in 1054 and its consequences and assured them of his loving endeavor to remove the remaining hindrances to reunion, as well as his contacts with other church leaders, such as his recent meeting with the Archbishop of Canterbury—all these are a complete novelty in the history of the Roman church. Paul was also no less friendly in his approach to the observers from non-Roman churches. Thus at his initiative a joint service of bishops and observers, which was criticized by conservatives, was conducted at the end of the Council in the Pope's presence. At this service Catholic and non-Catholic theologians alternated in reading Scripture lessons and speaking prayers. One could say that all this need not contradict the Pope's conservative theological convictions, inasmuch as in these encounters the Pope was concerned about establishing initial contact, not about clarifying the dogmatic differences existing between the churches, and that the primatial position of the pope remained completely safeguarded according to the protocol. But Paul VI met the "separated brethren" with a warmth and cordiality which transcended conventional limits and expressed his yearning for fellowship with them in a manner permitting one to look for further spontaneous steps of a kind foreign to conservative thinking. This fact is also supported by the first address to the Council, which Paul VI delivered at the beginning of the second period and in which he impressively supported and deepened the progressive trends of the Council.

Remembering all of this must make one cautious about prognoses, especially since the present pope feels himself obligated to his so different predecessors, John XXIII and Pius XII, and at the same time looks to them as his models. It is, of course, completely impossible to predict what conclusions later popes will draw from the resolutions of Vatican II.

Objections from Non-Roman Churches

The dogmatic definition of Vatican I concerning the papal primacy and the infallibility of his teaching office was rejected, as is well known, by all non-Roman churches, including the Orthodox, even though the latter acknowledge the superior rank of the bishop of Rome as a matter of principle. This rejection did not rest on the remembrance of many unworthy representatives on the papal throne and of the times when popes abused worldly power to fight against these churches; their objection was based on principle. The plenipotentiary power and infallibility of the pope can be supported neither by New Testament references to Peter nor by the ancient position of the bishop of Rome in the fellowship of the patriarchs. Every church order, it must be remembered, is subject to historical changes. In this view of primacy, however, people everywhere saw a violation of the basic spiritual structure of fellowship which belongs to the essence of the church —quite apart from other important dogmatic differences.

Vatican II has not removed these objections to the papal primacy. Even though there is cause for hope that in practice the structure of fellowship will increase in importance, the pope's position of power remains dogmatically and canonically unchanged.

In addition to the historical and dogmatic objections, which cannot be discussed further at this place, there are also some considerable practical misgivings. Without a doubt the plenary power given to the pope is incomparably greater than any one man can exercise. Though in this century a number of unusually outstanding personalities succeeded each other on the papal throne, not one of them was equally outstanding as theological teacher and as pastor, as liturgist and as canonist and as diplomat, to mention just a few areas in which the pope must constantly make normative decisions. It cannot be otherwise. According to the New Testament the various spiritual gifts of teaching, prophecy, administration, etc., are distributed among different members of the body of Christ, and only in the community of their reciprocal service does the spiritual fullness manifest itself. Already this variety of gifts leads to practical limits for the independent activity of every pope, whereas the authority granted to him, and hence also his responsibility, is universal. There are further reasons why he must rely on co-workers. In view of the worldwide size of the Roman church it is, naturally, completely impossible for him to be himself informed on all areas, problems, and personalities to the extent that on the basis of his own concrete analysis he can make the required decisions, even if it were only the appointment of bishops. He must constantly resort to the information, proposals, and outlines of his co-workers, including their elaboration of his encyclicals and speeches.

This raises the problem of the Curia. In its teaching on the hierarchy (pope, bishops, priests, deacons) the Constitution on the Church does not mention the Curia, for dogmatically it has no special existence. It is to be nothing more than the executive organ of the pope. In fact, however, the pope does not rule alone but with the Curia; indeed, in many decisions the Curia rules in the name of the pope. In practice, therefore, the Curia participates in the pope's plenary power and together with the pope stands over against the bishops and the entire Roman church.

The Reform of the Curia

During the Council there was frequent, at times extremely severe, criticism of the Curia, and this not only by bishops of Eastern churches united with Rome, whose tradition led them to find the curial centralization particularly strange and offensive. The criticism was made that the Curia was outmoded and still held captive by the courtly forms in vogue when the Curia came into being; that the Curia knew too little about the reality of the church in different parts of the world and ruled in a way that was bureaucratic, fussy, and out of touch with reality; that the Curia was staffed one-sidedly by Italians and that other areas of the church were insufficiently represented and their substantive concerns inadequately dealt with; and that the Curia treated bishops as "subjects," etc. There was demand for the creation of a council of bishops superior to the Curia, for a reduction of the Curia's responsibility in carrying out the decisions of the pope and the college of bishops, for a sharp decrease in the number of curial bishops and priests employed there, and for assigning many of the Curia's functions to laymen, etc. Cardinal Frings was especially severe in his criticism of the Holy Office. No one could be condemned by this body in matters of faith without first granting the accused and his bishop a hearing and an opportunity to explain and amend his utterances. Behind all this criticism was the bishops' desire for direct association with the pope in the government of their church and the entire church.

Paul VI did not turn a deaf ear to these criticisms. At a meeting of all the members of the Curia on September 21, 1963, he announced a thoroughgoing reform of the Curia. In his address he clothed his obvious criticism of this body, as inclined to autocracy and as being extremely sensitive, in words of praise and thanks for its work. The Pope began the reform itself cautiously and sparingly. He created the legal basis for a synod of bishops, in which, to be sure, only the leading cardinals of the Curia are to hold permanent membership, while the elected representatives of the territorial conferences of bishops will constantly change. He approved of a reorganization of the Congregation for the Propagation of the Faith (*de propaganda fide*) by adding bishops and counselors from the mission fields. He brought about a change in the name of the Holy Office which is now to be known as "Congregation for the Doctrine of Faith." It will still have the same functions, but henceforth it is not only to act as a court but is also to stimulate theological discussion in the church. Furthermore, in the future, every accused person is to have the right to defend himself. In addition, the Pope confirmed the Secretariat for Christian Unity as a permanent institution and established the Secretariats for Non-Christian Religions and for Non-Believers. Further reforms may be expected. Much will depend on whether these reforms will enable the bishops to work together with the pope directly, and whether they will permit the pope to gain a more realistic insight into the problems prevailing in various areas of the church.

There is no doubt that much can still be improved in fixing the limits of competence, in the personnel, and in the work-methods of the Curia. The question remains, however, whether some of the expectations of those who impetuously call for reform are not unrealistic. Even though far-reaching reforms should be carried out, the old centralization would be maintained and therefore the need for a large curial board would continue. For practical reasons the functions of this board cannot be reduced to the mere implementation of the decisions of the pope and the synod of bishops. Such a reduction would result only if the pope, following the precedent of the ancient church, would structure the Roman church into relatively autonomous patriarchates and confine himself to the exercise of his primacy of jurisdiction within the association of patriarchs as an honorary primacy with clearly defined legal limits. The pope could exercise such a primacy directly to a much higher degree. There are, however, no indications that this will be done.

12

The Significance of the Council for Other Churches

Vatican II is extremely significant for the Roman church. Beyond a doubt it signifies a considerable strengthening for this church. There is strengthening already in the fact that at the Council Roman Catholic bishops from all over the world came together for a living exchange of views. There is strengthening in that the deliberations led in large measure to the abandonment of a defensive stance and to a concern for the problems of the present. Above all, there is strengthening in the wide consensus with which the resolutions of the Council were finally promulgated. Thus, the men assembled in Rome had every reason to return with new optimism to their work at home.

The significance of this Council for the non-Roman churches is a different matter. Here the reactions in part diverge considerably. Naturally, this difference resulted from the different expectations with which men initially looked to the Council. Those who originally thought that, because of Vatican I, a genuine conciliar experience was impossible in the Roman church were agreeably surprised. Those who hoped, on the other hand, that the Council would remove major barriers to church union were disappointed in their expectations and were in danger of failing to see at the end of the Council what progress had been made. It will not be possible in what follows to discuss the full scale of the manifold evaluations of the Council. By analyzing only a few widespread critical replies, we intend to seek to clarify what the Council meant for non-Roman churches.

SIGNIFICANCE FOR OTHER CHURCHES

Unchanged Differences and New Approaches

What can the Council mean for other churches since the Council rescinded or expressly toned down no dogma and no dogmatic condemnation with which the Roman church once fenced herself off? This is true, for example, of the definition of papal infallibility. This is true also of the condemnation of the Reformation teachings concerning justification and the Lord's Supper. Not only by means of the solemn pledge given by all Council Fathers at the opening session, but also by means of the Council's observance of the four hundredth anniversary of Trent, the Council committed itself explicitly to the resolutions of the Council of Trent. This is true also of the Marian dogmas of Pius IX (Immaculate Conception of Mary) and of Pius XII (Bodily Assumption of Mary), through which the Roman church had widened the gap between herself and all other churches. The Orthodox churches, too, reject these dogmas, although in contrast to the Reformation churches they in their piety make similar assertions. They refuse, however, to elevate such pious opinions to dogmatic statements, the acceptance or rejection of which involves man's salvation and the boundaries of the church. The Council also expressly declined the irenic gesture of toning down the dogmatic obligations in force. Hence the dogmatic bases for the historic Counter-Reformation, as well as for Roman mission work among the Orthodox, have been maintained. In view of the central significance of the dogmas, some conclude that everything remains as it was and that the Council has no significance for non-Roman churches.

Yet the Council is not fairly judged if one looks only at the dogmatic differences that have in fact remained unchanged. A series of new approaches have become manifest, and these approaches can have an impact even upon the fundamental structures of the Roman church. It is a matter of shifts which become more evident in the practical directives than in the basic dogmatic explanations but which are not absent even in the dogmatic constitutions. These changes in accent, which were illustrated by means of numerous examples in the earlier chapters, have opened up new possibilities and justify certain hopes, and in any evaluation of the Council these must by all means be taken into account. In any case, these changes are so important that the traditional descriptions of the Roman church in texts on comparative symbolics are no longer adequate. It must be noted further that this Council consciously refrained from establishing new dogmas so as not to increase the differences among the separated churches. The rest of Christendom ought to interpret this fact in a positive way, all the more since there were definitely forces at the Council which pressed for new dogmatic definitions and condemnations and which could appeal to the history of councils for support of their positions.

To be sure, the new trends, accents, and approaches are nothing new for some non-Roman churches, to the extent that much of this new material has long been clear to them. Not only in the Reformation churches but also in the Eastern church, the Bible in the hands of the people and the sermon have always played a much larger role than in the Roman church, which at times had even forbidden the use of the Bible by the laity. The Eastern churches and the Reformation churches have always distributed the Lord's Supper under both kinds and celebrated the liturgy in the vernacular. Furthermore, the Orthodox and the Reformation churches have always preserved the fellowship structure of the ancient church to a much higher degree and have rejected a centralization that demanded uniformity. Also, the statements about the priesthood of all believers and the acknowledgment of religious freedom are nothing new for most of the other churches. Hence, many judge that the Council merely satisfied the need of the Roman church to catch up, but that it had nothing new to offer other churches. At the most, one should be surprised that the Roman church was so late in deciding for this new undertaking, that there was so much resistance to it, and that it is being approached so timidly.

Such an evaluation, however, does not do justice to the Council, and it would be a mistake to conclude for the stated reasons that these new conciliar approaches had no significance for other churches. We surely have every reason to be thankful that through the Reformation the Bible, the vernacular in worship, the cup in Communion, and other things were restored to us. Yet it cannot be a matter of indifference to us that through the introduction of the vernacular in the liturgy the biblical message also meets the members of the Roman church in a more intelligible and personal way and enables them to participate in worship in far richer measure. Should this not be for us a cause for joy and a new stimulus zealously to make our own what we have inherited from our fathers? Undoubtedly it will mean a change in relationships between the churches when the Bible and biblical proclamation will play an increasing role in the consciousness of the people in the Catholic church, and when one day the Roman Mass will appear to the layman at first glance as hardly distinguishable from the combined preaching and communion service in the Reformation churches, after the vernacular is introduced and further liturgical reforms already in preparation are carried out. It is, furthermore, of great significance for the communal life of the churches that this Council treated the same questions and in part offered the same answers given by other churches in the association of the World Council to questions of Christian responsibility in today's world, specifically to questions of the rapid social upheaval, atomic warfare, and racial differences. Is it not also cause for joy that in this way the scandal which a divided Christendom offers the world is diminished?

The Significance of Roman Ecumenism

Moreover, the Council, especially in its Decree on Ecumenism, led to a conscious approach to other churches, an approach which meets the pressure of these churches themselves. In this encounter, common elements between the ecumenism of Vatican II and the ecumenism of the World Council became apparent, and these elements are highly significant. On both sides the movement originated with elementary spiritual impulses which opened the eyes for the brethren and aroused yearning for unity. The origin of the ecumenical movement at the beginning of this century did not result from the external situation of the churches, and its progress in the last decades is not to be derived from the increasing secularization, from totalitarian atheistic systems, and from the persecution of Christians. There was here, rather, a spiritual awakening in which the separated churches became sure of their oneness in Christ and felt the separation as a sin and disgrace. Thus the ecumenical movement is a penitential movement which grips hearts in a way that shatters and blesses, destroys and builds up. I have no doubt that elementary spiritual impulses also led Pope John XXIII to assign the theme of ecumenism to the Second Vatican Council, and that identical impulses also made themselves felt in the discussions during the Council.

One can, of course, raise an objection: What do these common elements mean in view of the differences existing between the ecumenism of Vatican II and the ecumenism of the World Council of Churches? Surely the goal of ecumenism is not the same on both sides. This goal is indeed the visible unity of the churches now separated, and, to be sure, it is unity of faith, fellowship in the reception of the Holy Supper, and fellowship in the church's offices. Yet in this consensus there is the significant difference that the World Council explicitly leaves the form of this desired unity open, while the ecumenism of the Roman church seeks to achieve union in the form already existing in the Roman church, that is to say, through acknowledgment of the Roman Catholic dogmas and the primacy of the pope. To a much larger degree the World Council leaves room for the structure of fellowship as it is in the New Testament and the ancient church and for the churches' growing together in mutual turning to each other. These differences in the understanding of the goal can hardly fail to affect the way ecumenical methods are handled. The ecumenism of the Council is, then, a specifically Roman ecumenism. It is a synthesis between the narrow sense of the ecumenical, as when the Roman church labels all her own general synods as ecumenical councils because she claims to be in herself the one, holy, catholic church, and the current understanding of the ecumenical, as concern for bringing the separated churches together and uniting them. In view of this state of affairs it should come as no surprise that some churches—for example, the Greek Orthodox Church—have not yet lost their fear that Roman ecumenism in the end could only seek submission, not fellowship. This distrust was also aroused by the fact that the Decree on Ecumenism did not deal with the World Council of Churches and that the interest of the Roman church is directed largely to bilateral negotiations with the individual non-Roman churches.

The specifically Roman limitations of the Decree on Ecumenism are indeed obvious. It must be borne in mind, however, that every church can be open toward other churches only on the presupposition that the one, holy, catholic, apostolic church is a reality in that church. The Toronto Declaration of the World Council likewise assures each member church the freedom to retain her self-understanding and her evaluation of other member churches. Within the World Council there are, therefore, different kinds of ecumenism converging on each other. True, most churches do not present their identity with the one holy church in the same exclusive sense as the Roman church does. Yet, at the beginning, we should not compare the presuppositions of the various churches with each other, but rather seek to determine the degree of intensity with which a church proceeds on the basis of her own presuppositions to be open to other churches. From this point of view, however, we can recognize a thoroughly imposing ecumenical breakthrough in the Roman church within the short space of the last four years—a breakthrough that is all the more imposing since it came about in spite of the well-known dogmatic and canonical fixities of this church. Furthermore, it must not be forgotten that the churches of the World Council also do not all take joint counsel and make joint decisions with each other, but that within this association a variety of bilateral negotiations between members takes place.

The Practical Consequences

The church members on both sides are less interested in the concept of ecumenism than in its practical effects. They judge the value of the Decree on Ecumenism and the significance of the Council in general on the basis of the removal of factors that impede living together as Christians. There are still areas of the Roman church (even in Germany) where the baptisms of other churches, though administered in the name of the Triune God, are not acknowledged, even though the Decree on Ecumenism has its basis in the common baptism. Mixed marriages performed by Evangelical pastors are still declared invalid by the Roman church, and the Catholic marriage partners are excluded from the sacrament even though, according to the Decree on Ecumenism, the Evangelical Christian has become a member of the body of Christ through baptism. There are still mission fields of Evangelical churches, indeed, even national Evangelical churches, as in Indonesia (NIAS), where the Roman church conducts counter missions at great expense in personnel and means, even though the Decrees on Ecumenism and on the Church's Missionary Activity summon other Christians to a common witness to the faith. In spite of the Declaration on Religious Freedom, the legal situation of the Evangelical church in Spain has not yet been changed. It is true that in individual cases the laws are no longer applied with their former severity, and yet the Evangelicals are still not permitted to call their houses of worship churches or to publish the time of services. Even in the areas of the Orthodox churches complaints continue, in spite of the special approach of the Council to these churches and the mitigation arranged in the treatment of Roman-Orthodox mixed marriages performed in the Orthodox church.

It would, however, be premature on the basis of such facts to deny the Council and its ecumenism a positive significance for other churches even at this time. In its resolutions the Council was concerned exclusively with elaborating and activating the basic principles which are in the future to determine the concrete activity of the Roman church. Thus, the Secretariat on Unity is currently occupied with developing an "ecumenical directory" which will contain the provisions for implementing the Decree on Ecumenism; for example, provisions for recognizing baptisms performed outside the Roman church and provisions for dealing with the possibility of conducting joint worship services between Catholic and non-Catholic Christians. Furthermore, in spite of the disappointing and inadequate Instruction of March 18, 1966, definitive regulation of the question of mixed marriages is still to come. A change in the circumstances in Spain depends not only on the Spanish episcopate and the Curia but also on the Spanish government. We must therefore alertly and patiently await the practical consequences which the Roman church will draw from the fundamental resolutions adopted in the Council. Much will, of course, depend on these consequences. If they are not drawn, the Decree on Ecumenism will for many Catholics and non-Catholics become discredited and meaningless. The same will happen with the conciliar Declaration on Religious Freedom if the Evangelical church in Spain does not receive her due freedom. In that case, this decree would merely reflect the Roman church's claim to her own freedom.

The Council as a Question Addressed to Other Churches

What does the Council mean to other churches? The answers discussed here are the product of a critical analysis of the Council and its achievements. We are obligated to make such a critical analysis. Yet non-Roman churches would neglect something decisive if they were not to understand the Council as a critical question addressed to them. Only by so doing will they be able really to grasp its significance.

Considering the course of the Council, the emergence of a variety of antitheses among the Council Fathers, and the completion of the deliberations down to the final votes, one can have only the highest respect for the care with which they listened to each other and learned from each other, for the open-mindedness of most bishops to the far-sighted questions and insights of the theologians, for the perseverance in the search for common formulations, and for the outstanding accomplishments of the commissions and their sub-commissions in digesting the widely diverging opinions of the Council Fathers. The consensus which emerged in the final voting was, therefore, the result of an exemplary synodical effort. Especially noteworthy is the fact that these resolutions contain many statements which would have been impossible before the Council, and the fact that the consensus extends to extremely differentiated questions and assertions. It is self-evident that a consensus, so differentiated and now binding, is possible only in a general synod of a confessional church, but not in a plenary assembly of the churches in the World Council. Churches of diverse confessions can never jointly speak in so differentiated and binding a manner as a single church; it is rather to be marveled that the churches of the World Council have jointly made the important decisions they have already made. But if we compare the Second Vatican Council as a general synod of the Roman church with corresponding general synods of the Lutheran or Reformed churches, or even with the Lambeth Conference, we cannot evade the question whether an equally far-reaching and differentiated consensus would be possible in these churches by means of new dogmatic decisions on the understanding of the church and the church's offices and in the questions concerning the relationship between church and world.

It was particularly striking that in spite of all the dramatics in the Council's negotiations a disintegration of the groups and formal opinions into false alternatives was almost entirely avoided. Such false alternatives were posed in some areas of the Reformation churches—as, for instance, seeing the church either as called to be not of the world or as sent into the world. The Council viewed both together, as the New Testament does. The Council avoided the false alternative of either liturgy or service to the world. Both were viewed together, while elsewhere those who stressed responsibility for the world looked with suspicion on an emphasis on liturgy. The sacrament and the sermon, too, are now more correctly coordinated in the Roman church, and more correctly than in Protestant circles, also, when the sacraments are neglected in favor of relevant preaching. Nor did the Council permit the office of the ministry and lay activity to disintegrate into an alternative which not infrequently confronts us, namely, that whoever wants to take the universal priesthood seriously thinks he must repudiate the ministerial office as clericalism. This is true in a similar way of the relationship between missions and a world come of age, and further examples could be cited. This peculiar disintegration which can often be observed in Christendom was noticeably avoided by the Council, without neglecting serious consideration of either side of the alternative.

Obviously, the Reformation churches cannot affirm some important doctrinal statements of the Council. The Council has not yet attempted to get at the questions of the faith which caused the division of the church in the sixteenth century. For that matter, the synods of the Reformation churches have not yet attacked these questions by means of the new methods of historical and systematic research which are available today. In spite of the divisive dogmatic differences that continue to exist, we cannot evade the question whether the Roman church has not retained confessional statements which belong to the elements of the Christian faith and which the Reformation could not dispense with. This includes confessional statements about which there is no consensus among Protestants today, such as the physical resurrection of Jesus Christ and his return at the end of history, or the incarnation of the eternal Son of God and, therefore, the confession of the eternal Trinity, God the Father, Son, and Holy Spirit. We cannot accept the Roman definition of the relationship between Scripture and tradition. However, is it not something to think about that confidence in the Holy Scriptures as the word of God has often been more solid in the Roman church than with many a theologian and layman in the Evangelical church of today?

Should not also the persistence in prayer, the firmness of commitment, and the willingness to make sacrifices (elements so impressively in evidence at the Council) be felt as a question addressed to us?

Perhaps such counter-questions will be offensive to some readers. Yet in the assembly hall of the Council so many humble and courageous voices of criticism were raised against conditions in the Roman church by Council Fathers that it would be pharisaic on our part to try to suppress the critical questions addressed to our own church. I have no doubt whatsoever that the Council did not relieve the Reformation churches of the task God gave them. I do have serious doubts that the Evangelical church is today performing her task as God expects her to.

Vatican II will be taken seriously only when non-Roman churches view it as a question addressed to themselves. Some of the questions which arise specifically for the Evangelical church have been mentioned. It will be up to the representatives of other churches to express the ways in which the Council represents a question addressed to their churches. It should not be doubted that the Council poses questions for them also—for the Anglican communion in a manner similar to the Lutherans, the question concerning doctrinal consensus; in a different manner for the Eastern churches, the problems of *aggiornamento*. The Council also poses a question for the World Council, which is in danger of being satisfied with cooperation among separated churches. With its doctrine of the church and with its ecumenical program, in spite of its inherent weaknesses, the Council issued an inescapable call to visible unity and rightly warned against being satisfied with mere cooperation.

13

A Fearful Christendom

Before we proceed to ask how non-Roman churches should now, after the Council, conduct themselves, it will be necessary to engage in some basis reflections concerning both the relationship to the Roman church and the relationship of the non-Roman churches to each other.

In 1929 Karl Barth created a sensation with his address "Roman Catholicism as a Question Addressed to the Protestant Church," and the Catholic theologian Robert Grosche, for his part, used his periodical *Catholica* in an exemplary new way to take up questions of Reformation theology for the purposes of a dialogue on areas of theological controversy. Since then, as the opinions expressed by Council Fathers show, the number of those taking other churches seriously as questions addressed to their own church has increased considerably. Yet the fear remains that the position of one's own church is weakened and that other churches are provided with arguments against her if one demonstrates weaknesses in one's own church, discovers something exemplary in other churches, and openly calls attention to it. This is, of course, not true in the same measure of all churches and their relationships to each other. In the history of the ecumenical movement many things have changed in this respect. Yet this fear can be observed again and again not only over against the numerically stronger Roman church but also in the mutual relationship between member churches of the World Council. It may be stated that a peculiar anxiety still characterizes Christendom today in spite of its ecumenical breakthrough. But where the relationship of Christians to each other is controlled by anxiety, their concern for the world is also inhibited. The fear Christians have of each other increases their fear of the world.

Causes of Anxiety

This anxious reserve has many causes. It would be not only an historical and theological task but also a task in depth-psychology to analyze these causes individually. The analysis would show that the causes of which people are conscious are by no means always the causes that actually predominate. Moreover, in the relationships of the individual churches to each other the same kinds of causes were by no means always in the foreground.

One important cause of anxiety is the memory of the history of divisions in the church, a series of events with traumatic effects on the subsequent relationship of the churches involved. Not infrequently, the division was linked with recourse to violence and bloodshed, and always with conflicts and pain, and these experiences continued in history, especially in attempts to compel the other side to return. This memory exerts itself in fear of further threatening situations, although most of the churches no longer have the resources of civil power at their disposal. What such memories signify becomes clear when, for example, a comparison is made between the relations of the Reformation churches and the Eastern church to each other, and the relations of both to the Roman church. The separation of the other churches from the Roman church was direct and immediate, while the separation between the Reformation churches and the Orthodox church is only an inherited situation; it was not brought about by them directly and was therefore less encumbered. The memory of the griefs mutually inflicted in history can be rendered innocuous only by mutual forgiveness.

A second cause lies in the images of the other church, images created through the conflicts involved in the separation for the purpose of justifying the separate status of one's own church by emphasizing the differences as clearly as possible and for the purpose of repelling the attacks of the other church. Arising during the painful process of separation, these images are wont to be accompanied on both sides by an exaggeration of differences and a toning down of what they have in common. These images have a peculiar molding effect and prove themselves beyond the time of their origin as singularly constant in the consciousness of each church. This is true even after changes have meanwhile taken place in the thought and life of both churches and many an abridgment and bias from the time of separation have been removed. Every church is inclined in an unhistorical way to preserve these images in their catechisms and in interdenominational discussions. They must, however, be re-examined and corrected through the study of the past and present of the churches.

Undertaking a study of the present reality of the other churches leads to a further cause of anxiety, namely, an experience of their strangeness, and this is increasingly true the more one is rooted in the piety and the dogmatic, liturgical, and legal structure of one's own church. Even though both churches have overcome much that was one-sided at the time of their separation, their further development nevertheless proceeded from the special presuppositions of each church, and for that reason these often appear at first glance not so much as *rapprochement* but as further differentiation. Great care in research is required here. It is not enough simply to search for those items of dogmatic formulas, ritual, etc., of one's own church that may be discovered in the other church; translations will have to be made. Frequently one discovers in other churches the same things under completely different forms. So, for example, the content of the Reformation formula "righteous and sinner at the same time" is rediscovered within the Roman church, not indeed in its dogma, but in its piety, especially in the believing reception of absolution in the face of death.

There is the further fear of causing confusion among one's own people if one dispenses with the current images of other churches and becomes too deeply involved in uncovering what they have in common. Being reminded of what happened when the churches separated and clinging to the images then formed constitutes an aid to preserving well-ordered church bodies. The fear of relaxing the church's doctrine and order plays a far smaller role today among the Christian youth and many active laymen than among those who bear the responsibility of church administration. This anxiety is heightened by the activity of ecumenical enthusiasts who think that the differences among the churches have become meaningless today. In this way, however, these enthusiasts not only lose their churchly roots themselves but also lead others into an uncertain no-man's-land between churches and thus hinder more than promote the *rapprochement* between the churches. Such enthusiasts are today a fringe phenomenon in nearly all churches. Careful reflection is, in fact, required to see how the danger of confusion and chaos may be avoided when men attempt to make the necessary corrections in the way their own churches see themselves and in the understanding of other churches. Yet linked with every correction of one's own church there remains a risk, and this risk must be taken.

The valid cause for holding back in relation to other churches may ultimately be only the fear of apostasy from the revealed truth, that is, of denying the Lord to whom the church belongs and whom she must serve. Where this danger exists, the issue is not only the memory of the history of separation but also the validity of the Fathers' witness to the truth; not only the images of other churches but also the distinction between truth and error. At stake is not only the preservation of a closed sociological structure but salvation itself. When it is a matter of confession or denial, separation is not only permitted but demanded. It is, therefore, not an accident that separations which resulted originally from other causes, such as political or jurisdictional ones as in the case of the separation between Rome and Byzantium, came to be understood in the course of controversy as differences in the truth.

Since a separation is ultimately justified only for the sake of the truth, every church seeks to justify her separate existence on the basis of the truth. The causes of separations, however, are undoubtedly very complex and they have by no means been sufficiently clarified in a systematic way. Thus, for example, separations arose because a dogmatically and legally entrenched church did not make room in her structure for newly gained insights in the faith and for charismatic gifts but rather excluded vital forces and drove people to establish a separate churchly existence. We must therefore ask in a new way today whether and to what extent the delimitation against false teaching was and still is in every case actually the cause of the separation. In any event, the yearning for unity calls for a new questing and searching, a renunciation of convenient notions, and an intensive pastoral concern.

Church Tradition as Protection and as Hindrance

A church's confession is the center of all affirmations of the faith. The confession is based on the message concerning God's saving deed in Jesus Christ. In the confession the believers commit themselves to Christ as the Lord and thus give glory to God the Father, the Son, and the Holy Spirit. The confession is expressed before God and man. In it are concentrated the statements of prayer and worship addressed to God and the statements of witness and doctrine addressed to fellow men. The confession is voiced by the community of believers, and the individual lives as a member of the church by assenting to the church's confession. As the confession of the church it determines the prayer and witness, the worship and teaching, of each individual member. Hence the confession is of central significance for the unity of the church.

The confession in its roots is confession of Christ. In the course of the history of dogma this confession has been made more precise and thematically more extensive over against historical threats to the faith. In the process, there were shifts in the structure of the confessional statement, depending on whether the dogma was formulated primarily in the structure of doxology (Orthodox church), of teaching (Roman church), or proclamation (Reformation churches). There have also been shifts in understanding about the authority and enforcement of the dogmas, especially since the establishment of the imperial church under Constantine caused conformity in dogmatic formulation to be regarded as necessary for the church's unity and the dogmas were received into the legal order of the state as fixed elements. Above all, differences in content resulted from differences in historical fronts, against which the confession was made more precise by means of further dogmas, the shifts in content and structure reinforcing each other. Also, these later dogmatic statements occupy a central position in the life of the church. They determine both the unstructured, personal prayers and testimonies of the believers and the polity and the liturgical propers in the parishes. In addition, they shape the order of the churchly life and offices, for in all her words and acts the church wants to abide by the truth to which her confession bears witness, and all of the church's regulations and customs are designed to help the church abide in this truth. Thus dogma, piety, regulations, and life are experienced as a unit.

If we call this unit churchly tradition, the separated churches exist side by side as different traditions. These traditions may be more or less explicitly fixed by law down to individual items, or they may leave room for freedom in expressing the faith. They may also be the result of more or less reflection, and even be urged in a basic way as the principle of tradition. In any event the individual believer is always a member of a totality of churchly life, and he lives within the totality of a specific tradition whether he is clearly aware of it or not. Even the common elements which the separated churches have retained are now in contexts of a different totality, and in times of crisis, as history shows, men regard as a violation of the truth the raising of questions about matters once left open, such as, for example, employing the concepts of a certain philosophy, or using leavened or unleavened bread in the Lord's Supper, or even making the sign of the cross in a certain way or placing crosses on the altar.

Tradition is without doubt important in preserving the churches. The more tradition is expressly formulated and legally secured, the more it becomes an important aid in preserving and further safeguarding the fellowship of the faithful as a fellowship of the contemporary brethren with the fathers who have preceded them in faith, that is, the continuity of the church in the vicissitudes of history and her unity at all places in the present. It is especially the identity of dogmatic formulas and constitutional regulations that make it easy to establish and maintain the reality and boundaries of a church. From this perspective we can understand why the Roman church at the Council proceeded so cautiously with innovations and why the Council Fathers tried so hard to demonstrate, even when a former position was amended (as for example, in the question of religious freedom), that the Roman church has always supported religious freedom (as in the presentation which Bishop de Smedt made to the first draft of the Declaration). Corresponding procedures can be established in other churches also.

The more comprehensively tradition embraces the thought and life of the faithful, the more it also constitutes a hindrance to the life of the church. One need only recall, for example, the extent to which Aristotelian philosophy, which Thomas Aquinas once employed in a missionary advance, has in modern times hindered Roman Catholic theology as well as classical Protestant orthodoxy from coming to grips at the proper time with the questions raised by the natural sciences and by historical modes of thought. Consider, too, how much the tenacious adherence to the state church conception of the unity of church, culture, and state has hindered the churches from recognizing the changed obligations within the social and political upheavals of recent years. Or consider how the traditional understanding of the ministry kept the universal priesthood of believers from waking from the slumber of a mere title and becoming effective in responsible action. Far too often the preservation of tradition resulted in keeping churches from getting through to the present situation of their environment by means of their reforms. Instead, they replaced the attitudes of the day before yesterday with those of yesterday, although it was their calling as God's eschatological people to be the vanguard of humanity. This is by no means true only of those churches that explicitly uphold a principle of tradition; it is also true of those who reject this principle and who, for lack of reflection on tradition, are in some cases held captive by tradition more obviously than the former and thus close their eyes to changed situations.

This double impact of church tradition becomes especially apparent as the separated churches confront each other. In the process of embracing and protecting the totality of the church's life, tradition at the same time hinders every church from understanding another church as a living whole and from bursting out of her own borders. Tradition holds understanding captive and prevents taking another church altogether seriously as a question addressed to one's own church. This results in timidity and a conflict between the yearning for unity among the separated churches and a clinging to the inherited unity in one's own church, a conflict between the will to be fully open to other churches and the fear of losing the heritage of one's own church.

The Relationship Between the Past and the Future

The relationship to the historical past for the churches of today is different from what it was for the congregations to whom the New Testament letters were written and of whom Book of Acts speaks.

Faith rests on the historical saving act of God in Jesus Christ. From the beginning, therefore, the eyewitnesses of the words, deeds, and fate of Jesus, and especially the appearances of the risen Lord on the basis of which his death was recognized as a saving act, have a basic significance for the churches. From the start it was necessary to preserve and transmit these testimonies. These transmitted testimonies served to hold the people to God's saving act in Jesus Christ. This in turn led to the writing of the Gospels and the kerygmatic formulas contained in the New Testament letters, and subsequently to the whole of the New Testament proclamation and exhortation. The Christians were entirely concerned with the content of the transmitted material and intent on preserving it. At that time, however, there was as yet no reflection on the process of transmission itself. The interval in time between them and the original event was small, and the apostolic eyewitnesses and their immediate pupils were still alive or temporally close.

The further the church's present is removed from its historical beginnings, the more tradition must become a problem. As the gospel advanced into ever new areas, it became necessary to make use of new images and concepts, and at the same time to hold fast to the identity of the original message concerning Christ. It became necessary to isolate the original transmission from others which falsely made the same claims, to collect the original written witnesses, and to add a canon of New Testament writings to the Old Testament Scriptures. The greater the distance from the beginning, the more urgent became the task of guaranteeing the identity of the message concerning Christ by means of further confessional statements and regulating the church's offices. To the transmitted foundational historical saving deed was added the history of this transmission, that is, the variety of interpretations placed on the original tradition on its way through history in preaching and teaching, in liturgy and the ordering of church offices, etc. Although the church is always concerned only with abiding by the saving deed which occurred once and for all time and with preserving its original attestations, the need arose to take into account this process of transmission that moved through many centuries for the purpose of understanding the original event. Thus the process of transmission itself, as well as its history, received a specific importance which weighs all the more heavily since this process was consummated in different areas of the church, in different historical situations and intellectual confrontations, and was embodied in different churchly traditions which then stood in part side by side and in part in opposition to each other. Consequently, there is today a change in the relationship of the churches to the past as compared with the first congregations, and this change has been produced both by the history of one's own church tradition and by a confrontation with the traditions of other churches.

Moreover, the church's relation to the future is today quite different from what it was in the early years. Paul had written to the Romans, "Salvation is nearer to us now than when we first believed; the night is far gone, the day is at hand" (Rom. 13:11 f.). He awaited this day of the Lord not only as a day of salvation but also as a day of judgment, and this not only as judgment of the world but also as judgment of the Christians. "For we must all appear before the judgment seat of Christ, so that each one may receive good or evil, according to what he has done in the body" (II Cor. 5:10). For that reason Paul labored in "the fear of the Lord" (5:11) and admonished the faithful to work out their salvation "with fear and trembling" (Phil. 2:12). This corresponds to Jesus' announcement of the separation of the good from the evil which the returning Son of Man will undertake, and to his admonition to watchfulness. "On that day many will say to me, 'Lord, Lord, did we not prophesy in your name, and cast out demons in your name, and do many mighty works in your name?' And then will I declare to them, 'I never knew you; depart from me, you evildoers' " (Matt. 7:22 f.).

If the day of the Lord had come closer for Paul in the course of the few years since his conversion it must in the course of centuries have come close far more distressingly for the consciousness of later Christendom. All churches indeed confess Jesus Christ as the one who "shall come to judge the quick and the dead." In general, however, they have not clung to the expectation that he will come soon. Apart from special periods of crisis, in which this expectation surged anew, the day of the Lord has receded into the distance, and the urgent sense of its approach has faded away. Within the original dialectic of "already" and "not yet" the weight has shifted, as the expectation of the coming reign of God was largely supplanted by statements about the presence of God's reign, and as the history of the church was understood as the history of God's reign. All in all, the eschatological messages of Jesus and Paul did not prevail, and the indications expressed in Luke's Acts were unfolded instead. The coming day of the Lord, a day of judgment and consummation which as the end of the world and the structure of the church and as a comprehensive new creation will shatter and transcend every conception, could in this way be incorporated in comprehensive theological systems dealing with the acts of God. Neither the salvation-history systems of the newer Protestantism nor the salvation-history conception of Vatican II are free of the danger of scaling down the Lord's imminent return to the level of a predictable course of church and world history.

The tradition of the primitive church was closely linked to the very recent history of the earthly Christ and his soon-to-be-expected return in glory. Then all men will see him whose saving deed is now transmitted and proclaimed in words. In contrast, the process of transmission and its results through the course of church history have taken on an increasing importance of their own which has been strengthened once more because men have relaxed their expectation of the Lord's nearness and have adapted themselves to a longer-lasting history of the church. As a result, the churches often look backwards rather than forwards. While God's saving deed accomplished in the death and resurrection of Jesus calls to the future and exhorts to life issuing from this future, the fear of losing the past—not only the beginning but also the results of the centuries—is often greater than the fear of the coming day of the Lord. Instead of hastening out to meet the Lord, the churches, burdened with the shell of traditions, often move ahead at no more than a snail's pace.

If the different traditions of the separated churches are to have an encounter, it will be necessary to consider them not only in the retrospect of their genetic history but also in the prospect of the end. The apostolic message calls not only for the preservation of what was transmitted but also for the expectation of him who is approaching at the end of time.

We must unconditionally hold fast to the normative primacy of the original message of the eyewitnesses over the testimonies of every succeeding period of church history, as well as the primacy of the decision made by the coming Christ over all decisions that were made or are still to be made in the history of the church. Indeed, the expectation of the coming Lord is so much a part of the apostolic message that the message cannot be retained without this watchful expectation. From the perspective of this memory and this expectation, the preponderance of the church's traditions is reduced and their juxtaposition and opposition broken up. The memory of Jesus makes it impossible to miss his woes on the scribes and Pharisees, woes that strike also our theology and our piety. The expectation of the Coming One makes it impossible to miss the threats which the Lord calls out to entire churches in the seven letters of the Apocalypse. For the coming Christ will separate the good from the evil and will cut more deeply than the separations of this age. His separation will cut diagonally across all the separations existing in this world. The expectation of the coming Christ will make it altogether impossible to regard the frailties and sins of one's own as more harmless than those of the churches separated from us. The real problem is not the self-preservation of the churches in the rivalries of this time, but the ability to stand in the day of judgment.

The Common Norm

As the different traditions of the separated churches begin to confront each other as questions, it is of decisive importance that these questions be determined by the common origin and the common future. If each church were simply to compare the other church with herself, such a dialogue would make no progress. If churches would become nothing more than questions addressed to each other, without giving glory to the Lord who calls them all into question, this experience would have not a cleansing and edifying effect but a relativizing and disintegrating one. But where have the message of the saving deed, accomplished once and for all, and the promise of the divine act that is still coming been transmitted in a manner binding for all churches? Is there a norm jointly acknowledged by all churches?

All churches agree that the apostolic message and its echoes in the first congregations are of foundational significance for the church of all times They agree in acknowledging this irreplaceable norm for all further words and deeds on their part. But they diverge on the question of where this norm confronts them, and they give different answers concerning the relationship between the Holy Scriptures and tradition; and here there is controversy not only on the relationship between these two but also on the limits of the biblical canon, and above all on the concepts as well as the concrete content of tradition. Furthermore, there are divergent definitions of the relationship between Scripture, tradition, and teaching office.

In view of this state of affairs we must not, however, overlook the fact that the Holy Scriptures are common to all churches in spite of existing differences and that the differences in the limits of the canon are of so little moment that they play no compelling role in the discussions between the churches. The churches do indeed differ in the way they define the relationship between Scripture and tradition, and therefore they do not accord the Holy Scriptures the same normative position. Nevertheless, in the worship of all churches the Scripture lessons occupy an incomparably prominent position. Even where the apostolic tradition is derived not only from the Holy Scriptures but also from the church's tradition, Scripture enjoys the unchallenged advantage that it transmits unchanged the authentic words of the apostolic and primitive Christian witnesses. The oral apostolic tradition, on the other hand, has entered into the church's life, participates in its historical vicissitudes, and can therefore no longer be recovered in its authentic wording. The separated churches are further linked by the fact that even where tradition is regarded as normative alongside Scripture, the principle that there can be no contradiction between Scripture and tradition is accepted. This principle of the absence of contradiction is also very important especially for the dialogue between the Reformation churches and the Roman church. It provides a broader base for common discussion than the antithesis between the Scripture principle and the tradition principle leads us to expect—no matter how both principles may have been modified in present theology. An arbitrary use of the content of tradition is also excluded by the principle of no contradiction, though it leaves room for diverging expositions of Scripture.

It would seem natural, then, for the churches to subject themselves to the Holy Scriptures as they address questions to each other and allow each other to be questioned. The Scriptures have, in fact, succeeded everywhere in being accepted more and more as the common norm in the course of the ecumenical conversations of the last decades. This actual recognition of the Holy Scriptures as the common norm in all churches has not decided the controverted basic question concerning the significance of tradition and teaching office alongside Scripture. The questions whether, in what sense, and to what extent the church's tradition contains authentic oral apostolic tradition are left open and surely require further clarification. Yet even in the history of theology and dogma *contents* of the *Credo* were clarified before thought was given to the *act* of faith, and certainly before the questions regarding a theory of dogmatic principles were clarified. The witness to Christ in the Holy Scriptures is, however, clear and overwhelming. Consequently, an acknowledgment of Scripture as the actual common norm has made possible an exceedingly fruitful exchange of questions, a new mutual understanding, and even a joint witness.

The Decree on Ecumenism also points to this great actual significance of the Holy Scriptures. Even though the churches do not agree on the basic definition of the norm, what the decree says is valid: "Nevertheless, in [ecumenical] dialogue itself, the sacred utterances are precious instruments in the mighty hand of God for attaining that unity which the Savior holds out to all men" (Art. 21).[1]

In this respect, the newer historical-critical research is highly significant. This method has uncovered a far greater variety of

[1] *Documents*, p. 363.

perspectives in Holy Scripture than had hitherto influenced the individual churchly traditions. This research has discovered a far greater variety of theologies within the Scriptures than earlier times had recognized. The same saving deed in Jesus Christ is proclaimed in the New Testament writings in ways that make use of greatly differing concepts and contexts of interpretation. Within the Scriptures we may therefore recognize far more suggestions for possible dogmatic developments than the theologians of the separated churches had realized or the history of dogma in the past had actually developed. We see clearly that the dogmatic formulations are the result of a selective decision, through which several biblical concepts from among a great variety were given prominence for the purpose of a systematic synthesis of that variety. It was inevitable that differences should arise when, for example, the saving activity of God was summarized in the Orthodox church predominantly by means of the New Testament concept of sanctification or in Western Christendom mainly by means of the concept of justification. In the West, moreover, the Reformation churches emphasized the forensic aspects, while Rome spoke in terms of renewal. These different concepts, used side by side in the New Testament, witness to one and the same saving activity of God. But in a dogmatic preference for one there is the danger of a narrowing and the danger of ultimately viewing the differences in dogmatic formulations as differences and antitheses in the faith.

Much the same could be said of the variety of approaches to church government contained in the widely divergent statements in the New Testament concerning prophets, teachers, rulers, shepherds, bishops, etc., as well as concerning the free emergence of charismatic services, and concerning the commissioning for service through the laying on of hands. Here, too, there are more approaches than have been adopted in the polity of the individual churches. The question concerning the historical situations which led to the further development and constitutional establishment of the one or the other approach needs to be investigated.

The varied approaches for later dogmatic and canonical decisions are not found in the New Testament in timeless juxtaposition. On the contrary, they manifest historical developments that already occurred in early Christendom. We must take into account not only the content of the New Testament witnesses but also the historical and forward-looking acts of witnessing—not only the ordering of the community but also the execution of service, government, and order. Furthermore, we must work out the basic structures in which the life of the church, her address to God and man, as well as her other services, are carried out. Thus a clear recognition of the unity of different liturgies can be gained only from an understanding of the basic structures of worship, and the question concerning the unity of dogmatic formulations can be undertaken in depth only on the basis of an understanding of the basic structures of theological discourse, if this involvement is not satisfied simply with comparing the wording of the dogmatic formulations.

Proceeding from the common basis and the common future of all churches, rather than from the particularity of one's own tradition, will, to be sure, not eliminate the various churchly traditions, but it will lead to a new understanding of these traditions and open them up for each church. It is impossible in any case to bypass the churchly traditions since, in fact, every church—with or without a principle concerning tradition—lives in a specific tradition, and above all, since the apostolic gospel must by an inner necessity be not only preserved as letter, but continue to be announced by word of mouth and proclaimed in new terms to the ever changing historical situation. The New Testament would not be truly revered as norm if in the encounter of the separated churches men were to reject everything that cannot be documented in so many words in the witnesses and regulations of the Bible. The word of God is "a light to our path." By this light we must endeavor anew to understand the variety of ways the churches have gone in the course of the changing times.

Overcoming Fear

As we examine ourselves by the witness of the Holy Scriptures, all of us without exception are placed in question. We are put in question both by the warnings with which the earthly Jesus confronted the pious and upright of his time and by the fate they prepared for him on the cross, as well as by the proclamation of the coming Christ who will judge the Christians also. The certainty with which we isolate ourselves from other churches will be shattered and all self-glorification will be destroyed. "If we say we have no sin, we deceive ourselves, and the truth is not in us" (I John 1:8). In fact every church has every reason to pray, "Lord, have mercy!" Instead of being afraid of other churches and of losing our own particular church traditions, we should be fearing the day of the Lord.

Jesus' *proper* mission, however, was not to judge, but to save, to forgive, to heal. He pronounced his woes on the pious, the righteous, the rich, and the satisfied that they might recognize their poverty and sin and be saved along with the sinners, harlots, and publicans, and the poor, the hungering, and the thirsting. In like manner he will come not only as judge but also as Savior. As he crushes and annihilates the rebellion of human self-righteousness, he will at the same time redeem the wretched, the poor, the yearning, and those who hunger and thirst for righteousness, and he will make all things new. The proper message of the gospel is not the judgment according to works but the justification of the sinner through faith in Jesus Christ. And that gospel not only announces the word of pardon in the coming judgment but declares and makes the believers righteous now and grants them the new life. "If we confess our sins, he is faithful and just, and will forgive our sins and cleanse us from all unrighteousness" (I John 1:9). Thus the last thing is not fear of the judgment but rather "confidence for the day of judgment" (I John 4:17). This joy is granted to those who in repentance affirm the deserved judgment and believe in Jesus Christ who has borne the sins of the world and was judged in place of the sinners.

If fear of the judgment causes the hardened boundaries between churches to be shattered, joy for the day of judgment will open hearts for that love which seeks not its own but reaches out to the brethren and meets them in reciprocal giving and receiving. This love rests on God's deed of love, his delivering up his Son for the world. This love also rests in the confidence we are permitted to have in the future on the basis of God's deed of love. In repentance and faith we are permitted to feel embraced by this love. Consequently, "there is no fear in love, but perfect love casts out fear" (I John 4:18).

Who, then, are the brothers we should love? The answers the New Testament writings give to this question are as precise as they are broad, putting the churches existing side by side today to shame: "No one can say 'Jesus is Lord' except by the Holy Spirit" (I Cor. 12:3). "Every spirit which confesses that Jesus Christ has come in the flesh is of God" (I John 4:2). "He who confesses the Son has the Father also" (I John 2:23). Paul could even transcend envy and rivalry and say, "What then? Only that in every way, whether in pretense or in truth, Christ is proclaimed; and in that I rejoice. Yes, and I shall rejoice" (Phil. 1:18 f.). To be sure, the name of Christ is abused too, but the Christ who is at work is greater than such abuse.

But if the fears of the churches in their relations to each other yield to love their fear of the world will also disappear. How much energy the churches waste in isolating themselves from each other and in debating with each other! Love to the brethren, however, will set men free for service to the world. If God loved the world, then brother-love cannot be held back but must penetrate into the world.

14

Necessary Steps

What should be the attitude of non-Roman churches toward the Roman church since the Council? In answering this question we must firmly keep in view the fact that in our century a deep-seated yearning for unity has sprung up in all churches on the part of all who believe in Christ. This yearning is the work of the Holy Spirit. For the will of the Lord that "they may all be one" has become an inescapably great obligation for Christendom. But opening hearts for the will of Christ is the work of the Holy Spirit. Jesus prayed to God that his own would be united in a unity of love, "so that the world may know that thou hast sent me and hast loved them even as thou hast loved me" (John 17:23). The Lord wills that no assignment and no spiritual gift he has given the individual churches be lost, but that all these gifts be put to use in the fellowship of worship and service to the world.

Wrong Reactions

If we take this seriously, certain forms of behavior found here and there over against the Roman church will be impossible.

Under the impact of the Council some Evangelical Christians have become afraid that the Roman church will overwhelm them and suffocate them in her ecumenical embrace. For this reason they react with an often unconscious tendency to belittle what has newly emerged in the Roman church, to become more critical, to set forth as evangelical what the Evangelicals and the Roman church do not have in common, and to adopt an anti-dogmatic, anti-liturgical, anti-sacramental stance. In this way, however, the fullness of the biblical message cannot be brought to bear, and the special service which the churches of the Reformation are to render the rest of Christendom cannot be realized. Thus their ecumenical responsibility would be denied.

Others permit themselves to be influenced by the Council to such an extent that they equate the avant garde phalanx of the movement toward renewal with the Roman church as a whole and thus miss the real situation. In their enthusiastic expectations they overlook the limits the Council has imposed on the ecumenical activity of the Roman church and thus are remiss in their obedience to the assignment God has given them as members of the church of the Reformation—an assignment which they are also to carry out with respect to the Roman church.

In openness and sobriety we must seek and follow the way leading between these two extremes.

There is a third attitude toward the Roman church which is quite common and which does not do justice to the present situation. This is the attitude of mere spectators who guard against every involvement and from a safe distance criticize what is going on in the Roman church today. Such people are nothing but detached observers. Yet the role of a mere spectator over against another church should be impossible for a Christian in any case. Having the name of Christ in common calls for a decision in every case. It is, indeed, easy to demonstrate that the Council did not create the presuppositions for a reunion of the separated churches. Already the fact that the Council retained the affirmation of all dogmas of the Roman church, together with all their accompanying condemnations of the teachings of other churches, as a prerequisite for church union indicates a narrowness in the understanding of unity, a narrowness which makes it impossible for other churches to contribute to such a union all that God has entrusted to them in insights of faith and in other gifts. Were they to accept these conditions, the impoverishment of Christendom would result, and this in the last analysis would be of no benefit to the Roman church either.

NECESSARY STEPS

The union of churches can ensue only after the churches have drawn closer to each other. To that end the Council in its Decree on Ecumenism has furnished a series of highly significant impulses. These impulses coincide in large measure with what the ecumenical movement of the non-Roman churches has in recent decades come to recognize as the necessary first steps. These possibilities now opened up for the Roman church must not only be observed and noted critically but utilized as well. The newborn ecumenism of the Roman church can grow in a truly ecumenical fashion only if it finds an echo in other churches.

Which steps must be taken? This question will be answered in detail differently by the non-Roman churches, depending on the historical, dogmatic, and constitutional presuppositions which determine their relationship to the Roman church. In spite of differences, however, we may point to certain basic requirements for moving ahead that apply to all churches. I shall illustrate these requirements by using the Evangelical church as an example.

Necessary Presuppositions

The first requirement for drawing closer is penitential self-reflection. Our own repentance must stand at the beginning, not the demand for repentance on the part of others. We may not evade this repentance by boasting of the upheaval brought about by the sixteenth-century Reformation—the rediscovery of the message of the sinner's justification by faith, the restored reception of the Lord's Supper under both kinds, the opening of the Bible for the members of the church, the stimulation of the priesthood of all believers, etc. We must rather examine the *current* state of our church. What is the state of the preaching of the pure gospel, church attendance, communion attendance, and actual Bible reading in Evangelical Christianity today? We cannot answer this question concerning our real situation by reciting the formula "Christ alone, grace alone, Scripture alone" any more than we can answer the question concerning the *reality* of the universal priesthood by pointing to the *principle* of the priesthood of all believers.

Furthermore, what is the consensus of believers today about those things that were so important to the Reformers? But as we thus examine ourselves we must not stop with a comparison with the Reformation. On the contrary, we must transcend the tradition of our church and move on to the historical basis of the apostles and primitive Christianity. We must examine our present state and the history of our church in the light of the word of Scripture. We must not expect the New Testament message simply to confirm the Reformation; we must also ask whether this message was perhaps proclaimed with bias or in an abridged form dictated by the conflicts at the time of the Reformation. We must also ask, for example, whether the establishment of the ministerial office, as it was formulated during the Reformation age in the conflict with the Enthusiasts, permitted the universal priesthood of the believers the free exercise that Paul acknowledged in his statements concerning spiritual gifts and services. Are the spiritual gifts and the power of the universal priesthood being exercised in reclaiming those who have fallen from the faith? Do we not have many reasons for a penitent return and renewal on the basis of the church's origin?

In connection with this penitent self-examination we must be concerned about a new understanding of the Roman church and go in quest of the truth even where its witness meets us hidden under strange forms. We must not see only the legalistic, ritualistic, and superstitious phenomena in the Roman church, but must keep in view the totality of the church's life and especially the renewal being carried out in worship, in biblical and theological studies, and in the attitude toward the rest of Christendom and toward the world. Similarly, as we look back into history, we must not see only the shape in which the Roman church at the time of the Reformation and in the Counter-Reformation confronted the Evangelical upheaval, but must also have an eye for the great historical breakthroughs which have at various times occurred in the Roman church's piety and theology and in her reforms and missionary advances. It is of decisive importance, however, that we not look at the past and the present of this church in isolation but that we go back to the witnesses of the New Testament and, on the basis of the variety of Christologies and ecclesiologies found there, as well as the liturgical impulses and the church orders, attempt as far as possible to interpret the tradition of the Roman Catholic Church. With eyes of love and the humility of questioning we must be concerned with a new understanding of the Roman church, discover the treasures hidden there for us under strange forms, and thank God for the knowledge of the truth, faithfulness, and devotion which he has produced through the Holy Spirit in that church also. Undoubtedly, we shall have to get rid of many misunderstandings, caricatures, and too easy conceptions, by means of which we are accustomed to evade the question which the Roman church poses for our church.

Repentance before God and the search for the brethren under the word of Holy Scripture are the indispensable prerequisites for all further ecumenical steps. If we will penitently strive for our renewal, our encounter with the Roman church will be genuine, that is, free from fear and enthusiastic fanaticism. Then we will be in a position to speak of our own shortcomings openly and without fear of suffering loss of prestige, and with equal frankness we will be able to bear witness in humility and freedom to the truth that lies concealed in the other church.

Ecumenical Dialogue

The next step is engaging in dialogue with the Roman church. This dialogue already had its beginning many years ago at various places as a result of the spontaneity of individual Christians, and it has since been kept alive among young people, student communities, and a number of study groups composed of laymen and theologians. The time has now come to conduct this dialogue also in official encounters between the church leaders and in various areas of the church's work.

For an ecumenical dialogue it is essential that all participants consciously confront each other as members of their respective churches. Only as they feel committed to the doctrine and order of their churches can there be an encounter between churches. The dialogue must be conducted with full readiness to listen to the other man as a brother committed to the same Lord. All attempts at glossing over existing differences must be avoided. Rather, the depth and importance of these differences must be re-examined, and the participants must strive to overcome the differences in their common faith in Christ and in their joint study of the Holy Scriptures.

The fact that the churches exist side by side within the same world situation will furnish more than enough topics for the dialogue. It would seem natural to begin with a joint analysis of the Decree on Ecumenism and the Toronto declaration of the World Council of Churches as well as the Pastoral Constitution on the Church in the Modern World, along with the corresponding reports and resolutions of world assemblies of the churches. We should ask the Catholic participants to explain what in their opinion the decisions of the Council mean for the common life of the separated churches, and they in turn should ask us what conclusions are to be drawn from the documents of the World Council. The participants must jointly clarify not only the traditional differences among the churches but also the spiritual climate of the environment in which the churches perform their services, as well as the problems of proclamation and religious instruction in this environment. Thereby, the history of the church cannot, of course, be bypassed. If in the treatment of relevant questions of the moment the traditions of the church are ignored with the thought of achieving results more quickly, it will sooner or later prove to be a mistake. The church's tradition is bound to assert itself in any event and will put the results of such dialogues in question. The traditions must be included in the dialogue; they must be understood anew and opened up to each other in the light of the Holy Scriptures. The unity of the church must remain the central theme of dialogue.

Initially, every dialogue is informative in character and seeks to promote better understanding. The dialogue, however, cannot stop at one's own self-understanding or at understanding the other churches, nor confine itself to practical questions. Rather, there must be careful research in order to achieve a more profound self-understanding in the light of a common basis and to bring to light the areas of agreement contained in the antitheses. Alongside the top-level dialogues, therefore, the cooperation of competent experts is needed. Such groups should be appointed by the church leaders and should devote themselves for longer periods of time to clarification of specific questions dividing the churches in the area of dogma as well as sexual and social ethics (such as, for example, questions concerning the understanding of marriage and the laws pertaining to mixed marriages). These research scholars should also prepare common translations of biblical and liturgical texts. Yet, however important the dialogues conducted or sponsored by the church leaders have become in our time, they should by no means seek to hold rein on the ecumenical spontaneity of the church's members or even to supplant it. It must not be forgotten that the ecumenical dialogue in most cases owes its origin not to the church leaders but to unusual awakenings in the churches.

No matter on which private or official levels the ecumenical dialogue is conducted, the principle *par cum pari*, recognized also by the Decree on Ecumenism, must in every case be observed. That is to say, the participants in the dialogue must have equal rights in alternating chairmanships, the choice of meeting place, the selection of topics, the corresponding makeup of the groups in terms of interested laymen, experts, bishops, theologians, etc. Insisting on the principle *par cum pari* does not mean mutual distrust but provides the form in which exchange of ideas can take place in the most frank and most free manner.

Furthermore, we cannot ignore the fact that the non-Roman churches have long been in dialogue with each other as member churches of the World Council. To be sure, the churches of the

World Council are not yet united. Yet they are on the way toward union, and by means of joint worship, consultations, resolutions, and activities have grown together into a spiritual community. This community could not yet be grasped in dogmatic definitions but it has nevertheless become an undeniable reality. It would not be consonant with this reality if the ecumenical dialogue with the Roman church were conducted in isolation as a bilateral dialogue in an exclusive sense. The presence of the other churches today belongs to a fruitful bilateral dialogue. This is particularly true of churches having the same confessions, as they are united in denominational world federations such as the Pan-Orthodox Conference and the Anglican Communion. It is, therefore, important that the dialogue between the Roman church and the World Council of Churches has meanwhile also been inaugurated and that an attempt is made here to establish a common formulation of the nature and the rules of ecumenical dialogue.

Joint Prayer

The ecumenical dialogue is more than just a conversation supported by rational arguments. It is here a matter of an encounter which embraces the total Christian existence. It is a matter of churches encountering each other in all the dimensions of their spiritual life. Hence the dialogue cannot be divorced from prayer, for in our commitment to God we are also rendered open to his operation in the brethren.

We must ask God for the terms on which the dialogue will be conducted. How could a penitential self-examination and the quest for the truth in another church be possible without the Holy Spirit who opens our eyes to our own reality and grants a new understanding of the separated brethren?

Moreover, prayer must accompany the dialogue itself. How could we ourselves keep this dialogue from relapsing into contentious and sterile debates in which each party seeks only his own self-justification? How could we by our own powers break through the strangeness and cause the truth by which we all live to shine forth?

Many people, individuals and congregations, are praying for the unification of the churches. Such prayer should also be spoken by the separated brethren jointly. For some time all churches have concurrently been praying for union during Prayer Week. Where Christians assemble for ecumenical dialogue, however, there is the opportunity to hear the word of Scripture in joint worship and to thank God for what he has already granted and to ask him to supply what is still wanting. Every church knows the prayer "Lord, have mercy!" and the doxology "Glory to God in the highest!" For that reason Christians should also sing them together. Every church prays the Lord's Prayer; for that reason Christians should also pray it together. The high-priestly prayer of Jesus for the unity of his own has been given to all churches as a promise that God will hear their prayers for this unity. The joint invocation of God should always be the first joint word before the participants in the ecumenical dialogue speak to each other.

Easing the Life Together

Ecumenical dialogue cannot be an end in itself. It must result in changes in the churches' relations to each other. A first important step beyond the dialogue would be the removal of the most serious hindrances keeping separated Christians from life together.

This is true especially of the existing regulations of canon law regarding mixed marriages. Such regulations have painful repercussions, by no means only in Germany. Unfortunately the Council produced no changes in this matter. It is true that the Council considered a draft proposing relaxation in the spirit of the Decree on Ecumenism and transmitted it to the Pope with the request for setting up new regulations. However, according to reports, objections were voiced by English and American bishops. This could account for the fact that the Instruction of March 18, 1966, fell considerably short not only of the expectations of the Reformation churches but also of the draft considered by the Council and caused extensive disappointment in Catholic circles generally. This problem is a burning issue for many Catholic Christians as well and it has led many to become embittered and to leave the church. The Council created important presuppositions for establishing new regulations in the treatment of mixed marriages. The Decree on Ecumenism also acknowledges non-Catholic Christians as members of the body of Christ on the basis of their baptism, and the Declaration on Religious Freedom emphatically upholds a man's personal dignity and insists that his free decision in religious questions is to be respected. Important, furthermore, is the revision which the Council undertook with regard to the practice affecting mixed marriages with members of the Orthodox church. Henceforth the validity of a mixed marriage performed by an Orthodox priest is acknowledged, even though the Orthodox church (like the Evangelical) affirms the possibility of divorce and the marriage of divorced persons by the church as distinct from the Roman church. Hence the problem of divorce cannot be the obstacle to a new canonical treatment of mixed marriages between Evangelicals and Catholics. On the basis of these presuppositions it would seem impossible for the Roman church to continue to declare Evangelical-Catholic mixed marriages invalid if they were performed by an Evangelical pastor. Rather, on the basis of the aforementioned new presuppositions, the conclusion suggests itself to me that the churches involved might well continue to warn their members of the special dangers connected with a mixed marriage, but ultimately leave it up to the consciences of their members to decide whether they want to be married in a Catholic or an Evangelical ceremony and how they want their children baptized and reared. The churches should acknowledge these marriages and refrain from imposing penalties. This view is shared by the Council theologian Hans Küng and several other Catholic theologians, but at the moment they constitute a very small minority. One may, however, assume that the Instruction of March, 1966, does not represent the definitive regulation.

The removal of other hindrances to life together that have already been mentioned will also have far-reaching implications for the approach of the churches to each other. This is true especially of proselytizing practiced by one church among the members of another and of resorting to governmental force in the suppression of another church. Both methods not only prevent ecumenical approaches between churches but also promote agnosticism among those who were converted by material means and ignoble propaganda and those who are hindered by the state in the free exercise of their faith.

The removal of existing hindrances cannot, of course, be expected only of the Roman church. There are hindrances to which the Roman church is subjected from our side. Every church will have to do her part in making a fraternal life together possible.

Cooperation

A further step is the coordination of the churches' charitable and social work at home, in foreign lands in the process of developing, and in disaster areas. Some approaches to coordination are already in existence. Beyond this, the churches should develop forms of cooperation in planning and implementation. There are also situations involving decisions in the history of individual nations and the world where the churches dare not remain silent. In those cases they should consult one another, coordinate their procedures, and strive for a common message in which to proclaim God's will in a warning, exhorting, and consoling manner. Also, in cultural endeavors, especially in the educational system at home and in the developing nations, an attempt should be made to achieve a greater degree of cooperation in planning and execution than has hitherto been the case. Who knows how much has been neglected or done only halfway, to the detriment of the needy, that could have been accomplished with proper cooperation?

Who knows how much has remained ineffective because the church leaders on both sides entrusted too little to the responsibility of the laity and expected too little of their initiative and cooperation?

Joint Witness to Christ

The Decree on Ecumenism exhorts Catholic Christians not only to cooperation with the separated brethren in social, cultural, and other areas, but also to a united witness to the faith. "Before the whole world, let all Christians profess their faith in God, one and three, in the incarnate Son of God, our Redeemer and Lord. United in their efforts, and with mutual respect, let them bear witness to our common hope, which does not play us false" (Art. 12).[1] These words do not say *how* this profession of faith is to be made jointly—whether each Christian himself is to confess the same God and Savior, or whether, in addition, the separated Christians are to confess him *together*. The latter was done repeatedly by the churches united in the World Council—Orthodox, Lutherans, Reformed, Anglicans, and others—by means of public declarations and messages as well as in the constitution of their federation. It would be an impressive witness to the one Lord before the world if it would be possible on special occasions for all Christian churches, including the Roman Catholic Church, to confess Christ jointly and to sound the glad tidings to the world.

These might be the first steps of an approach between the Evangelical church and the Roman church. They would not constitute a union of these churches. Quite a number of further steps would be necessary for that. These are, however, the inescapably necessary first steps if the will of the Lord that "they may all be one" is taken seriously. Even though the Roman church is not a member of the World Council of Churches, she will be welcomed as a partner in the common search for unity.

---

[1] *Documents*, p. 354.

15

The Mystery of Unity

All Christians believe that God created the church. The church has come into being and is preserved not because men have decided to associate together but because God has gathered them together. All Christians confess the church to be "one, holy, catholic, and apostolic": one, as belonging to the one Lord Jesus Christ who imparts himself to her; holy, as sanctified by the Holy Spirit who prepares her for service; catholic, as sent into the world by him who has overcome the world; apostolic, as built upon the foundation of the apostles. Every Christian is sure of being a member of the one, holy, catholic, apostolic church because he is a member of the church through whose message he was brought to faith in Christ, through whose baptism he was buried in Christ's death and raised in his resurrection and at whose table he receives Christ's body and blood. Indeed, he is certain that this church, in which he has received and continues to receive these gifts, is the one, holy, catholic, and apostolic church.

This church in its historically conditioned status is the center from which each Christian looks at other churches and judges them. As he looks at other churches, he seeks first of all what they have in common with his own church, and he inquires about people in these other churches who think and act as he does. Such an approach is also suggested for individual churches. No matter what view a particular church may hold about the possibility of the church's existence beyond the confines of a particular church —whether she will exclude this possibility or leave it open—each church will, as a rule, reflect on this question from its own point of view. In the certainty that Christ is active in her and that the

Spirit is alive in her, she looks for the same effects and gifts in other churches. Thus as a matter of course there results a quantitative evaluation of other churches, their grasp of the truth, their means of grace, and the grace granted to them. "Traces" and "elements" of what one's own church possesses whole, and parts of the "fullness" present in one's own church, are discovered.

Yet, however much this way of thinking may commend itself, the other churches will not feel that they are being correctly understood in this way. As a matter of fact, this approach does not do justice to the self-understanding of other churches. For *every* church lives in the certainty of Christ active in her and the spiritual gifts alive in her. Every church understands herself not primarily from the point of view of another church, but on the basis of the origin of God's historical saving deed in Jesus Christ and the outpouring of the Holy Spirit through whom Jesus Christ is present in her midst today. Thus by this approach the churches justify to each other their separate existence.

The Turning Point in the Understanding of the Church

Chapter One proceeded from Christendom's loss of security, from its being torn out of its accustomed imbeddedness in its cultural and political environs, from the disruption of the accustomed shape of its status.

But the church-consciousness was also shattered, that is, the idea which equates the church to which one belongs with the one holy church and on the basis of which the rest of Christendom had been judged. Especially in times of upheaval and times of suppression it becomes evident not only that elements of our church are present in other churches but also that Christ himself is at work in their midst and manifests himself to the world through them. The evaluation of other churches on the basis of one's own church does not correspond to the spiritual experiences which we have today as we encounter other churches. For there we are confronted by Christ, who in the freedom of his grace is not bound to any presuppositions regarding human boundaries. In his freedom he may cause weak and despised churches to be the light of the world, and reveal strong and esteemed churches to be powerless components of this world.

The church-consciousness has also been shattered as the inadequacies of one's own church became apparent in the loss of security. Particularly in periods of upheaval and persecution one's own indolence and smugness, which have kept us from putting the talents entrusted to us to work and from serving men before they turned away from Christ in disappointment or despair, become evident.

Thus the shaking of church-consciousness implies both shame and blessing. There is an increasing number of Christians who are dissatisfied with the traditional condition of their church. At the same time there is an increasing number of those who live spiritually no longer merely by the tradition of their own church, but also by what has emerged in spiritual gifts in other churches. Thus the witness of suffering in the Russian Orthodox Church after the First World War, or the liturgical movement in the Roman church, or the fruits of biblical scholarship in the Evangelical churches became gifts for all churches. This shaking of church-consciousness is today moving more or less strongly through all churches, including the Roman church.

Without these shake-ups the Council's statements concerning other churches are also unintelligible. While the first form of the Constitution on the Church had in an exclusive manner identified the one, holy, catholic, apostolic church with the Roman church, the final text (by substituting "subsists in" for "is"; cf. above, p. 87) opened up the possibility of thinking of the one, holy, catholic, apostolic church that reaches beyond the borders of the Roman church. To be sure, the constitution itself makes extremely restrained use of this possibility in that it speaks only of "elements of sanctification and of truth" outside the Roman church. The constitution is less reticent, however, in enumerating the items that interpret the meaning of this statement concerning the "elements": baptism, honoring sacred Scripture, religious zeal, faith in God the Father and in Christ, the Son of God, in some places the recognition of other sacraments, the episcopate, and devotion to Mary.

> They also share with us in prayer and other spiritual benefits. Likewise, we can say that in some real way they are joined with us in the Holy Spirit, for to them also He gives His gifts and graces, and is thereby operative among them with His sanctifying power. Some indeed He has strengthened to the extent of the shedding of their blood (Art. 15).[1]

As "elements or endowments" which "can exist outside the visible boundaries of the Catholic Church" the Decree on Ecumenism lists "the written word of God; the life of grace; faith, hope, and charity, along with other interior gifts of the Holy Spirit and visible elements" (Art. 3).[2] This list is supplemented by numerous other references in chapters i and iii of the decree. "It is right and salutary to recognize the riches of Christ and virtuous works in the lives of others who are bearing witness to Christ, sometimes even to the shedding of their blood" (Art. 4).[3] While the Constitution on the Church had spoken only of persons who share in such elements outside the Roman church, the Decree on Ecumenism goes further and speaks of "churches and ecclesial communities" beyond these boundaries (cf. above, pp. 102 f.).

It is true that all of these statements were made unequivocally from the Roman church as the center. The reality of the Roman church is the yardstick for evaluating other churches (cf. above, pp. 118 ff.). What is recognized in other churches as constituting elements of the church are elements of what is present in the Roman church in its fullness. In this sense it can be said of these elements that "as gifts properly belonging to the Church of Christ" they "possess an inner dynamism toward Catholic unity" (Art. 8),[4] and in the same sense it can be said of non-Roman churches that their efficacy is derived "from the very fullness of grace and truth

---

[1] *Documents*, p. 34.
[2] *Documents*, p. 345.
[3] *Documents*, p. 349.
[4] *Documents*, p. 23.

entrusted to the Catholic Church" (Decree on Ecumenism, Art. 3).[5] In this sense we must also understand the Roman church's claim of jurisdiction over every baptized person beyond her borders. In the same conciliar texts, however, there is an unambiguous acknowledgment of the activity of Christ and the Holy Spirit beyond the borders of the Roman church, even though these Christians do not resort to the mediation of the Roman church. By baptism "they are united with Christ," and the Holy Spirit with "His gifts and graces" is "operative among them with His sanctifying power" (Constitution on the Church, Art. 15),[6] "the riches of Christ" are present in their lives (Decree on Ecumenism, Art. 4).[7] If we compare these statements with the encyclical *Mystici Corporis Christi* of Pius XII, and if we remember the Council's explicit emphasis on the necessity of renewal for the Roman church, we see clearly that the shaming and blessing shake-up of church-consciousness which our time has experienced has also left its mark on the resolutions of the Council.

If we go as far as the Council went, the question must be raised whether the point of departure in one's own church ought to be retained in this way, and whether it is sufficient to recognize "elements" of one's own church in other churches. Our only concern is no longer whether such statements do justice to the way other churches see themselves but whether they are appropriate to the activity of Christ and the Holy Spirit in the other churches, an activity which is expressly acknowledged. It is acknowledged that "all those justified by faith through baptism are incorporated into Christ" (Decree on Ecumenism, Art. 3).[8] Surely the reception of "the riches of Christ" (Art. 4)[9] is not merely the reception of a part of Christ. And surely sanctifying grace (Constitution on the Church, Art. 15)[10] is not merely a preparatory grace. In view

[5] *Documents*, p. 346.
[6] *Documents*, p. 34.
[7] *Documents*, p. 349.
[8] *Documents*, p. 345.
[9] *Documents*, p. 349.
[10] *Documents*, p. 34.

of the fact that such activity of Christ in the power of the Holy Spirit is acknowledged outside the borders of the Roman church, should this not bring about a change in thinking about the church? Instead of beginning with one's own church and viewing Christ's activity in the other churches as "elements" of one's own church, should one not begin with Christ's activity and view one's own church as a part of Christ's total sphere of activity?

Every church is in danger of understanding herself as the center around which the other churches orbit as planets. This lies close at hand because every Christian is sure that the church whose message brought him to faith, in which by baptism he was incorporated with Christ, and where through word and sacrament he is nourished ever anew, is the one, holy, catholic, and apostolic church. But the activity of Christ is not confined to one church. He works freely, without being confined to the boundaries of our churches. We must not be content to measure other churches by ourselves but must start with Christ, by whom we are measured together with all churches. He is the sun around whom we, together with other churches, orbit as planets and from whom we receive light. A kind of Copernican revolution in ecclesiological thinking is needed.

Now, every church might retort that she is one with Christ and that therefore there is no difference between her view of herself as the center of all churches and her acknowledgment of Christ. Here, however, we must with due care take seriously the great variety of relationships between Christ and the church of which the Scriptures bear witness. We may not one-sidedly claim God's covenant with his people for ourselves, for God can raise up children for himself from stones and he can call those his people who were not his people. Nor may we one-sidedly claim the unity of Christ with our church, nor his being in her and her being in him; we must at the same time take Christ seriously as the one who confronts our church in a forgiving, demanding, and judging way, and who is at liberty to "spew" out of his mouth churches which make their appeal to him (Rev. 3:16). Taking the biblical variety of relationships between Christ and the church seriously (cf. pp. 91 f.) will make impossible the security of a quantitative evaluation of the grace he has given other churches.

The Mercy of Christ

What will be the result if we consider the "elements and endowments" mentioned by the Council as the deeds of Christ, and if we seek to understand our own church and other churches from the point of view of Christ's activity?

Although Christ desires the unity of all believers, he is active in separated churches. Even though these may deny each other the right to forgive sins, he forgives their sins. Even though they do not acknowledge each other as the body of Christ, he through their baptism incorporates them into his body. Even though they do not treat each other as members of one body, he gives them his sacramental body. Even though they deny each other the fullness of spiritual gifts, he is active in them in the power of the Holy Spirit. And even when they deny the authority and legitimacy of each other's ministry, he makes use of these offices to build and to govern the churches. So low does the Lord stoop to the churches that he serves them even when they are not one. As the exalted one, Jesus Christ did not cease to be the same one who humbled himself, became the servant of all men, and died for them on the cross. As we look at the activity of Christ in the separated churches his mercy looms overwhelmingly large.

There are separations which God demands. In such cases the boundaries between salvation and disaster, between the confession and the denial of Christ, are involved. There are also, however, separations springing from lovelessness, lust for power, dogmatism, and narrowness, which have arisen among those who confess Christ as Lord and yet fail to see the universality of his activity. If we cannot recognize "the riches of Christ" and "the gifts of the Holy Spirit" beyond the borders of our church, then this signifies that Christ will not permit every separation brought about by the churches to be a separation from him. By the operation of the same Lord a unity of the separated is preserved, a unity unaffected and undissolved by their schism. Through the reception of the gifts of the same Christ a unity remains which is concealed under the schisms—concealed from the eyes of the churches and from the eyes of the world. So low does Christ stoop to the churches that he takes their schisms upon himself and permits the separated to be one in him.

This hidden unity is beginning to come to light in our generation. We are beginning to be aware of it. We are overwhelmed by the riches of the gifts of Christ which confront us where formerly we had neither seen nor expected them. We begin to sense how antitheses which we regarded as irreconcilable belong together, and how biases which seemed intolerable to us are necessary correctives for our own bias. From the contrasts, the riches of the one Holy Spirit's activities begin to emerge, and we begin to sense that even through the scandal of schisms God has preserved a universal whole—a whole which has not been fully unfolded in any one church—and continues to unfold it.

If, thus, the present of Christendom is drawn into a new light, the same is true of her past history. We begin to suspect how enigmatically, in a manner surpassing all our conceptions, the activity of Christ and the culpable conduct of Christians permeate each other. Throughout the scandals of church history he has held fast to his saving will. By means of the sorrows of schisms he has judged the church and at the same time has not ceased calling, admonishing, and endowing her, and using her service for the salvation of the world. Again and again his grace was greater than his judgment. Indeed, even through schisms he has brought to flower insights and gifts which had been suppressed and stunted before. Even through the churches' opposition to each other he has attested to the riches of his grace and has increased the number of his people. Just as God's omnipotence appears as weakness in the face of the crimes and catastrophes of world history, so Christ's rule appears utterly futile in the face of the history of the schisms, the fights, and the failures of Christendom. Yet just as

God by his world-rule encompasses even the evil and causes it to serve the welfare of his own, so Christ takes even the schisms into the service of his rule.

The mystery of unity is thus the mystery of Christ's mercy. The churches' unity is contained in the fact that Christ never ceases to have mercy on the churches and to accomplish his saving work through their so questionable service. Though the mystery of unity makes its shattering and blessing appearance today in the midst of a separated Christendom, it does not cease to be a mystery. On the contrary, it comes into view precisely as a mystery. For the mercy of Christ transcends all our limits and ideas. Just as the church came into being as a result of God's action and not because men decided to join together and establish the church, so it is also with the church's unity. Just as the church is indestructible, so also is her unity. The church may be suppressed and kept from expanding, her membership may be reduced, and she may even be pushed back into concealment. Nevertheless, God will preserve her in the midst of this world so that she cannot perish. Even so, her unity may be disfigured by the disunity of her members and concealed by her schisms. Nevertheless, in spite of her contentions God will not cease to be the one who will deal with her in a saving, purifying, and judging way, and who will preserve her unity even though it be hidden under schisms.

Does the recognition of Christ's activity in the separated churches justify their separation? It does not. The scandal and the guilt of separation become particularly noticeable when Christ's activity becomes visible even beyond the borders of our own church. May we be soothed by the certainty that there is a unity hidden under the separations? By no means. Just the opposite. If we are one in Christ it is impossible to remain disunited. "Are we to continue in sin that grace may abound? By no means! How can we who died to sin still live in it?" (Rom. 6:1 f.). The very greatness of the mercy by which Christ gives himself even to separated churches is the most powerful impetus for unification. Such unification cannot mean that we are to create unity. This unity is given in Christ. But we are expected to provide room for this unity and to put off all that disfigures and conceals it. What is true of all New Testament imperatives is true also of the command to be one: God demands nothing that he has not already granted in Christ.

The Recognition of Unity

Where shall we find this unity for which we are to provide room? We sense it more than we are clearly aware of it. We are sure that Christ is active beyond our own church, but we do not yet see clearly just where he is at work there. We know there are separations in the church which are not separation from Christ, but we cannot yet distinguish them from those other separations necessary for the sake of salvation. Christendom lives today in a time of astonishing discoveries, but we are not yet able to distinguish clearly between impressions, hopes, illusions, and realities. Clarity is made more difficult by the fact that, together with the "riches of Christ" and the "gifts of the Holy Spirit" outside one's own church, dimensions of the one, holy, catholic, and apostolic church are beginning to unfold; past doctrines of the church are inadequate for the comprehension of these dimensions for which there are as yet no appropriate concepts. This situation leads not only to the danger of fearing Christ's universal activity and retreating to one's own church, but also to the opposite danger of forsaking in a fanatical way the reality of the church on earth. But we are dealing precisely with the visibleness of the universal church. Where shall we begin in order to move from premonitions and impressions to achieving a clear understanding of the unity concealed by schisms? Where do we find the one church on earth beyond the borders of our own church?

Here, too, we start with the concrete references by means of which the "elements and endowments" outside the Roman church have been illustrated in the Council's resolutions, namely, Holy Scripture, religious zeal, faith, baptism, episcopate, the life of grace, virtuous works, etc. In comparing the sequence of such references in the Constitution on the Church (Art. 15) and the Decree on Ecumenism (Art. 3), and by adding further scattered statements, we are struck by a certain element of chance in the arrangements. Assembled here were various items of what was noteworthy in other churches, and in the course of the Council's deliberations other points were added. In the casualness of the listings we may perhaps rediscover the element of surprised discovery that is characteristic of the churches as they contemplate each other anew. These "elements" lie on very different levels. This is true, for one thing, in view of their recognizability. Not all of them are visible to the same degree. So, for example, the use of Scripture, the administration of baptism, and the episcopate are visible. This is not the case in the same measure with regard to religious zeal, faith, love, virtues, etc., and, especially, the "life of grace" and the "inner gifts of the Holy Spirit" are peculiarly incapable of empirical verification. Even determination of a genuine martyrdom must ultimately be left to God, though a man visibly and publicly suffered martyrdom. Furthermore, the listed elements are on different levels in view of their functions. Some are instruments of the grace by which Christ is active in the power of the Spirit. Others are operations—spiritual gifts, which are imparted through the means of grace. But where must we start in order to achieve a clear understanding of the activity of Christ and thus achieve a clear understanding of the church's unity?

We are now struck by the fact that in lining up a variety of references, both in the Constitution on the Church and in the Decree on Ecumenism, special prominence is given to *baptism*. The Christians separated from the Roman church are through baptism "honored with the name of Christian" and are "united with Christ" (Constitution on the Church, Art. 15).[11] They are "justified by faith through baptism" and are "incorporated into Christ" (Decree on Ecumenism, Art. 3).[12] "By the sacrament of

[11] *Documents*, pp. 33 f.

[12] *Documents*, p. 345.

baptism, whenever it is properly conferred in the way the Lord determined, and received with the appropriate dispositions of soul, a man becomes truly incorporated into the crucified and glorified Christ and is reborn to a sharing of the divine life . . ." (Art. 22).[13] In this way one such "element" is given prominence, one that is at once visible and a means of grace. Also, Holy Scripture is especially emphasized. "For there are many who honor sacred Scripture, taking it as a norm of belief and of action" (Constitution on the Church, Art. 15).[14] "The written word of God" is mentioned also by the Decree on Ecumenism at the beginning of its enumeration. These two emphases suggest the following reflections.

Since the question concerning unity involves the visible church or, more precisely, the recognition of the one holy church which is becoming visible also outside our own church, we must start with the *visible* "elements" through which Christ bestows the inner gifts. The Council properly emphasized baptism as a visible means of grace through which the faithful are justified, incorporated into the body of Christ, and reborn to the new life. The gospel must be equally emphasized, for it is "the power of God for salvation to every one who has faith" (Rom. 1:16). Through the proclaimed message of Christ's saving deed God not only *summons* to faith and *announces* justification and the new life but *creates* faith and *bestows* righteousness and new life on the believers. We must further emphasize the second chief sacrament of all churches, the Lord's Supper, in which Christ under the visible forms of bread and wine grants participation in his body and blood and thus establishes the believers as his body. In whatever manner in the life of the churches these means of grace may be developed in the various forms of preaching, absolution, benediction, or further "sacraments," Christ is active here in a clearly recognizable way—in such a way that we can hear, see, and taste his working.

---

[13] *Documents*, p. 363.
[14] *Documents*, p. 34.

But by what means can we know that here the pure gospel is preached and the sacraments are administered in truth? In their enumeration of the "elements" the Council documents justly give precedence to the Scriptures "as a norm of belief and of action," for the historical saving deed in Jesus Christ and its attestation through the apostles and the earliest community is of basic and normative significance for the church's speaking and acting in all ages. The gospel and the sacraments are to be recognized by their agreement with the Holy Scriptures. Now, the gospel in its essence is not a book but an oral message. The conferring of baptism not the biblical texts on baptism, the reception of the Lord's Supper not the New Testament texts on the Lord's Supper, these grant participation in the body of Christ. Though the Holy Scriptures are given normative precedence over all the church says and does, they point beyond themselves insofar as their statements must be constantly proclaimed and actualized anew in the change of the historical situation. To that extent we must not test the proclamation and the sacraments in a biblicistic-legalistic way. We must take into account the full range of possibilities that are contained in the biblical witnesses and that have been actualized in one way or another in the history of proclamation and of the administration of the sacraments. The question concerning scripturalness has often been answered unhistorically, and for that reason Christ's activity in the other churches has often gone unrecognized.

Through the gospel and the sacraments, Christ justifies, sanctifies, and renews the faithful, draws them into his death and resurrection, and establishes them as his body. Through the gospel and the sacraments he gives them the Holy Spirit with a variety of gifts and produces the "virtuous works" as fruits. The inner life of Christians is hidden from us. We are forbidden to differentiate between believers and hypocrites and to pronounce final judgment on their works. God knows the hearts and the works and he will one day make them manifest. But the gospel and the sacraments are to be clearly recognized on the basis of Holy Scripture, and we may be sure that wherever the gospel is preached and the sacraments are administered there will be believers. For the gospel is not an empty word and the sacraments are not empty signs; Christ is active in them to awaken and to renew. Thus the unity of the church is recognized by the gospel and the sacraments.

In the midst of the differences and contrasts in the churchly traditions we must fix our gaze on this event through which Christ builds the church. By this criterion we must evaluate the weight of individual components of the churchly traditions. We dare not underestimate the significance of the dogmas and the necessity of clarifying the dogmatic differences. Yet salvation comes not through dogmatic statements about word and sacrament but through the proclamation of the word and the administration of the sacraments. The dogmatic statements are in the service of this event, but they are not yet the event. Also, the significance of the ministry and the settlement of existing differences in this matter are very important. Yet the office of the ministry is attached as a service to Christ's activity through word and sacrament and cannot be called a means of grace in the same sense as word and sacrament. We must not simply assemble and compare the various components of the churchly tradition and of the present life of the churches. We must also take into account the structure of the operational contexts. In this structure every one of these components is coordinated to the activity of Christ through word and sacrament as a service. Then we shall recognize the unity which encompasses many differences. We shall recognize it when we recognize the one Christ, who through word and sacrament builds up the one church in the multiplicity of churchly traditions.

The Manifestation of Unity

Once we have recognized the unity of the church, which encompasses the boundaries of the individual churches and their traditions, we cannot stop there. The unity which has been recognized must be manifested, and the separations disfiguring and concealing that unity must be removed. The separated churches may be ever so considerate in their relations to each other; they may have gone beyond this and developed a cordial fraternal affection, and in their understanding of the other church they may have come to a spiritual participation in its life. Yet neither tact nor friendship nor spiritual empathy, nor even a partial cooperation can substitute for the unity in which the God-given unity of all believers is to become visible in this world. This bodily unity in full fellowship may not be treated as a remote goal or even only as an idea. The Council quite properly laid great stress on the extreme urgency of unity.

Since the believers in Christ are one, they must strive for union. It is not up to them to establish unity, but they must provide room for it. Since we are one in Christ, we are to be united. Providing room for unity demands intensive common work in questioning and searching and furnishing answers. Here we must make use of the most diverse methods of exegetical and historical scholarship, and also of the most modern questions and insights of logic, linguistic science, psychology of thought, sociology, and anthropology in the broadest sense. In rethinking the dogmatic differences, we must push forward to the point where the churches can jointly confess the mighty acts of God. In the process of rethinking the problems of jurisdiction, autonomy, autocephalism, etc., we must find the form of fellowship in which the unity of all churches will become visible. But what good is all searching if it is not done in love, the love that feels responsible for seeing to it that nothing of what God has entrusted to another church is lost? The believers must concern themselves with this union "with fear and trembling" (Phil. 2:12), the way they must be concerned about their salvation.

Nevertheless, this union will not be the result of human desire, effort, and accomplishment. Just as the unity in Christ is given by God, so, too, can the union of churches be produced only by God, who "is at work in you, both to will and to work for his good pleasure" (Phil. 2:13). Therefore, in the midst of all ecumenical endeavor the churches pray that God would grant unity in the freedom of his grace. In the first stage of the ecumenical movement various models of a united Christendom and its order were constructed. But there has been less and less talk of such constructive anticipation. It has been increasingly recognized that the union of the churches and the form of the united church can be expected only from God. Thus Christians from all churches observe the annual Prayer Week and simultaneously, often in joint worship, pray for "the unity of the church of Jesus Christ, as he wills it and when he wills it." In this prayer, composed by the Catholic priest Couturier, all glory is given to God, since the praying Christians do not act proleptically but await everything from God. More than ever the churches today are aware of their reliance on the miracle of divine guidance, which is able to show the way even where human efforts come up against insurmountable obstacles.

Whatever form God has predestined for a united Christendom, however, it is clear to all in this praying and working that the unity of the message of Christ, the unity of baptism, the fellowship of the Lord's Supper, and the mutual recognition of each other's ministry are irreducible elements of the church's unity. This is not a humanly devised notion but a divine necessity imposed on the churches from their origin. In the assembly of the World Council of Churches in New Delhi (1961), the assembled churches expressed this concern in the following words:

> We believe that the unity which is both God's will and his gift to his Church is being made visible as all in each place who are baptized into Jesus Christ and confess him as Lord and Savior are brought by the Holy Spirit into one fully committed fellowship, holding the one apostolic faith, preaching the one Gospel, breaking the one bread, joining in common prayer, and having a corporate life reaching out in witness and service to all and who at the same time are united with the whole Christian fellowship in all places and all ages in such wise that ministry and members are accepted by all, and that all can act and speak together as occasion requires for the tasks to which God calls his people.[15]

---

[15] *The New Delhi Report* (cited above p. 13), p. 116.

The statements of the Augsburg Confession, the principal confession of the Reformation, share this understanding of unity.

> For it is sufficient for the true unity of the Christian church that the Gospel be preached in conformity with a pure understanding of it and that the sacraments be administered in accordance with the divine Word. It is not necessary for the true unity of the Christian church that ceremonies, instituted by men, should be observed uniformly in all places. It is as Paul says in Eph. 4:4, 5, "There is one body and one Spirit, just as you were called to the one hope that belongs to your call, one Lord, one faith, one baptism."[16]

Here, too, one could attempt to point to first steps which will not only lead to mutual approaches but, beyond that, are necessary for union. We must here confine ourselves to a few basic principles, and in view of the great significance of the confession we emphasize the question concerning the dogmatic consensus that belongs in essence to unity.

(a) Union will be impossible if each church insists on all her dogmatic statements, regards them all as equally binding, and demands their full acceptance by the other churches as prerequisite for union. The Decree on Ecumenism of Vatican II has properly pointed out that the dogmatic statements constitute a sort of hierarchy and must be interpreted from their controlling center. All dogmas are in fact and ultimately an unfolding of the central confession of Christ. The distinction between central confessional statements and their further concrete explications is of great importance not only for *understanding* the dogmas of other churches but also for *union*. Then, indeed, this hierarchy must be understood not only as a hierarchy of contents but also as a hierarchy in the degree of obligation in the various dogmatic statements. As surely as oneness in faith is the prerequisite for union, this is not true with regard to undiscriminating acceptance of all dogmatic statements. For in the course of church history the one confession

---

[16] Article VII, cited from *The Book of Concord,* trans. and ed. Theodore G Tappert (Philadelphia: Fortress Press, 1959), p. 32.

of Christ has been expounded in different statements as it met a variety of special fronts and concepts, which are not important for all of Christendom in the same way and which cannot be imposed on all in the same way. Within the structure of canon law a distinction is made between what is "by divine right" and what is "by human right," that is, between the unalterably valid divine command and the alterable concrete application of canon law. Similarly the central dogmas should be distinguished from the variableness of their concrete expression.

(b) But even if there can be no reduction in the *substantive* unity of the central dogmatic affirmations required for the union of the churches, this unity need not be a unity in the same dogmatic *formulas*. We must not forget that in the ancient church a large number of territorial baptismal creeds were used side by side, and that the unity of the church was expressed not in the same confessional formulas but in the same Lord who is confessed, and in the reciprocal acknowledgment of different confessional formulas. In its statements on liturgy the Council rightly moved away from a centralized uniformity in the direction of the structure of fellowship. The Council's statements on the theological traditions and legally prescribed orders in the particular churches contain similar indications. However, an understanding of unity as a fellowship in reciprocal recognition must, in addition, be expanded to include an understanding of dogmatic unity, if the riches of what God has granted the churches in insight and doctrine are to be brought along to the union.

The Roman church could perhaps agree to the second principle, for this principle is only an extension to the expressions of dogma, an extension of her affirmation of the variety of rites and theologies. Thus the Decree on Ecumenism states with regard to the Eastern church, that "these various theological formulations are often to be considered as complementary rather than conflicting" (Art. 17).[17] To be sure, the document is here speaking only of a

---

[17] *Documents*, p. 360.

different way of proclaiming doctrine, not specifically of solemn dogmas. Nevertheless, when the Roman church attempted reunion with the Greek Orthodox Church at Florence (1439) she did not demand that the Greek church insert the previously rejected *Filioque* in the text of her creed but contented herself with an expression of consensus with the content of the Western formula. The first principle would, however, already represent a correction of the Roman church's former demand that all her dogmas be universally and equally binding.

(c) Beyond this it is correct to say that none of the churches can remain exactly as she is. In every case there is need for a renewal and an unfolding of catholicity, hence, of a return to God and a turning toward the other churches. One-sided elements must be removed, stunted elements must be made whole, errors must be corrected, and anathemas must be expunged. Church history shows that all attempts at achieving union by having one church absorb the others have failed. Such attempts were bound to fail because no church as it is can provide room for everything that God has produced in the others. Union will not be possible without sacrifices. But where the sacrifice is offered to God, there is no loss but only an act of self-surrender to a treasure richer than what we possessed before.

Type, 11 on 13 and 10 on 11 Garamond
Display, Cloister Bold
Paper, White G. M. Antique